To Tim.

2

RAFFLES AND HIS CREATOR

Previous publications:
The Last Liberal Governments: The Promised Land, 1905-1910
(Barrie & Jenkins, 1968)
The Last Liberal Governments: Unfinished Business, 1911-1914
(Barrie & Jenkins, 1971)
Lloyd George (Barrie & Jenkins, 1975)
The Disappearance of Edwin Drood (Constable, 1991)
The Life and Times of Thomas Day, 1748 – 89:
Virtue Almost Personified (Edwin Mellen Press, 1996)
My Early Times (Aurum Press, 1997)
(revised edition of a Dickensian compilation originally published by the Folio Society in 1988)
Just Stylish (Nekta, 1998)

ೞ৪

Compilations for the Folio Society:
Macaulay's History of England in the Eighteenth Century (1980)
Macaulay's History of England from 1485 to 1685 (1985)

ೞ৪

Forthcoming:
The Elegy Man: the life and rhymes of Thomas Gray

E. W. Hornung.

RAFFLES AND HIS CREATOR:
the life and works of E. W. Hornung

❧

Peter Rowland

NEKTA PUBLICATIONS

First published 1999 by Nekta Publications,
PO Box 18514, London, E11 2YH

ISBN 0 9533583 2 1

Produced in Great Britain by
Axxent Ltd,
The Short Run Book Company,
St Stephen's House, Arthur Road,
Windsor, Berkshire SL4 1RY

Frontispiece: Illustrated London News Picture Library

ACKNOWLEDGEMENTS

I am much indebted, for his valuable advice and information on sundry family matters, to Mr Stephen Hornung, not least for his having kindly made available to me the privately-printed biography of his grandfather (*J.P. Hornung, A family portrait*) written by his aunt, Mrs B.M Collin, in 1970, and copies of letters and Press cuttings. Others to whom I am indebted for advice on various matters are Mr H.R.F. Keating, Mr Peter E. Blau, Mr Otto Penzler, the Rev. Charles Jeffries, Ms Virginia Murray, Mr John Riley of the British Film Institute and Mr David Tyrell, Archivist of Middlesbrough Borough Council – not to mention Don Hardenbrook and the Trained Cormorants for advice and encouragement, their howls of protest at the conclusions reached in Chapter 11 notwithstanding. For their zeal in helping to track down a copy of *At Large* at the New York Public Library to carry out an interim identification check, my heartfelt thanks go out to Enola Stewart and her husband, and I am tremendously indebted to the University of Ohio for actually forwarding a copy for my perusal (especially since a copy previously despatched by the University of Texas appears to have disappeared somewhere in the region of the Bermuda triangle). I am also very grateful to Ms Libby Chenault of the University of North Carolina at Chapel Hill for supplying me so speedily with a copy of Hornung's Preface to the 1919 edition of *Fathers of Men*, which is equally unobtainable in England. My thanks go, as ever, to the staffs of the British Library and the London Library for their unstinting assistance, and to Richard and Mo Hubbard ("RichMo") for patiently reading and commenting on the stuff as each instalment was churned out in its original unvarnished state.

Contents

"Vanity of Vanities! We know what we meant to do, we know how hard we aimed, we judge by results, we very seldom give ourselves or each other the credit of the good that was in our hearts and in our heads, but just out of reach of our poor human hands; and yet, 'God weigheth the intention', always; of nothing in this life or the next one are we surer than of that."

E.W. Hornung, July 1914

INTRODUCTION

IN the mid-1890s there was published, in a magazine yet to be identified, a story entitled 'After the Fact'. It told the experiences of a young man, ex-public school type, visiting Geelong, a small town in Australia where, as it happens, a number of banks have been robbed by "a second Ned Kelly", adorned with a black beard. En route, for interest's sake, to the scene of the latest crime, he encounters, much to his astonishment, an old schoolfellow.

"Deedes Major!" I cried.... My man turned and favoured me with the stare of studied insolence which had made our house-master's life a burden to him some ten years before that night ... although the dark eyes were sunken and devil-may-care, the full lips hidden by a moustache with grey hairs in it, and the pale face prematurely lined...

"We were at school together," I explained. "I was your fag when you were captain of Footer. To think of meeting you here!"

"Do tell me your name," he said wearily; and at that moment I recollected (what had quite escaped my memory) his ultimate expulsion; and I stood confounded by my maladroitness.

"Bower," said I, abashed.

"The Beetle!" cried Deedes, not unkindly; a moment later he was shaking my hand and smiling on my confusion.

They stroll on, reminiscing about old times, and Bower is astonished to learn that, by a remarkable coincidence, Deedes is a clerk at the bank where the robbery had been carried out. There follows a most extraordinary yarn with bags of action, in the course of which (surprise, surprise!) the mysterious bank robber turns out to have been none other than Deedes himself. Seeking to make his escape, and pursued by armed constables, he viciously locks up both his old friend and his ex-girl friend, Miss Enid I'Anson – although Enid, even after a volley of shots has been exchanged for two or three pages, still thinks kindly of him. "He is not fit to die," she tells Bower; "he has fine qualities – you know it yourself – he could play a man's part yet in the world." But the game is up. Deedes bursts into the room – "I'm done for!" he cries – and flings out his arms to Enid. "A great look lit his face, half mocking, half sublime", he collapses in a heap, blood trickling from the fatal wound, and Bower promptly becomes engaged to Enid. (Having been locked in a room with her for at least three hours, he obviously had to do the decent thing.)

Virtue had triumphed but the author was attracted by the character of Deedes Major and evidently troubled (like Enid) by the thought that retribution had struck far too soon. He had prematurely killed off, he decided, a goose that might have laid a good many golden eggs. So Deedes was resurrected, transformed from an ex-captain of footer into a brilliant cricketer and shunted back to England to become A.J. Raffles, the debonair man about town whose leisure time pursuits are principally those of breaking and entering. And Bower (still his ex-fag) becomes Manders, otherwise known as 'Bunny', his partner in crime. Raffles and Bunny won instant fame and a fortune for their creator (becoming as well known, indeed, as the immortal creations of his brother-in-law, Conan Doyle). Raffles eventually atones for his misdeeds by dying for Queen and country on the South African veldt. Deedes Major and Bower were meanwhile entombed in a book of short stories called, most fittingly, *Some Persons Unknown*.

Ernest William Hornung, the creator of Raffles, is overwhelmingly a Person Unknown so far as posterity is concerned. It must be instantly acknowledged that A.J. continues to enjoy a faithful following, with his exploits being periodically rediscovered by fresh generations of delighted readers, but – thanks to the indefatigable Inspector Mackenzie of Scotland Yard – the gentleman burglar was unmasked a century ago. E.W.H., on the other hand, has become a true

Man of Mystery. One sought him in vain in the *Dictionary of National Biography* – or did, at any rate, until 1993, when a supplementary volume entitled *Missing Persons* was published. In a contribution penned by G.H.L. Le May we encounter, once again, the same bare handful of much-recycled facts that has done such sterling service to those, such as M.R. Ridley, Anthony Powell and Peter Haining, who have been called upon to produce Introductions to compilations of the Raffles short stories. Our quarry is also granted a few lines in *The Oxford Companion to English Literature*, which – after mentioning *The Amateur Cracksman* (1899) – refers us to Orwell's essay on 'Raffles and Miss Blandish' and then hastens on to the next entry.

All the ascertainable facts about Hornung currently in print barely exceed the data that was utilised by *The Times* obituary writer on 24 March 1921 – although that writer was able to state, presumably from personal acquaintance, that "in private life Mr Hornung was a man of large and generous nature, a delightful companion and conversationalist. He leaves many deeply attached friends to mourn him." The casual reader knows that Hornung was writing at the turn of the century, and may also be aware of his relationship to Conan Doyle, but this is virtually the full extent of general knowledge. To have disappeared into such obscurity, after creating (with what seems, in retrospect, effortless ease) one of the most engaging characters in popular fiction, is a lamentable fate. On the *prima facie* evidence alone, he deserves reinstatement in a more prominent position on the literary scene – if not on a pedestal, then at any rate on a sizeable plinth.

But the biographer is faced, at the outset, with what appears to be an insurmountable problem, namely this almost total absence of information about the man. There are, it seems, no "Hornung papers" – or, if they exist, then they are extremely well concealed. Of his private life we know virtually nothing. We know when and where he was born, what public school he went to, what books he wrote, the name of his wife and the name of his brother-in-law, his great distress at the death in action of his only son and, finally, when and where he died. Is it conceivable that, at this present late date, a little more flesh might be put on these very bare bones? What follows, while primarily an assessment of his skills as a writer, is an attempt to do just that – aided, it must be said, not only by information in the public records but by autobiographical material that is scattered throughout most of his novels. In *Young Blood*, for example, published in 1898, the young Harry Ringrose obviously has very much in common with the young Willie Hornung. (As much, at any rate, as the young David Copperfield had with the young Charles Dickens – for such material must obviously be used with caution.)

What emerges from this investigation is, like the character of Raffles himself, somewhat electrifying. For there was one particular episode in his life whch, until now, has remained totally unknown.

1

A VISITOR TO DOWN UNDER

IT MIGHT, perhaps, be regarded as a classic instance of wish-fulfilment that a slim, clean-limbed, athletic and amazingly resourceful young Englishman (albeit with one or two disturbing little idiosyncrasies) should have been conjured into existence by a small, short-sighted, asthmatic and self-effacing pen-pusher of Hungarian extraction.

Ernest William Hornung, the creator of A.J. Raffles, cricketer *extraordinaire*, was born on 7 June 1866 in the Yorkshire town of Middlesbrough, located on the southern bank of the River Tees. He was the eighth and last child of John Peter Hornung and his wife Harriet (née Armstrong) but his wealthy father was something rather more than the usual self-made north-country tycoon – for he hailed from Transylvania (which formed, by that time, part of the Austro-Hungarian Empire) and had been christened Johan Petrus.

Born in the little town of Mediasch on 4 October 1821, in a region in which the Hornungs had been landowners for several generations, Johan Petrus Hornung studied at the University of Vienna in the early 1840s and apparently took a degree in law. But he decided to emulate his own father, Petrus Hornung, who was a merchant, and engage in business. He worked for a shipping firm in Hamburg but grew frustrated at the lack of opportunity, and the head of the company advised him to try his luck in the north of England, where there was much industrial activity afoot offering far better scope for ambitious young men anxious to make their fortunes. He therefore crossed the North Sea, took up residence in Middlesbrough, became involved in the export of

13

iron and eventually found a partner prepared to join him in forming an independent company. He had meanwhile met a girl almost three years younger than himself whose father (Robert Armstrong) was a wine merchant. A courtship prospered and they were married in the parish church of Stockton-upon-Tees, in the county of Durham, on 30 March 1848. By this time he had Anglicised his name to 'John Peter', having decided to settle permanently in England, and his profession was declared (on their marriage licence) to be that of merchant. Harriet had been born in Newcastle-upon-Tyne on 6 March 1824 but was living in Stockton at the time of their marriage.

Their first child, a boy, was born in the spring of 1849 but lived for little more than three months. Then came, after a gap of four years, three sons and three daughters – Theodore (1853), Bertha (1856), Harriet Susan (1857), Ida (1859), John Peter (1861) and Charles (1863). Ernest William may have been something of an afterthought, for there was a time lag of three years before he appeared on the scene (by which time his mother was forty-two). So he was, as he described one his fictional characters in 1912, "the youngest of a large family, and that after a gap; in one sense he had been literally the only child".

John Peter Hornung had developed, by then, into a high-powered figure in the local community. Defined on Ernest's birth certificate as an "Iron & Coal Merchant", he had offices in Turton Street and was now deeply engaged in the export of both these commodities. But his business activities also encompassed the import of Scandinavian timber, another flourishing trade, and in this capacity he acted as the town's Swedish, Norwegian and Danish vice-consul. He was one of the local dignitaries present at the opening of Middlesbrough High School in June 1870. The town's Roman Catholic Cathedral Church in Sussex Street, completed in 1878, had side altars adorned with pictures presented by himself. He made three short trips home to Mediasch after settling down in England and on one of these, in the early 1880s, was accompanied by his wife and Ida. On this particular occasion he was honoured as town benefactor, having come there to formally open a Young Man's Institute and a club presented to it by himself. His eldest son, Theodore, had meanwhile spent part of his early manhood in Norway, and – having a gift for music – had received tuition from Grieg.

To begin with, the family had lived in Middlesbrough itself, but in 1860 they took up residence in the Grove Hill area of Marton, a short distance south of the town, in one of the four semi-detached houses known collectively as Cleveland Villas. It was here that Ernest – or 'Willie', as he would be called in the family circle – was born. He was baptised at St Hilda's church three weeks later. His father had meanwhile obtained planning permission to build a large house for his family on a nearby site and the Hornungs presumably took up residence in their new home in 1867. John Peter called it 'Erdely', the Magyar name for Transylvania. "It was well situated near unspoiled country stretching away to the Cleveland Hills,", wrote one of his grand-daughters, more than a century later, "yet conveniently close to Middlesbrough where the reflected glare from the blast furnaces set the sky on fire at night. There was nothing foreign about Erdely but its name, for it was designed in the latest Victorian Gothic style of red brick, complete with tower, and a large 'winter garden' or conservatory, which served as an extra drawing room. The grounds were ample and included every contemporary amenity, such as a lake large enough for boating."

It was at Erdely, therefore, that Willie grew up. There features, in a Raffles story entitled 'The Spoils of Sacrilege', the childhood home of its narrator (Bunny Manders), and at one point they take refuge in a tiny tower in the house, with a dormer window in each of its four sloping sides. "The fixed seats", he writes, "looked to me to be wearing their old, old coat of grained varnish; nay, the varnish had its ancient smell, and the very vanes outside creaked their message to my ears. I remembered whole days that I had spent, whole books that I had read, here in this favourite fastness of my boyhood."

A small and rather thin child, suffering from asthma and poor eyesight, Willie was sent to a dame school in the first instance. A dame school features in *Young Blood* (1898) and a small boy who is evidently a very young version of Hornung appears in it as Woodman, a "delicate little fellow", pale-faced and slender and permanently in a poor state of health but with a great passion for reading – especially the works of R.M. Ballantyne – and also with an interest in cricket. He was then transferred to a newly-established private school, St Ninian's, Moffat, to the north of Dumfries in the Lowlands of Scotland ("'Mid purple heather and brown crag", so he later recalled in 'Forerunners'), and was one of its nine founder pupils when it opened for business in the spring of 1879.

There was, it seems, the occasional family trip to London. "I remember as a little boy", he recalled in September 1918, "seeing Lady Butler's 'Charge of the Light Brigade' at my first Academy. I am not sure that I have looked upon that canvas since, but the wild-eyed central figure, 'back from the mouth of Hell', rises up before me after forty years." The highlight of such trips – perhaps, indeed, the main reason for them – was a visit to the Oval, to witness a test match between England and Australia. He would cherish memories of "the early Australian cricketers, of beardless Blackham, Boyles and Bonnors taking the field to mow down the flower of our English cricket, in the days when those were our serious wars. How I hated the type as a schoolboy sitting open-mouthed and heart-broken at the Oval!" "I was twelve, but I knew my *Lillywhite* off by heart", the narrator of 'A Bowler's Innings' recalls, "and all that season I cut the matches out of the newspapers and pasted them in a book. I have it still."

The family was meanwhile starting to break up. At Solihull, in November 1877, Theodore married Agnes Gillott (offspring of a well-known firm of pen manufacturers) and on 25 April 1878 a proud John Peter Hornung bestowed upon Samuel Clarence Lush, solicitor, son of a High Court Judge, the hand of his second daughter, Harriet Susan ('Hetty'). The latter event was described in the local Press as a "fashionable marriage" and an impressive guest list included Watkin Williams, MP. The Hungarian flag flew from the tower of Erdely Villa on this auspicious day and the name of "Master W. Hornung" also featured in the guest list.

Willie moved on from St Ninian's, in September 1880, to Uppingham, fifteen miles east of Leicester. He was an amiable lad who proved popular among his schoolmates and his interest in cricket grew ever more intense, although he was a player of only very limited skills – nourishing (like Harry Ringrose, another fictionalised version of himself) "a hopeless passion for the game". He played an amateurish form of cricket during the holiday times, with what he recalled as "snob-wickets" being painted on a certain buttress in the back yard and his-fellow players being members of his family and perhaps a servant or two. (If his asthma was particularly bad, a sister would act as runner.)

Perfect bliss, he later recalled, were those summer Saturday afternoons when school had ended at midday and there were only a few Latin verses to do before going up to the dormitory that night. "A match on the Upper, where you could lie on your rug and watch the game you couldn't play; call-over at the match; ices and lemon-drinks in a tent on the field; and for Saturday supper anything you liked to buy, cooked for you in the kitchen and put piping hot at your place in hall, not even for the asking, but merely by writing your name plainly on the eggs and leaving them on the slab outside!" And on Sundays there were chapel bells "that rang you down the hill at the double if you were late and not too asthmatical" and you would go puffing up the opposite hill to take your place for chapel call-over in the school quad, in Sunday tails or Eton jackets, with the masters in their silk hoods or rabbit-skins. "Then came the cool and spacious chapel, with its marble pulpit and its brazen candelabra, and rows of chastened chapel faces ... giving a swing to chants." After chapel he would go out for a walk with a friend, or else write his letter home and get it over with, and the day would end with cold boiled beef and apple-pie with cloves. Brian Belk, a master at the school who also came from Middlesbrough, would later recall that Willie had written a great deal for the school magazine, and an ex-classmate confirmed, in 1941, that he had penned some "very clever and amusing verses" for that august publication.

When did Hornung's schooldays come to an end? Ringrose leaves school at the age of fourteen, "in the form below the Sixth", although we may wish to note that young Parker, in a story called 'Jim-of-the-Whim', "had been sent away from his public school because the rudiments of Latin were still beyond him at seventeen". According to Shane R. Chichester (who became acquainted with him in 1896) it was in 1883, when Hornung had indeed been seventeen. It is clear, at any rate, that his asthma had become so bad by this time that any thought of going into the Upper Sixth, let alone moving on to University, had been abandoned. "You cannot sit up half your nights with asthma and be an average boy," he observed in 1911. The schoolboy hero of a little book he wrote that year entitled *The Camera Fiend*, who is almost seventeen and in the Middle Fifth, puffs asthma cigarettes at times when the attacks are particularly bad and is granted permanent exemption from attending the first lessons of the day. (Needless to say, he too is intensely interested in cricket.) The school-mate quoted above also recalled that he "had some papers which he used to set burning at all hours of the night and thereby create a cloud of smoke", much to the intense irritation of the other boys in his dormitory.

One thing emphatically clear is that, even if he was at Uppingham for no more than three years, Hornung thoroughly enjoyed his schooldays and remembered them with much affection. He came to regard Edward Thring, the headmaster of Uppingham, as "one of the great headmasters of the nineteenth century", and would recall him "addressing the whole school of three to four hundred boys one morning and urging us to read a little book which he had just been reading himself. The little book was Mrs Ewing's *Jackanapes* – the story of a little boy who was killed at Waterloo". Ernest read *Jackanapes* and also another tear-inducing book by the same author called *Story of a Short Life*. "Had my own Uppingham life extended to the normal span," he wrote in 1919, "annual pressure from below must have hoisted me at last into the Upper Sixth; and I might have more and seemlier recollections to draw upon. As it is I see Thring plainest in his pulpit – no longer a little old man [sixty-two in 1883], but majestic, noble, and austere; or limping down the street – frock-coat flapping, top-hat inclined to the back of his head, a snowy spread of tie and whisker joining in his wide, radiant, out-of-door smile; or jabbing a copy of elegiacs with his formidable pencil, or looking cold steel at the morning's offenders, one blue-veined hand in rest upon his awful armoury of canes. He really was a flogging judge! ... One memorable morning he beat a batch of over fifty of us for coming back after the summer holidays with our 'holiday tags' unlearnt; it was said that he required a glass of water before the end, but my turn came too early for personal corroboration of that sardonic detail."

Uppingham, he adds, "was actually the first English school of its class to be equipped with a gymnasium; it was probably the first where music was taken seriously and most efficiently taught; there were gardens for boys who cared for gardening, aviaries for those who fancied birds, and in my own time a blacksmith's forge was added to the regulation carpenter's shop. Constitutionally open to the new idea, it may be that our unconventional Head at times lent himself and us to strange procedure... We were the first school to start a London Mission, and it was Thring himself who initiated the Headmasters' Conference. What he apparently never would countenance, and what we were probably the last school in England to possess, was anything in the shape of the Rifle Corps of those days or the O.T.C. of these."

In joyous and emotional mood in 1913 (the year after writing *Fathers of Men*) Hornung looked back at his schooldays and celebrated them by writing 'Uppingham Song', extracts from which run as follows:

Ages ago (as today they are reckoned)
I was a lone little, blown little fag:
Panting to heel when Authority beckoned,
Spoiling to write for the Uppingham Mag.!

ॐ

Ages ago that was Somebody's study;
Somebody Else had the study next door.
O their long walks in the fields dry or muddy!
O their long talks in the evenings of yore!

ॐ

O but the ghosts at each turn I could show you! –
Ghosts in low collars and little cloth caps –
Each of 'em now quite an elderly O.U. –
Wiser, no doubt, and as pleasant – perhaps!
That's where poor Jack lit the slide up in tollies,
Once when the quad was a foot deep in snow –
When a live Bishop was one of the Pollies –
Ages and ages and ages ago!
Things that were Decent and things that were Rotten,
How I remember them year after year!
Some – it may be – that were better forgotten:
Some that – it may be – should still draw a tear.

ॐ

Repton can put up as good an Eleven.
Marlborough men are the fear of the foe.
All that I wish to remark is – thank Heaven
I was at Uppingham ages ago!

By December 1883 Willie's schooldays were over. He
returned to a household somewhat diminished in size. In
addition to the departures of Theodore and Harriet, the
second John Peter – known in the family circle as 'Pitt' – was
now working in Lisbon, where he had just become engaged to
Laura Paiva Rapozo, the daughter of a very wealthy

businessman. (They were married four months later.) Two junior members of the family still living at home were Charles and Ida – and they had been rejoined, in all probability, by Bertha, who had been widowed within a few months of her own marriage in 1879.

Willie was apparently taken into his father's business in the first instance but showed no aptitude for the work. His health, in any case, grew steadily worse and his parents were advised that he should be sent to gentler climes to recuperate. The climes decided upon were those of Australia, and it was in a clipper bound for New South Wales that he set sail in 1884 – "ordered south", just as Robert Louis Stevenson had been ten years earlier. He later wrote a graphic account of the three-months' voyage from Liverpool to Melbourne in a short story entitled 'The Star of the *Grasmere*', in which it is fairly easy to separate fact from the fiction. A young man whose wrists were "many sizes too small", he spent much of the first half of the voyage lying on the berth in his cabin. "For four hours one's berth was at such an angle that one could hardly climb out of it; for four more the angle was reversed, and one lay in continual peril of being shot across the cabin like clay from a spade.... I think my single joy during those three weeks was one particularly foul morning on the skirts of the Bay [of Biscay], when I heard that all the ham and eggs for the cuddy breakfast had been washed through the lee scupper-holes. Ham and eggs in a sea like that! Most days, it is true, I did manage to crawl on deck, but I could never stand it for long. I had not found my sea-legs, my knees were weak, and I went sliding about the wet poop like butter on a hot plate."

Then, the weather improved and the sea died down. "The heavy canvas was taken down, the ship put on her summer suit of thin white sails, and every stitch bagged out with steadfast wind.... There was an end to our miseries, and the pendulum swung to the other extreme. I never saw so many souls in spirits so high or in health so blooming. We got to know each other; we told stories; we sang songs; we organised sweepstakes on the day's run. We played quoits and cards, draughts and chess. We ventured aloft [on the rigging], were duly pursued and mulcted in the usual fine. We got up a concert. We even started a weekly magazine" – of which Hornung was co-editor. Eventually, the ship was within one day's sail of Port Phillip Heads. There was a final ship's concert, much cheerful leave-taking, and everyone turned in – but Hornung was unable to sleep.

> We had seen no land for eighty days. We expected to sight the coast at daybreak. I desired to miss none of it.... So I flung back my blankets at two bells, and I slipped into my flannels. In another minute I was running up the foremast ratlines.... I had acquired a sure foot aloft, a ready hand, and, above all, a steady head. I climbed to the cross-trees without halt or pause, and then I must needs go higher....
>
> I sat close to the mast, with my arm (so to speak) round its waist; and it is extraordinary how much one sees from the fore-royal yard. There was no moon that night, the sea seemed as vast as the sky and almost as concave. Indeed, they were as two skies, joined like the hollows of two hands: the one spattered with a million moonstones; the other all smeared with phosphorus; both inky, both infinite; and, perched between the two, an eighteen-year-old atom, with fluttering heart and with straining eyes, on the edge of a wide new world.

Sixteen years later, Hornung wrote a short story entitled 'The Jackeroo on G. Block'. Bestowing the curious name of 'Tahourdin' upon a very slightly fictionalised version of his earlier self, he looked back with wry amusement – somewhere between compassion and contempt – at those early days of the intrepid explorer of this wide new world, with his wild preconceptions and his great expectations:

> Tahourdin went out to Australia for his health, but in his secret soul he cherished other projects. Cursed by a distressing delicacy, and neither physically nor mentally robust, he had nevertheless an incongruous and quite unsuspected hankering after violent experiences in wild places. In part this was due to much early reading in a well-worn groove, in part to a less worthy stimulus. Tahourdin had a big brother, who had once ... [returned home] in

romantic rags, thereafter to thrill all callers with graphic accounts of his more respectable adventures by flood and field. This had fired Tahourdin with an ignoble ambition, not so much to do and see and suffer in his turn, as to lay in a stock of yarns which should one day compare favourably with those of his brother. An unerring arrival in Hobson's Bay, after no more than eighty days under canvas, fell proportionately flat upon the bold spirit that had spent half the voyage in wistful day-dreams of coral islands and of pirates' lairs. But there was one dream whose fulfilment nothing could prevent, and Tahourdin set foot on Australian soil with the fixed determination to plant it forthwith in the very heart of the Bush.

Tahourdin's preconception of the Bush (the capital was his in all his letters) was a mental picture of singular detail and definition. He saw huge and sombre trees in the bowels of some vast ravine, with perpetual noon above and perpetual night below – in the cool bed of an ocean of unchanging leaves. He picked out the shadows with horsemen in jack-boots and red shirts (himself among them), now feasting round monster camp-fires, now caracoling behind orderly flocks and herds. Then there were the gold-diggings; you pegged out your claim and dug away until your pick harpooned a nugget. Then there were bushrangers and wild blacks, and Tahourdin had hopes and fears of an encounter with one or the other. Perhaps the hopes predominated; they certainly did in the case of the bushrangers. Tahourdin had read much of these gentry; he intended to go prepared for them, with very little worth stealing about his person at any one time. With their well-known magnanimity they would probably hand him that little back again, and he would have it to talk about for the term of his natural life.

It will be seen that this egoist did not fly too high. He did not aspire to astonish the world, but only his friends, and he kept his aspiration to himself. Moreover, there was one excuse for him. He was not quite eighteen when he landed at Williamstown. His letters of introduction made him several friends, who did their best to deter the escaped schoolboy from plunging into a life for which he was obviously unfitted. They assured him that there were no wild blacks within a thousand miles; that bushrangers had been stamped out years since with the Kellys; that the single digger was obsolete and his claim an anachronism. Tahourdin was sorry to hear all this, but he merely refrained from buying a horse and riding forth to seek adventures as he had originally proposed to himself. Instead, he pushed for introductions to squatters, and finally succeeded in discovering one who at length consented to feed him for his services, if he chose to present himself at the station at his own risk and expense, prepared to do anything he was told, and to pay his own way back if he could not do it well enough to be worth his rations.

In other words he was to be given a trial in the untranslatable capacity of 'jackeroo'.

Hornung remained in Australia for just over two years and, for at least part of this time, was employed by Cecil Joseph Parsons, owner of a sheep-station at Mossgiel in the Riverina, as tutor to his children. Those years were the making of him and, in a sense, the making of his career as a writer, for he was excited by what he saw and developed a love and enthusiasm for this incredible new country, with its wide open spaces, wonderful fresh air and pioneering inhabitants which never left him. Australia, in the mid-1880s, was a land of golden opportunities – still only partially civilised, and with adventures galore beckoning for those with the courage, the zest and the fortitude to undertake them. Melbourne, admittedly, had much in common with English cities, which was not necessarily any great recommendation: he would scarcely mention it in any of his subsequent writings, although one of his books refers to the "deep-cut channel between road-metal and curb-stone, whereby you shall remember the streets of Melbourne" and he recalls strolling in Fitzroy Gardens and looking at the statues. But when one had escaped from its confines there opened up a totally new landscape – the land of the bush, where squatters staked their rights and set up 'stations', much as the Norman warriors who followed in the wake of William the Conqueror had staked out their claims to English estates. But Australia was vastly bigger than England and, potentially, a far greater country.

It was also, of course, a country where Englishmen who had failed to make the grade at home might make a fresh start – or, failing that, disappear into quiet oblivion without causing their relatives any embarrassment. "You know, Evelyn," exclaims Bishop Methuen to his daughter in a tale entitled 'Strong-Minded Miss Methuen', "this country is full of educated young men who have gone hard down hill until reaching the bottom here in the bush. I have come across I can't tell you how many instances up country, of men from our Universities and public schools, living from year's end to year's end in lonely huts, mere boundary-riders and whim-drivers."

It must be remembered that Hornung was a short, dark-haired youth with a slightly foreign name, and a slightly exaggerated self-portrait appears in *The Boss of Taroomba* (1894) when a shy young Englishman called Hermann Engelhardt, with artistic yearnings (and bearing the initials H.E. rather than E.H.), seeks to establish himself among the rugged landscape and its rugged inhabitants. "He was a little bit of a fellow, with long dark hair and dark glowing eyes.... He was a very sensitive young man, with a constitutional desire to please, and an acute horror of making a fool of himself... To get on with older and rougher men was his great difficulty, and one of his ambitions.... [He] had as profound a scorn for himself as any he was likely to meet with from another. His saving grace was the moral courage which enabled him to run counter to his own craven inclinations."

He feared, later, that he had "failed to give signal satisfaction" as a tutor. "He taught us Latin grammar and sentences," he imagined one of his ex-pupils subsequently saying (in a story entitled 'The Poet of Jumping Sandhills'), "and a lot of extraordinary rhymes about Latin genders. I remember some of them still, but I can't say they come in extra handy in the back-blocks." The only retrospective defence he could offer was that, having only just escaped from school himself, he was obliged to teach his pupils something he actually knew.

Having arrived (so he later recalled) "as a hobble-de-hoy in the bush", and initially rather timid of the "supercilious confidence" of the home-grown article, Hornung seized every opportunity to widen his experience that he could. He returned to England in 1886 determined to convey, to his fellow-citizens, some small sense of the delight and wonderment which had overcome him. One is surprised, in fact, that he came home at all: would he not have been better employed, perhaps, in working on one of those vast stations which he would soon be describing so graphically, and helping to muster a herd of wandering sheep? The answer may be found (if we carefully exclude all other considerations, for the moment) in *The Belle of Toorak* (1900), which introduces us to a bespectacled young jackeroo called Ives – an Englishman educated at Rugby and a 'new chum' (i.e., a fresh arrival in Australia, very much a novice) who has been working on a such a station but has reluctantly decided that he is not suited for the life. He escorts Moya, fiancée of his boss,

> along the fluted yellow ribbon miscalled a road, between tufts of sea-green saltbush and far-away clumps of trees.
>
> "I wish I wasn't such a duffer in the bush," said Ives, resolved to make the most of the first lady he had met for months. "The rum thing is that I'm frightfully keen on the life.... It's so open and fresh and free, and unlike everything else; it gets at me to the core; but, of course, they don't give me my rations for that."
>
> "Should you really like to spend all your days here?"
>
> "No, but I shouldn't be surprised if I were to spend half my nights here for the term of my natural life! I shall come back to these paddocks in my dreams. I can't tell why, but I feel it in my bones; it's the light, the smell, the extraordinary sense of space, and all the little things as well. The dust and scuttle of the sheep when two or three are gathered together; it's really beastly, but I shall smell it and hear it till I die."
>
> Moya glanced sidelong at her companion, and all was enthusiasm behind the dusty spectacles. There was something in this new chum after all. Moya wondered what.
>
> "You're not going to stick to it, then?"

Ives laughed.

"I'm afraid it won't stick to me. I can't see sheep, I'm no real good with horses, and I couldn't even keep the station books; the owner said my education had been sadly neglected (one for Rugby, that was!) when he was up here the other day."

(Harry also knows nothing about book-keeping and confesses to a disapproving uncle that maths are his "weakest point".) But the bespectacled Hornung, alias Ives, had become, for all practical purposes, an Anglo-Australian. Clearly, therefore, he *did* work on a sheep station in the Riverina for some months, either at Mossgiel or elsewhere, gathering experiences which would stand him in good stead for the next decade or so. The opening words of a story entitled 'The Luckiest Man in the Colony' probably reflect one such experience:

> That is never a nice moment when your horse knocks up under you, and you know quite well that he has done so, and that to ride him another inch would be a cruelty – another mile a sheer impossibility. But when it happens in the bush, the moment becomes more than negatively disagreeable; for you may be miles from the nearest habitation, and an unpremeditated bivouac, with neither food nor blankets, demands a philosophic temperament as well as the quality of endurance.

Almost certainly, it was in the early summer of 1886 that Hornung arrived back in England. For this is what happens in the second chapter of *At Large* (1902) when Dick Edmonstone, a "reserved and quiet" young man, returns to his native shores after four years in Australia:

> One chilly night in June, 1886, the ship *Hesper*, bound from Melbourne to London, sailed into the Channel. She carried the usual wool cargo and twenty saloon passengers besides. When the Lizard light was sighted, the excitement – which had increased hourly since the Western Islands were left astern – knew no reasonable bounds. For the *Hesper* was a hundred and eight days out, and among the passengers were grizzled Colonists, to whom this light was the first glimmer

of England for thirty years; men who had found in the Colonial Exhibition at South Kensington an excuse to intrust vast flocks and herds to the hands of overseers, and to consumate that darling scheme of every proper Colonial, which they render by their phrase "a trip home". Sweepstakes on the date of sighting England, got up in the tropics, were now promptly settled; quarrels begun in the Southern Ocean were made up in the magic element of British waters; discontent was in irons, and joy held the ship. Far into the middle-watch festive souls perambulated the quarter-deck with noisy expressions of mirth, though with the conviction that the vessel was behaving badly; whereas the vessel was a good deal more innocent of that charge than the gentlemen who preferred it. But even when the last of these roysterers retired there was still one passenger left on the poop.

A young man leaned with folded arms upon the port rail, staring out into the night... This was one of the youngest men on board, and his years of absence from England were but a tithe of some his fellow-passengers.... He allowed no doubts to interfere with the pleasures of anticipation; no fears, no anxieties. If he thought of what might have happened at home during the past four or five months since he had received news, the catalogue of calamities was endless. He did not believe disappointment possible through any sort of a calamity. If those he loved still lived – as he knew they did five or six months ago – then he was sure of his reception; he was sure of hearts and hands; he was sure of his reception from every one – yes, from every one.

The future seemed so splendid and so near! Yet it was giving the future hardly a fair chance to expect as much of it as young Edmonstone expected during the last days of his homeward voyage.

The frame of mind in which Hornung returned home can also be gauged from the opening chapter of *Young Blood*, when Harry Ringrose arrives back in England – for "he had undertaken to be home for his twenty-first birthday" – after spending two years in South Africa:

The last two years of his life had been a joke from beginning to end: for in the name of health he had been really seeking adventure and undergoing the most unnecessary hardships for the fun of talking about them for the rest of his days. He pictured the first dinner-party after his return, and the faces of some dozen old friends when they heard of [his exploits].... They should perceive that the schoolboy they remembered was no longer anything of the sort, but a man of the world who had seen more of it then themselves ... and his mind [was] much too simple to be aware of its own egotism.

He boards the train at Euston and it bears him north, back to the city which he had left two years before:

Miles of green dales rushed past under a network of stone walls, to change soon to mines and quarries, which in their turn developed into furnaces and works, until all at once the sky was no longer blue and the land no longer green.... When he next looked out the train was running in the very shadow of some furnaces in full blast. The morning sun looked cool and pale behind their monstrous fires, and ... [he gazed at] his father's ironworks, though with a rather grim eye, which saw the illuminated squalor of the scene without appreciating its prosperity. Sulphurous flames issued from all four furnaces; at one of the four they were casting as the train passed, and the molten incandescent stream ran white as the wire of an electric light.

After the works came rank upon rank of workmen's streets running right and left of the line; then the ancient and historic quarter of the town, with its granite houses and its hilly streets, all much as it had been a hundred years before the discovery of iron-stone enriched and polluted a fair countryside.

One fancies from this description, if we equate Hornung with Ringrose, that the prospect of settling down in Middlesbrough, after two years in the bush, did not greatly appeal to the young traveller – and that he was anxious to escape to London and make his fame and fortune. And, if he was ready to talk about Australia for the rest of his days, it might be even more rewarding if he could write about it, and make his recollections (enriched by a fertile imagination) pay for his keep.

This is, however, only half the story, for it is necessary to record at this point that Hornung's father, John Peter Hornung, died on 11 November 1886 – and did so in an acute state of poverty. For, despite being described as "Gentleman" on his death certificate, his personal estate amounted to no more than £116 and three shillings. Clearly, something rather dreadful had happened.

In *Young Blood*, Harry Ringrose returns to his native town and is puzzled at being greeted rather coldly by people he had previously regarded as friends. Reaching the family home, however, he is astonished to find it empty and locked up, and very soon after this he learns that his father has fled the land and taken with him the sum of £10,000 outstanding to his creditors. His father, moreover, is an ironmaster – a professional status not far removed from "Iron & Coal Merchant". The theme of errant fathers who bring shame upon their sons is, indeed, a well-worked one in Hornung's subsequent fiction. In 'The Luckiest Man in the Colony' the hero is told by the man himself (albeit unrecognised by his son): "Your father robbed the bank of which he himself was manager. He had lost money in mining speculations." The plot of *Young Blood* itself is, of course, dominated by such a theme, as is *The Belle of Toorak*. "My poor father," says Cazalet in *The Thousandth Woman* (1913), "ought never to have been a business man at all; he should have been a poet."

All this suggests, of course, that Hornung's father had done something rather disgraceful, even though he had not been sent to prison, and had brought the family name into severe disrepute. The trouble was, of course, that it was a rather distinctive family name, for the Hornungs – however plentiful they may have been in Austria or Germany – were at this time very thin on the ground in England. Harry Ringrose reflects, rather bitterly, on the fact that his surname is an uncommon one, certain to stick in the memory, and this is precisely what Hornung must have felt.

In fact, however, Peter John Hornung had been a victim rather than a plotter, although Cazalet's reflections still hold true. What had actually happened was that the North Country iron industry in general had passed through some very difficult times in the 1880s and that Hornung's firm, in particular, had been dealt some very severe blows. "In 1885", wrote his grand-daughter in 1970, "troubles fell thick upon him. Two of the cargo boats belonging to his firm, boats that carried iron ore and pit props between the Tees and Norway or Hamburg, were lost at sea. About the same time he discovered that his partner, having defrauded him of a large sum of money, had absconded to South America with the proceeds. This double blow was more than his business could stand, and he found himself bankrupt."

Pitt, accompanied by his pregnant wife and baby daughter, had hurried over from Lisbon at the end of 1885 to take charge, for his father's health was now in so poor a state that the elder John Peter could no longer cope with the situation. A purchaser was found for Erdely in the spring of 1886 and Pitt moved the family as far away from the scene of disaster as he could. Fifteen years earlier he had attended a boarding school at Hampton Wick, which was an area that he was thus familiar with, and he now bought them all a house at 49 Waldegrave Park Road, near Strawberry Hill in Twickenham. Into this house he crammed his parents, his sisters Bertha and Ida, his wife and (now) their *two* babies, and a Portuguese maid. This was the state of affairs that confronted Willie on his return to England.

Young Blood gets off to a dramatic start, with the young hero arriving home to discover a family mansion that is shuttered and deserted. But it seems quite possible that, in reality, Hornung did not return to Middlesbrough at all (although his brother Charles was still there) but came to grips with the situation as soon as his boat had docked at Blackwall. Young Edmonstone, in *At Large*, is met by his brother the moment he arrives and the fact that his family is now living in straitened circumstances is, clearly, no surprise to him. (Despite the portentous final paragraphs quoted above, the only disappointment that awaits him is that his girl friend, with a rival suitor in the offing, is less excited by his return than he had expected.) He delights his mother, sister and brother by presenting them with some splendid souvenirs of his trip, much as Hornung must have delighted his own family: "There was a famous rug of Tasmanian opossum skins, a dozen emu eggs, the skin of an immense carpet-snake, a deadly collection of boomerangs and spears, and a necklace of quandong stones mounted with silver."

Hornung remarks more than once, in *At Large*, on how wet and cold it was in England in June 1886 and he wastes no time in sending his hero off to South Kensington, where the Colonial Exhibition had just begun:

> When he was in the vast place, and had found his way to the Australian section, his interest speedily rose to a high pitch. It is one thing to go to an exhibition to be instructed, or to wonder what on earth half the things are; it is something quite different to find yourself among familiar objects and signs which are not Greek to you, to thread corridors lined with curios which you hail as the household gods of your exile. Instead of the bored outsider, with his shallow appreciation of everything, you become at once a discriminate observer and intelligent critic, and sightseeing for once loses its tedium. Dick wandered from aisle to aisle, from stand to stand, in rapt attention. At every turn he found something of peculiar interest to him: here it was a view of some township whose every stick he knew by heart; there a sample of wood bearing on the printed label under the glass the name of a sheep station where he had stayed time out of number.
>
> The golden arch at the entrance to the Victorian court arrested him, as it arrested all the world; but even more fascinating in his eyes was the case of model nuggets close at hand.... [And a highlight of the Australian section, the Settler's Hut,] was a most realistic property, with its strips of bark and its bench and wash basin.

These sound like personal recollections. It is fairly safe to assume, therefore, that five months elapsed between Hornung's return to England and the death of his father from heart disease, degeneration of the kidney and general anascara – i.e., dropsy – at the age of sixty-five. What we do not know, of course, is whether he moved into the house in Waldegrave Park Road in the very first instance or whether he stayed elsewhere for a while. Clearly, the Hornungs' modest residence to the south-west of London would have been packed out for a time, which may explain the contemptuous tones in which the current home of Dick's impoverished family is described:

> The Edmonstones lived in a plain little house in a road at Teddington, in which all the houses were little, plain and uniformly alike. They called their house 'The Pill Box'; but that was a mere nickname, since all the houses in that plain little road were fearfully and wonderfully christened, and theirs no exception to the rule. Its name – blazoned on the little wooden gate – was Iris Lodge.... [Initially, the Edmonstones had not taken kindly] to road or house. And naturally, since five years ago, before Mr Edmonstone's death, they had lived in a great, square, charming villa.... But then Richard Edmonstone senior had dropped dead, at the height of his reputed success on the Stock Exchange, and of his undoubted popularity in the clubs. To the surprise of all but those who knew him most intimately, he had left next to nothing behind him ... [and the family] had bundled into as small a house as they could find in the neighbourhood.

In reality, Mr Hornung Senior delayed dropping dead until after the Hornung family had been bundled into the Waldegrave Park Road residence. This would have made a mite more space. In the summer of 1887 there was a fresh arrival on the scene, in the shape of Pitt and Laura's third child, but later in 1887 Pitt took his wife and children back to Lisbon, to live with his sister-in-law, while he himself went on to Portuguese East Africa to explore the various possibilities that might be pursued in the vicinity of Mopea. He and his family returned to the Twickenham house in the spring of 1889, by which time he was fired with the idea of growing sugar there. By January 1890 he had succeeded in floating the *Companhia do Assucar de Moçambique (C.A.M.)*, backed by friends and the Banco Lusitano, and in August 1890 Pitt and his family left England for a second time, with Bertha accompanying them to Africa as a companion for Laura.

The overcrowding at Waldegrave Park Road was eased after the first year, therefore, and whatever his initial feelings of chagrin might have been Hornung had an opportunity to settle down and became acquainted with the areas of Twickenham, Richmond, Teddington and Bushey Park, which feature in some of his books, and with Hampton Court and Richmond Park. Living in wondrous proximity to a picturesque stretch of the Thames, he would have picnicked on Eel Pie Island and strolled, from time to time, along the banks of the River Mole.

The playful opening paragraph of another Raffles story, 'A Bad Night', refers to the forthcoming marriage between a "bride elect living in some retirement, with a recently widowed mother, and an asthmatical brother, in a mellow hermitage on the banks of the Mole" – for Ida, at thirty-three, had become engaged to a clergyman from Blyth, Walter St John Field, whom she married on 27 April 1892. One suspects that Willie would not have been a permanent resident at Waldegrave Park Road by this time, for the indications are that by the early 1890s he had acquired some cheap lodgings in London (and his independence). But there would doubtless have been a bed for him there at weekends or at any other time prior to April 1892.

Thereafter the remnants of the family broke up and the Twickenham house was sold. Mrs Hornung took a flat in London and Willie may have lived with her there for a time, just as Harry Ringrose lives with *his* mother in *Young Blood*. Bertha joined her in 1894, after accompanying Pitt and his family in Lisbon. Later, Mrs Hornung returned to Middlesbrough, where she died in 1896. She was, writes Mrs Collin (Pitt's daughter), "a typical Victorian both in appearance and character. She wore stiff corded dresses of black or grey, with lighter richly embroidered panels down the front. Indoors, like the Queen herself, she wore an exquisite white tulle hat with allpets to the waist. A rather severe old lady, she was more respected than loved by Pitt's children".

In *The Unbidden Guest* (1894), Hornung would pen a description of the formidable wife of the weak-willed, improvident David Teesdale (and mother of John William, as distinct from John Peter) which owes something, perhaps, to the character of Harriet Hornung:

> Mrs Teesdale was a tall, striking woman who at sixty struck one first of all with all her strength, activity, and hard, solid pluck. Her courage and her hardness too were written in every wrinkle of a bloodless, weather-beaten face that must have been sharp and pointed even in girlhood; and those same dominant qualities shone continuously in a pair of eyes like cold steel – the eyes of a woman who had never given in. The woman had not the husband's heart full of sympathy and affection for all but the very worst who came his way. She had neither his moderately good education, nor his immoderately ready and helping hand even for the worst. Least of all had she his simple but adequate sense of humour; of this quality and all its illuminating satellites Mrs Teesdale was totally devoid. Yet, but for his wife, old David would probably have found himself facing his latter end at one or other of the Benevolent Asylums of that Colony; whereas with the wife's character inside the husband's skin, it is not improbable that the name of David Teesdale would have been known and honoured in the land where his days had been long indeed, but sadly unprofitable.

The Teesdales, like the Hornungs (and as the references to 'Tees' and 'dales' indicate), are a Yorkshire family. The action of *The Unbidden Guest* is set, unobtrusively but very carefully, in the year 1883. In it, Mrs Teesdale objects very strongly to the girl John William is proposing to marry. Could it be that Mrs Hornung had objected, in 1883, to John Peter's desire to wed a girl from Portugal, however illustrious her family?

It is reassuring to note, incidentally, that the wretched financial straits of John Peter Hornung at the time of his death would be in no way reflected in the fortunes of his sons. Theodore, another ironmaster, would leave £34,876 in December 1927, while the second John Peter Hornung ('Pitt') would become a country gentleman, the owner of West Grinstead Park in Horsham, Sussex, and leave £293,795 when *he* shuffled off the mortal coil in February 1940. Charles, surviving until 1952, would leave effects totalling £17,817. Ernest William Hornung, by comparison, would leave the more modest sum of £11,907 in March 1921, and the question of what he did to earn that money (plus the respect and affection of a few million readers) will be considered in the pages that follow.

2

DÉBUT

HORNUNG had realised, by the late 1880s, that he had a natural talent for writing fiction, for spinning a yarn which (all being well) would hold the attention of a vast range of readers – and if he could quietly educate them in the process, why then all well and good. He would act as a bridge between the mother country and her gigantic offspring on the opposite side of the globe. He was in the unique position, among the writing fraternity of that day and age, of having a foot in both camps – and this would prove to be, in a sense, his personal trademark, or 'gimmick'. Certainly, there was a great deal of ignorance about the offspring among his contemporaries: "colonial geography," noted Hornung in 1912, "unlike that of Ancient Greece, was not then a recognised item in the public-school curriculum."

But how, exactly, did he did develop into an author? M.R. Ridley tells us that, on his return to England, "he resolved to devote his time to journalism". According to Peter Haining, he was "particularly attracted to the subjects of social conditions and crime" and "most of his early writings appeared anonymously in London newspapers and journals, including the *Cornhill Magazine* and *Temple Bar*".

In an early short story entitled 'An Idle Singer' we encounter a young writer called Bertram Adeane, who, at the age of twenty-two, has a job on a slightly disreputable comic magazine and lives in what we would now call a bed-sitter. "He was at this time beating round the financial Horn, and not yet out of dangerous waters; in fact, his income was trembling between two and three figures a year. He was a literary freelance, and more or less a poet; more by inclination, by necessity less. At present he could afford to mix very little verse with his assorted prose. Verse supplied but a doubtful tithe of that extremely doubtful hundred a year. On the other hand, more than half of his income was derived from [the magazine]."

Adeane is almost certainly a fictionalised version of Hornung himself. Certainly, Hornung wrote poetry, and sometimes quotes the odd verse or two in the context of his stories albeit in disparaging tones. He tells us, feelingly, of the creative difficulties experienced by young poets. "It is one thing to get a poem into your head, and another to get it out again on paper. The fitting together of any form of verse is the soul-possessing employment to be found; but its hard and fast requirements render the sonnet the greatest strain of all." Two hours' hard work might result, if one were lucky, in a cheque for ten shillings and sixpence. But Adeane, like Hornung himself, does not pursue his poetry in a true spirit of dedication. "He had neither the qualification nor the temperament of a professional prophet. He was no Thinker; he could simply sing.... He was a minor poet to the marrow; he never tried to be anything better."

Turning to *Young Blood* for an alternative fictionalised account, we find that Harry, at the age of twenty-one, has joined his widowed mother in London and is hard pressed to find a job. His handwriting and maths are poor, which disqualifies him for office work, and he doesn't have the necessary experience to qualify for a decent teaching post. But his mother reminds him that he had shown, while at school, a talent for writing – and, in particular, for writing pastiches – and a girl to whom he holds forth about his African experiences urges him to write them down. Inspiration of another kind strikes, and he pens a poem and sends it to a magazine. It is accepted, for (once again) the princely sum of half-a-guinea. He pens some more. They are rejected. He then tries his hand at writing a factual account of one of his African experiences, but this too is rejected.

Momentarily losing heart, he takes no further action until purchasing, for a railway journey and for the sum of one penny "a comic paper with considerable vogue" which contains "a number of sets of intentionally droll verses on topics of the week". Harry sends in some comical verses of his own, they are accepted by the editor, and he becomes a regular contributor. This brings him ten to fifteen shillings a week. The fictional name of this journal is *Tommy Tiddler*: presumably the magazine in question (assuming that this is a genuine account of how Hornung's career started) was *Ally Sloper*, which had been going strong since 1867 Thereafter, presumably, one thing led to another, although it is always conceivable that Hornung (like his alter ego) did indeed do a spot of teaching in a rather poor-quality prep school until his career was properly established.

He came of age in the year of Queen Victoria's Silver Jubilee. It is tempting for Hornung's biographer to assume that his subject was proud to be British – and proud, too, of being a member of that far-flung governing race on whose Empire the sun never set. But his ancestry was East European and there is, it must be confessed, a notable absence of strident Imperialist sentiments in Hornung's books. (Raffles, admittedly, would celebrate Queen Victoria's Diamond Jubilee in 1897 but in a spirit of light-heartedness rather than veneration.) Hornung certainly wrote adventures stories set in Australia, because this was a place which fired his imagination, but his fiction was never of the *Boy's Own Paper*, gung-ho variety.

During this year, and the two that followed, he must have been honing his skills, in unsigned articles which passed into kindly obscurity well over a century ago. But from articles he moved to short stories, of which some at any rate would *not* be forgotten, and it was now that he seems to have mapped out a conscious plan of campaign for the future. It would be his mission to narrate, in the main, tales of Englishmen plonked down in Australia, just as he himself had been, and (conversely) of Australians plucked from their native surroundings and brought back to the old country. The two civilisations, ostensibly so different from one another, would be seen through the puzzled eyes of immigrants. There would be some comical clashes, some misunderstandings, and, ultimately, some emotional reconciliations. And, quite often, the Australian hearty and the well-bred Englishman would find common ground in despising the Dago and the Jew.

"So far as his writing methods were concerned," a nephew and godson (Brigadier Foley) would later be quoted as saying, "he took great pains over checking and correcting manuscripts which were all written in full in his neat hand."

Hornung's very first book, *A Bride from the Bush*, is an assured, graceful comedy of manners. It was published by Smith, Elder & Co. in October 1890 (after being serialised by them in *The Cornhill Magazine*), when the author was only twenty-four years old. Into the genteel household of Sir James Bligh, an intensely dignified judge, his sweet-tempered wife, and his supercilious second son Granville, a young barrister, there suddenly returns his eldest son, Alfred, bringing with him the girl whom he has met, wooed and married in Australia at breakneck speed – an Amazon of a woman, whose twang and slang grate dreadfully on the nerves of her hosts. Gladys is immensely good-looking but takes some getting used to. Her boisterous high spirits, her unrestrained praise of all things Australian and her lukewarm attitude towards most things English, and an episode in which she brandishes a stock-whip to startling effect, leave her husband's family rather dazed. Throughout most of the book she is constantly referred to as "the Bride", in much the same way as Mary Shelley might have referred to her most famous creation as "the Monster". Realising, after a time, how much she is distressing her hosts and embarrassing her husband, she falls silent. Her relations with her in-laws gradually improve, but then comes a crowning incident in Hyde Park when she brings irrevocable shame upon them. For, from an elegant carriage parked near Rotten Row, and despite the presence of Royalty (to whom she remains oblivious) she spots an old Australian acquaintance riding past and lets out a deafening cry of "Coo-ee!" before leaping out and charging after her. This, alas, is the most heinous of all her misdeeds. The family return home in silence and her extraordinary behaviour is the talk of fashionable London. Dreadfully aware of her shortcomings, overhearing some contemptuous remarks by Granville, and convinced that Alfred would be better off without her, Gladys decides to make herself scarce by faking her suicide and heading back to Australia to be a boundary-rider on a sheepfarm (closely akin to becoming a lighthouse keeper or joining the ladies' branch of the Foreign Legion). But her distraught husband, following some enquiries by a moderately-repentant Granville, sets off in hot pursuit and they are reunited in the midst of a sandstorm. They decide to remain in Australia (which is, so Alfred writes to his mother, "a bigger and a better Britain" with a perfect climate) and all ends happily.

It was, for such a young author, a marvellously cool, calm and accomplished production. Primarily a comedy, but with a spot of drama and a dollop of pathos thrown in, and with sympathetic, well-rounded characters, Hornung displayed an admirably deft touch. Not a word had been wasted. He plunged his readers into the story without a moment's hesitation, held their attention from start to finish, brought his tale to a speedy conclusion and left them wanting more.

And more was speedily forthcoming.

Before moving on to consider *The Bride*'s successors, however, it is necessary to take note of Harry's account of how his first book came to be published. For he makes it clear that his first book was really not produced quite so effortlessly as it seems to the reader. It had been the fruits of many hours' work at his desk, with only his mother present to encourage him, and time and again it had been sent off to publishers and time and again it had been returned. Their flat had no knocker, so the postman's ring at the bell, before he thrust a letter through the door, was, for both of them, a moment of tension. Harry Ringrose developed an incredibly fine ear for what came through. He was never deceived in the thud of a rejected manuscript. He used to vow that a proof fell with peculiar softness, and, later, that a press-cutting was unmistakable because you could not hear it fall. He had an essay on the subject in his second book, published when he was twenty-five.

His first book had been one of the minor successes of its season. It had made a small, a very small, name for Harry, but had developed his character more than his fame. It is an ominous coincidence, however, that in conception his first book was as barefaced and as cold-blooded as his first [published] verses....

For nearly three years he had been writing up, for as many guineas as possible, those African anecdotes which he had brought home with him for conversational purposes. In this way he had wasted much excellent material, to which, however, he was not too proud to return when he knew better.... One would have thought – he thought himself – that he had squeezed the last drop from his African orange, when one fine day he saw the way to make the pulp pay better than the juice. It was not his his own way. It was the way of the greatest humorist then living. Harry took the whole of his two years abroad, and eyed them afresh from that humorist's point of view, as he apprehended it. He saw the things the great man would have seized upon, and the way it seemed to Harry he would have treated them. The result was a [more light-hearted production].....

The book ... earned him an ambiguous compliment from various reviewers who insisted on dubbing him the English So-and-so; but it was lucky for Harry that the new humour was then an unmade phrase. His humour was not new, but that would not have saved it from the category. It was keen enough, however, in its way, and not too desperately subtle for the man on the knifeboard. Yet Harry's first book, after "going" for a few weeks, showed a want of staying power, and was but a very moderate success after all. A few papers hailed Mr Ringrose as the humorist for whom England had been sighing since the death of Charles Dickens, and predicted that his book would be the book of the season and of many seasons to come. Such enthusiasm was inevitable from organs which let loose at least one genius a week; but

Harry did not realise the inevitability all at once. For a week or two he could not give his name in a shop without a wholly unnecessary blush; while he took his mother to look at empty houses in West End squares, thanks to indiscriminate praise from irresponsible quarters. On the whole, however, Harry had no reason to complain of the treatment accorded to his first-born; and, to descend to lower details, he sold the copyright for a small sum, which was, nevertheless, quite as much as the publishers could possibly have made out of it.

The reviews for *A Bride from the Bush* had indeed been encouraging. "This is a delightful little work," declared the *Daily News*, "freshly conceived, freshly written, with a heroine so rarely piquant that every reader must fall head over heels in love with her." The *Daily Graphic* found it "clever and animated, bright and amusing, [steering] admirably clear of the commonplace" while the *Glasgow Herald* thought the characters "clearly and firmly drawn, the incidents well chosen, and the dialogue clever and characteristic.... Mr Hornung's style possesses distinction and grace." These words must have been music to the young author's ears. And there were, moreover, the august sentiments of the *Court Journal* to revel in. "There is something", it proclaimed, "very pathetic in the story of the big-hearted, beautiful, blundering girl, whose society shortcomings and personal charm are described so cleverly in Mr E.W. Hornung's capital tale.... The loyal love of her husband for his beautiful, uncultured wife, the dignified kindliness of the old Judge, the cynicism of the smart young barrister brother, and the motherly solicitude of Lady Bligh, are all admirably done; and the volume is not only thoroughly readable, but written in a kind, manly tone, which is refreshing and wholesome to a degree." Mr Hornung had, in short, made quite an impression.

But it was in indirect ways [continues *Young Blood*] that this book did most for [its author]. It made new friends for him at a time when his acquaintance was badly in need of some fresh blood. Years of immersion in solitary work must narrow and may warp a man; and the almost exclusive companionship of his dear mother ... tended to monopolise his sympathies, and it did not increase his knowledge of the outside world....

His book was not a huge success, but it succeeded well enough to take him out of his corner.... It cannot be said, however, that he did anybody much credit; he had been too long in his corner, and had an awkward manner when not perfectly at home. Yet a number of [society] ladies asked him to go and see them, and one of them invited him to dinner at her smart house – where the wretched Harry distinguished himself by freezing into a solid block of self-consciousness and hardly opening his mouth.

But it was all very valuable experience, and, instead of two or three, he knew a good many people by the end of that winter. He became a member of a club, and got on intimate terms with men whose names and work had become familiar to him in these years. They enlarged his sympathies – they extended his boundaries on every side. And they made him know himself as he had not known himself before. All at once he realised that he had fewer interests than other men, that his nose had been too close to his own grindstone, that the mind he had been slaving to develop had grown narrow in the process.

Harry's books, we gather, purport to be fact rather than fiction, and his second is actually a collection of essays, but there is a ring of truth about this passage which – after mentally converting Africa into Australia – Hornung's biographer ignores at his peril. His subject's second book, it is scarcely necessary to mention, was published when he was still twenty-five (albeit well advanced into his twenty-sixth year). Most certainly, it was during the early 1890s that he became acquainted with Dr Arthur Conan Doyle, a prolific contributor to the *Strand* magazine and the creator of Sherlock Holmes. There is, moreover, that reference to the unnamed "greatest humorist then living" which it will be necessary to bear in mind.

Writing in 1892, making a candid assessment of Betram Adeane in 'An Idle Singer', Hornung presents what would appear to be a reasonably fair appraisal of himself:

He was self-centred, but not self-seeking: he was hard-working, and wonderfully persevering, though in many ways weak; and if he was not always quite admirable, he was very lovable – which is something. It is true he had lofty ideals which he made an enormous effort to realise, and principles which he did not exert himself to live up to personally ... but for all that there was good in Adeane, quite apart from his brains.... [Contemporaries thought he] must have known that there was freshness in his stuff. He did know it; only he was such an excessively modest young man. He heard that this also was being said about him, and the rumour amused his vanity.

And Adeane, like Harry Ringrose, is going up in the world:

He was enticed from his lodgings – which now consisted of two rooms – into certain drawing rooms further west. There his eyes were opened to many things – first of all to himself. He simply amazed himself by taking rather kindly to society, for all his life he had spoken of it with the loftiest scorn. His ignorant poet's prejudices died a violent death. He had his eyes opened, which did him good.

Two of the new acquaintances whom he made at this time can be identified. Both were Irish. The first, Frederick Whyte, was an editorial assistant at Cassells and approximately his own age. The second was Richard Dowling, a journalist and novelist twenty years older than himself who had written a number of romances and mystery stories, mainly of the three-decker variety, but who never became particularly well-known. According to Whyte, he was "a kindly and witty Irishman" who served as Hornung's "guide and mentor" in his earliest days but whose own career remained in the doldrums long after his pupil's triumphant début. Hornung dedicated *The Rogue's March* to him in September 1896 and acknowledged "his very kindly assistance" in the Preface to that book. Dowling died in 1898, but he may have been one of those responsible, almost ten years earlier, for enticing Willie Hornung from his humble lodgings into circles of a more select nature – particularly those of the literary Irish, of whom a good number were then resident in London. The house of

Fitzgerald Molloy, who knew virtually all of them, was a well-established venue for their gatherings. ("Met about a dozen men at Molloy's," George Bernard Shaw noted in his diary on 14 September 1886, "all strangers to me except Oscar Wilde and Dowling.")

"One of the earliest tributes to Hornung's success", Whyte recalled in 1931, "took the form of a suggestion from a woman novelist, then well known, now forgotten, that he and she should collaborate. Her letter, which was a great joy to him, contained the phrase that launched him as a lecturer on 'The Wrong Word'. He got together, in the course of time, a wonderful collection of specimens, but never anything again quite so good. 'I feel", wrote this lady, 'that my own novels are lacking in ballast, a quality in which yours abound.'" One assumes, since Whyte does not choose to be more explicit, that this is what the lady had *intended* to write but that her spelling of "ballast" had fallen short by a letter or two.

3

FOLLOW-ONS

HORNUNG's second book, published by A. & C. Black in 1892, was a collection of seven short stories and ran to about 60,000 words. It was entitled *Under Two Skies*, a conscious nod in the direction of Ouida's *Under Two Flags* (1867), and the skies in question (for anyone in doubt) were those of Britain and Australia.

The first tale, 'Jim-of-the-Whim' (an echo of Stevenson's 'Will o' the Mill'), was a sad little love story set in Australia, dealing with the irrevocable misunderstanding which resulted from a letter being opened when it should not have been. Jim's eyes, we may note in passing, were "slightly sunken, but extremely blue" and the eyes of Edward Nettleship, the unscrupulous hero of the second tale, "were blue, and keen, and searching". 'Nettleship's Score' introduces us to an embryonic Raffles, for Edward Nettleship is a well-known amateur cricketer but very hard up. At the 'Varsity match at Lords between Oxford and Cambridge he scores, for the former (which he had left the previous year), ninety-nine runs – "a record all to himself, for ninety-nine is the rarest of scores". Tremendous applause follows him as he leaves the field and returns to his seedy lodgings. A sharp-witted, cynical young man, he impishly discovers a chink in the armour of his beloved's formidable, hostile mother: her bowling is deadly, but he knocks her for six and thus gains access to the wealthy family of his choice.

In the third tale, 'The Luckiest Man in the Colony', we are back in Australia and encounter a theme which would dominate one of Hornung's novels (*The Belle of Toorak*) eight years later, namely that of a young man who has done well for himself but has a convict for a father: should the secret become known, then his prospects of a happy life will be ruined. Deverell, in this story, is lucky: his father, released from prison, comes in search of him but goes sadly away without revealing his identity, once he realises what an embarrassment his presence would be to his son.

'The Notorious Miss Anstruther' is set in England but with a faint Australian connection. The young lady in question is notorious for having rejected the proposals of a long line of suitors, after apparently leading them on, but she is really rather fond of the very first man she rejected, who had gone out to Australia to seek solace – and who she suddenly learns, after thinking wistfully of him, has been killed by a buck-jumper (a bucking bronco). Then comes, as a companion piece, 'Strong-Minded Miss Methuen', concerning the daughter of an English canon who has accepted "the least tempting of the Australian bishoprics". She is disdainful about most of the colonials she encounters but falls in love with the curate, a reformed alcoholic bushranger, which rather alarms her father: sent away to wealthy friends in Sydney for six months, to think things over, she becomes engaged to a wholesale manufacturer of jewellery. Jubilant, she comes home and jilts the curate. The latter turns white, abandons his clerical garb, goes back to the bush and drinks himself to death, much to the archbishop's horror.

'An Idle Singer' (set in London) charts the romance between the poet Bertram Adeane and a lady novelist, which encounters one or two rocks but comes right in the end. 'Sergeant Seth', based firmly in Australia, tells how the hero of this final tale is jilted by the girl he loves, how she in turn is jilted by the young Englishman who has supplanted him, how they finally come together and how the young Englishman (secretly returning to the scene of his misdeeds, having repented of his action, and determined to do the honourable thing) tiptoes away when he realises the latest state of play.

More than a century later, the stories still carry a remarkable freshness and some of them are, indeed, quite riveting – although one or two, it must be conceded, come perilously close to melodrama. Whether these were *all* the stories that Hornung had written for magazines at this time, or whether they were simply the best of the bunch, must remain a matter for speculation.

Written, once again, in a calm, confident and pleasantly detached manner, Hornung's second book attracted an even greater outpouring of praise than its predecessor. It was, as before, the freshness of his material that appealed. The *Daily Telegraph* referred to his "rich natural gift of narrative and description, as well as a pleasant vein of humour": every one of his stories, it declared, was "absolutely free from conventionality and affectation". "Mr Hornung", proclaimed the *Manchester Guardian*, "never fails to be bright and full of flavour. He has the artist's eye for things half-hidden in the background." Its rival, the *Manchester Examiner*, thought the stories attained "a very high standard of artistic excellence and literary worth" while the *Scottish Leader* decided that there was "as much skill in his reserve as there is freshness in his candour". And, from afar, the *Melbourne Argus* hailed them as "very good stories... especially 'Jim-of-the-Whim' and 'Sergeant Seth' – perhaps the best that have been written of Australian life, without exaggeration, with abundance of humour and pathos, and in a style which is pure and simple English".

A Bride from the Bush had run to approximately 45,000 words. Hornung's second novel, *Tiny Luttrell*, published in 1893, totalled approximately 80,000, and Cassells, his latest publishers, decided to issue it in two volumes. It is, in many respects, a rather curious tale for a man to have written: some of the early chapters, reminiscent of *Persuasion*, could well have been penned by a latter-day Jane Austen, while subsequent portions have a distinct touch of Ouida about them. At one point, admittedly, we seem to be gliding into *Portrait of a Lady*, but James is soon thrust aside by Edith Wharton.

And here, for the first time, it is possible to detect the influence of Thackeray (underlined, admittedly, by the fact that Tiny finds *The Newcomes* absorbing) – and also, perhaps, that of Trollope. Not only does Hornung periodically buttonhole the reader in amiable conversation, quite outside the scene of the action, but it is also clear that he is developing a predilection for the English nobility. Some of the upper crust had, admittedly, hovered in the background of *A Bride from the Bush*, and two or three Members of Parliament have had walk-on parts in his fiction prior to this date, but the presence of Lord Nunthorp in 'The Notorious Miss Anstruther' alerts one (retrospectively, at any rate) to the fact that Hornung rather liked the peerage. (It is better to draw a veil, on the other hand, over his laboured attempt to portray Bertram Adeane's cockney landlady.) By the third chapter of *Tiny Luttrell* we are at a ball given by Lady Almeric, and Lord Manister – who had wooed Tiny during his visit to Australia the previous year – takes up centre stage for much of the subsequent action.

In essence, the story is a simple one. Christina (or 'Tiny') Lutttrell, the daughter of a wealthy sheepfarmer, has been wooed by Lord Manister (aide-de-camp to the Governor-General) before the curtain rises, but his mother had summoned him back to England on learning of his attachment. Tiny and her brother Herbert pay a visit to the old country, staying with their sister Ruth and her husband, and her path once again crosses (by her sister's artful design) that of Lord Manister. His lordship woos her afresh, and his mother is impressed by her, but Tiny – having led him on by all the coquetry at her disposal – takes her revenge by brutally turning him down: and in front of his mother, too! Revenge is less sweet than expected, however, and when Manister pursues the family to Portugal she agrees to reconsider her rejection. But, while tempted, she decides that she doesn't really love him, and returns to Australia with her brother when he is sent down from Cambridge. On her father's sheep-station at Wallandoon she is proposed to, for the second time, by the *other* man in her life, Jack Swift, the manager of the station, and this time – when he adopts a masterful tone – she succumbs.

The tale begins and ends in Australia, but 85% of the action takes place in England and 5% in Portugal. The leading characters (especially Tiny herself) are well-drawn, and there is an element of suspense and uncertainty that persists until the very end of the tale, but it is very much a woman's book and marks, for Hornung, a distinct departure from his usual manner and *locale*. Clearly, he wanted to display his prowess in romance and psychological insight as well as in humour. (Some rather curious incidents, not strictly relevant to the main plot, will be considered elsewhere.) But it must be acknowledged that *Tiny Luttrell* contains some splendid descriptions. Here, for instance, are the two sisters relaxing in St James's Park in the early evening:

> They sat down with their eyes towards the pale traces of a gentle undemonstrative September sunset, and were silent. Already the lamps were lighted in the Mall, where the trees were tanned and tattered by the change and fall of the leaf; at each end of the bridge, too, the lamps were lighted and reflected below in palpitating pillars of fire; and every moment all the lights burnt brighter. Eastward a bluish haze mellowed trees and chimneys, making them seem more distant than they were; the noise of the traffic seemed more distant still, but it floated inward from the four corners, like the breaking of waves upon an islet; and here in the midst of it the stillness was strange, and certainly charming: only Tiny was immoderately charmed. She sat so long without speaking that Ruth leant back and watched her curiously. Her face was raised to the pale pink sky, with wide-open eyes and tight-shut lips, as though the desires of her soul were written out in the tinted haze, as you may scratch with your finger in the bloom of a plum. She never spoke until the next quarter rang out from Westminster and was lingering in the quiet air, when she said, "Why have we never done this before, Ruth?"

CঙৎৎO

Very wistfully her eyes wandered over the fading sky. The thin floating clouds, fast disappearing in the darkness, were not less vague than her desires, and not more lofty. Her soul was tugging at a chain that had been too seldom taut.... Then the sights and sounds of the place came suddenly home to Christina, and her eyes fell. A pleasure-boat villainously rowed passed with hoarse shouts through the pillar of fire below the bridge, and left it writhing. Her eyes as she lowered them were greeted with the smarting smoke of a cigar, and her nostrils with the smell that priced it. The smoker took a neighbouring chair, or rather two, for he was not without his companion.

And the magic is broken. A couple of pages on, and there is an even more masterly description, for Hornung had evidently visited Portugal (the native land of his sister-in-law) in the not-too-distant past:

There is in Cintra a good specimen of the purely Portuguese hotel, which is worth a trial if you can speak the language of the country and eat its meats. If you want to feel as much abroad as you are, this is the spot to promote that sensation. The whole concern is engagingly indigenous. They will give you a dinner of which every course (there must be nearly twenty) has the twofold charm of novelty and mystery combined; and you shall dine in a room where it is safe (if unsportsmanlike) to criticise aloud your fellow-diners, when their ways are most notably not your ways. Then after dinner you may make music in a pleasant drawing-room, or saunter in the quaint garden behind the hotel; only remember that the garden has a view, which is necessarily lost at night.

The view is good, and it improves as the day wears on, by reason of the beetling crag that stands between Cintra and the morning sun. So close is this crag to the town, and so sheer, that at dawn it looms the highest mountain on earth; but with the afternoon sunlight streaming on its face you see it for what it is, and there is much in the sight to satisfy the eye. Half-way up, the vast wall is forested with fir-trees, picked out with bright villas, and streaked with the white lines of ascending roads. The upper portion is of granite, rugged and bare and iron-gray. The topmost angle is surmounted by square towers and battlements that seem a part of the peak, as indeed they are, since the Moors who made them hewed the stones from the spot; and the serrated crest notches the sky like a crown on a hoary head. Finer effects may recur very readily to the travelled eye, but to one too used to flat regions this is fine enough.

Next day, the travellers climb this crag:

Low parapets were continually on their left, high walls on their right; and wherever there was a gap in the fir-trees growing below the parapets, a fresh view was presented of the town below. First it was a bird's eye view of the palace, seen to better advantage through the trees of the Rua do Duque Saldanha than before from the street; then a fair impression of the town as a whole, with its gay gardens and cheap-looking stuccoed houses; and then successive editions of Cintra, each one smaller than the last, and each with a wider tract of undulating brown land beyond, and a broader band of ocean at the horizon. They then plunged into mountain gorges; there were no more distant views, but mighty walls on either side and reddening foliage interlacing overhead, as though woven upon the strip of pure blue sky. And the atmosphere was clear as distilled water in a crystal vessel; but in the shade the air had a sweet keenness, an inspiriting pungency, under whose influence the enthusiasm of the party grew inevitably eloquent in the praises of Portugal....

The ascent, however, was steep enough to touch the breath, and conversation was for some minutes neither a pleasure nor a necessity. Then, above the firs, the palace of Pena reared hoary head and granite shoulders; for, like the ruined fort visible from the town below, the palace is built upon the summit of a rock. Still a steeper climb, and the party stood looking down upon the fir-trees which had just shadowed them, with their backs to the palace walls, that seem, and often are, a part of the rugged peak itself. For this is a palace not only founded on a rock, and on the rock's topmost crag, but the foundation has itself supplied so many features ready-made that Nature and the Moors may be said to have collaborated in its making.

But Hornung was also capable of unexpected banality on one or two occasions. Thus, at a garden party given by Lady Dromard, we encounter the following description:

The party of three wandered towards the band, admiring the scarlet coats of the bandsmen against the dark green of the shrubbery, and their bright brass instruments flaming in the sun. The music, also, was of much spirit and gaiety, and it was agreed that a band was an immense improvement to a rite of this sort.

But such passages, which could have been lifted direct from *The Young Visiters*, are mercifully rare.

The critics, on the whole, were again quite impressed. "[*Tiny Luttrell*]", enthused the *Westminster Gazette*, "is admirably told, and Tiny herself, with her swiftly varying moods, running through all the changes from cynicism to enthusiasm, is a study of the first order. Excellent, too, in their way are her sister Ruth, with her husband, and the young barbarian Herbert. Whether the scene is laid in Australia or England, Mr Hornung is at home." The *Daily Telegraph* found Tiny "a charming incorporation of contradictions and inconsistencies" and the book as a whole "in every respect worthy of its precursors". The *Bristol Mercury* thought it "a most artistic story", occupying "ground on which the author has no rival", and the critic of the *Weekly Sun* proclaimed that it was "a long time since we have read a novel so enthralling in its interest and so sprightly in movement".

Most if not all of Hornung's stories were featured or serialised in English periodicals before being published in hardback. *A Bride from the Bush*, for example, was serialised in the *Cornhill Magazine* from July until November 1890, and 'Nettleship's Score' had appeared in its January issue earlier that same year. But his fame had now spread even further afield than the British Isles, for a preparatory note to his *next* novel, *The Boss of Taroomba*, published by Bliss, Sands and Foster in 1894, explained that "at least a third of this tale has appeared already in a Christmas Number of *The Detroit Free Press*" but that the remainder was now published for the first time. Taroomba is a sheep-station and its boss, almost inevitably, is a girl – Naomi Pryse, who had inherited it from her father a year or so before the story starts. In theory, she is engaged to Monty Gilroy, the manager of the station, but we soon discover that he is a mean-spirited bully and she gives him his marching orders halfway through the tale. To Taroomba comes a piano-tuner, short in stature but plucky in spirit. Will Naomi succumb to him or will she marry good-natured Tom Chester, the overseer of the station? A horde of family silver and three horrible bushrangers, one of them intent on Naomi's defloration, pose additional problems. There's romance and villainy in ample abundance and, for the first time in one of Hornung's books, the odd murder or two. The tale leads up to an exciting climax, which – more than a century after it was first written – still grips the attention. And it is clear, by the final page, that Tom Chester will have to look elsewhere for a wife.

The Boss of Taroomba is a relatively simple adventure story and romance, far removed from the soul-searchings of *Tiny Luttrell*, although the piano-tuner does find time, admittedly, to give Naomi a crash-course in the subtleties of English poetry and to spout some of Rossetti's verses at her. Running to approximately 50,000 words, it probably attracted a wider readership than its immediate predecessor: a particularly blood-curdling account of the death of one of the bushrangers was designed to show, perhaps, that Hornung was fully capable of writing a man's book. Once again there are one or two verbal infelicities – "his eyes ran into her like bayonets", for example – but overall one is conscious, as ever, of the relaxed and accomplished style of the born story-teller.

The Unbidden Guest, published by Longmans, Green & Co. in 1894, following a six-month serialisation in *Longman's Magazine*, and running to approximately 60,000 words, comes across at first glance as no more than another agreeable yarn, with domestic humour and drama ladled out in roughly equal proportions. It is set in 1883 on a small farm nine miles north of Melbourne, for on this occasion we have come down rather sharply in the social scale. There are no rolling pastures of a sheep station, simply the surrounding fields, although the farm does, admittedly, command a splendid view of the Dendenong Ranges, twenty miles distant. David Teesdale and his martinet of a wife, established here since 1851, are hard strapped for cash, for David is an easy-going, gentle soul, incapable of making his debtors pay up on time. They have two unmarried children, John William and Arabella, both in their early thirties.

A letter arrives from one of David's old friends in England, stating that his daughter is arriving in Melbourne shortly and hoping that the Teesdales will make her welcome – although warning, rather mysteriously, that she is very modern in her outlook and may startle them on first acquaintance. Startle them she does, for Miriam Oliver arrives almost instantly and turns out to be a very hearty, boisterous girl with a pale face and red hair. She is surprisingly shabby, all her clothes (she explains) having been ruined by a wave that came through the open window of her cabin on the way over, and she doesn't care for the name Miriam: can they call her Missy, please? David and his son and daughter take to the girl, but Mrs Teesdale dislikes her on sight. The family (with the notable exception of Mrs T.) urge her to stay with them. She is oddly reluctant to accept the invitation, warning that they may find her more trouble than they expect, but promises to come back shortly – and arrives, indeed, a few days later, after secretly borrowing £20 from David so that she can buy a fresh wardrobe.

It is abundantly clear to the reader, her letter of introduction notwithstanding, that Missy is an impostor. But the father, for whom she develops a great fondness, is incredibly trusting and the son is smitten by her. Arabella is puzzled by sundry inconsistencies, and astonished by what are allegedly the latest fashions in London society. But she soon has cause to thank Missy (a woman-of the world) for preventing her from eloping with a ne'er-do-well. The ne'er-do-well is sent packing, but he has met Missy in the past and we now discover that she is nothing more than a chorus girl from the local theatre (and much worse besides, as the author delicately hints) who had chanced to find the letter of introduction and originally turned up in the rightful Miriam's place just "for a lark". A little while later the genuine Miriam arrives – a very supercilious young lady – and the impostor is violently sent packing by Mrs Teesdale, all her long-held suspicions having been confirmed. Missy has, indeed, long ago repented of her masquerade, and has endeavoured (without success) to confess all both to David and to John William, but she had developed a strong affection for the family and the farm and had been seeking to protect Arabella from the ne'er-do-well. She now makes herself scarce and John William scours the streets of Melbourne for her in vain.

The real Miriam stays no longer than she has to, regarding the Teesdale family with great contempt, and soon afterwards Mrs Teesdale develops a fatal illness. Missy meanwhile atones for her sins by a life of grim drudgery on a farm in the Dendenong Ranges, losing her looks and growing thin, but she comes back to the Teesdale farm as soon as she has saved up £20 with which to repay David. Mrs T., in a terrible scene, totters from her deathbed to order her out of the house for a second time and Missy heads for the river, determined to put an end to everything – but John William seizes her just as she is about to jump (for his mother's death has released him from a pledge not to pursue the girl in Mrs T.'s lifetime).

The book can easily be regarded, of course, as a down-market *Bride from the Bush*, for it relates the impact of a high-spirited, unruly girl from the opposite side of the world on an unsuspecting family. That too had had its moments of drama, but *The Unbidden Guest* is rather more serious. For on this occasion there has been deliberate deception, and Missy (whose real name of Ada Lefroy is only mentioned once) could have been sent to prison for her crime. But the author makes clear that her earlier life, both in London and Melbourne, had been a hard one and that there are, in effect, extenuating circumstances. The genuine Miriam, with all her advantages in life, is a much more unsatisfactory character, and Missy has undergone punishment enough by the end of the book. It has some genuinely comical scenes, especially when Missy performs a music-hall song-and-dance act in front of two visiting clergymen as part of the Christmas Day celebrations (and as a desperate means of alerting her hosts to her true identity), but Hornung sounds a deeper note from time to time and we become momentarily aware of his Christianity and compassion. In a sense, these are stock characters that he has been dealing with, but he has managed to give them some substance and the tale remains a gripping one down to the very last paragraph. It *is* a tract, but it is not until afterwards that we realise this.

4

TALKING STRINE

SO FAR AS the English-reading public were concerned, it seemed that Hornung was doing for Australia what Bret Harte had done for America – he was putting it on the map in a literary sense. Admittedly, he was not quite the first in the field, for Rolf Boldrewood's *Robbery Under Arms, A Story of life and adventure in the bush and in the goldfields of Australia* had been published in London in 1888 and had enjoyed a fair degree of success. Boldrewood, forty years Hornung's senior, was an English-born writer whose family had emigrated to Australia in 1830; he had taken up the pen in the late 1870s and would produce a steady stream of novels throughout the 1890s, but *Robbery Under Arms* – a boy's adventure yarn, which had originally been serialised in a newspaper in 1881 – was the one for which he would be remembered. It was a lively, action-packed tale in which Captain Starlight, the most gallant yet dastardly of bushrangers, dominates the scene and we follow his adventures through the eyes of Dick Marston (a slightly more mature Jim Hawkins). But, perversely, there would be a greater degree of authenticity about Hornung's stories – possibly because they were less excitable, and contained more reflective passages – than those of Boldrewood. Certainly, it was Hornung's tales which caught and retained the imagination.

A close friend of his, Gilbert Parker, who had been born in Ontario but emigrated to England at an early date, was meanwhile endeavouring to put Canada on the map in similar fashion: according to the *DNB*, the host of novels that he penned about that country were "sensational, unconvincing, inaccurate and turgidly written, [but] appealed to uncritical readers". Parker, four years older than Hornung, would become a Conservative MP in 1900 and acquire a knighthood in 1902. Hornung's books, in contrast, were usually non-sensational, convincing, accurate and extremely well-written, but a knighthood would never come his way. (It may be, however, that he was not unduly perturbed by this omission.)

His English readers, whether they realised it or not, were being subjected to subtle tutorials when they opened a Hornung book of the 1890s. There was a culture-gap to be bridged and they had to accustom themselves to new words – or, in some instances, to familiar words with strangely different meanings from what they were used to. Their vocabulary became enriched by such exotic pearls as wide-awake, pannikin, billy-can, johny-cake, grog-shanty, whattle-bush, verandah, station, travellers' hut, shed and whim, and they speedily made the acquaintance of new chums, jackeroos, cornstalks, squatters, swagmen, bushrangers and over-seers of back-blocks – and men who "knock down their cheque" at the nearest saloon as soon as they're paid – not to mention exercises such as mustering, sheep-shearing, buck-jumping and 'possum shooting. They would have been gratified to discover that England was still referred to as Home, but little by little it would be borne in upon them that they had entered a foreign land with different galaxies (such as the Southern Cross) and a National Poet whose name was Adam Lindsay Gordon rather than Alfred Lord Tennyson. (There were, on the other hand, almost no references to boomerangs and it was only on exceedingly rare occasions that a kangaroo bounded into view.) The two basic differences between the countries were, it seemed, that Australia had genuinely blue sky whereas England had genuinely green grass.

"[Englishmen] discover where I come from", exclaims Tiny Luttrell to her brother-in-law, soon after arriving in London; "then they show their ignorance. They want to know if there is any chance for a fellow on the gold-fields now; they have heard of a place called Ballarat, but they aren't certain whether it's a part of Melbourne or nearer Sydney. One man knows some people at Hobart Town, in New Zealand, he fancies. I never knew anything like their ignorance of the Colonies!"

Dick Edmonstone is questioned about Australia by a couple of old acquaintances, on his return to England in 1886, and speedily corrects "one or two notions entertained by them respecting that country. He assured them that the natives were frequently as white as they were. He informed them, in response to a question, that lions and tigers did not prowl around people's premises in the majority of Australian towns; nor, indeed, were those animals to be found in the Colonies, except in cages."

Starting from basics, Gladys the Bride briskly dismisses the notion "that everyone out there wears a big black beard, and a red shirt, a jack-boot and revolver" and that most of the legislators are convicts. But even people who think they have done their homework come a cropper – as does a bishop's daughter, for example:

> Miss Methuen's idea of that continent had been very vague, very elementary, and rather funny. Her timely reading gave shape and background to her ideas, but left them funnier than ever; it did not prepare her for the place she was going to; it did not prepare her, but perhaps it did not pretend to do so, for that romantic literature; but Miss Methuen had chosen to assume that all Australian scenery would be in the same style. She was prepared for gullies, gumtrees, caves, ranges, kangaroos, opossums, claims, creeks, snakes in the grass, and chivalrous robbers on the highroad; but she was not prepared for a dead level of sandy desert, broken only by the river-timber of a narrow, sluggish stream, nor for a wooden township where the worst weapons of men were strong drink in the head and strong language on the tongue; and this was what she found.

Given such ignorance, Hornung feels that the best thing he can do is to take his readers direct to Australia and show them precisely what it looks like. In the person of young

Tahourdin, avidly looking forward to exploring "the Bush" *en route* to a Riverina sheep station six hundred miles away, he transports us from Melbourne first by train, then by river steamer, and finally by coach, into "the real bush" which, much to Tahourdin's chagrin, does "not deserve a capital after all":

> The trees were not a bit high. They were uncommonly low. Rangers and gullies there were none. The whole country was as flat and arid as a rusty frying-pan. It whistled with crickets at night. It quivered in the heat all day. Night and day, Tahourdin had to jump down every five miles or so to open a gate, for he was the only passenger. It seemed that the whole country was in squares like a chess-board; it was as though a vast wire net had been cast across it. Tahourdin was thankful to see some cockatoos and parakeets, and once a snake, and more than once a kangaroo; they were the only points in common between the real and the ideal. In the end he was met by a lean and nasal lout in a 'spring' cart, and jolted forty miles back from the so-called road to a few log huts on a sandy pine ridge. Such was the Riverina station of his dreams.

Now comes an overall view of such a station:

> Picture the Great Sahara. The popular impression will do: it has the merit of simplicity: glaring desert, dark-blue sky, vertical sun, and there you are. Omit the mirage and the thirsty man; but, instead, mix sombre colours and work up the African desert into a fairly desirable piece of Australian sheep-country.
>
> This, too, is a simple matter. You have only to cover the desert with pale-green saliferous bushes, no higher than a man's knee; quite a scanty covering will do, so that in the thickest places plenty of sand may still be seen; and there should be barren patches to represent the low sand-hills and the smooth clay-pans. Then have a line of low-sized dark-green scrub at the horizon; but bite in one gleaming, steely speck upon this sombre rim.
>
> Conceive this modification of the desert, and you have a fair notion of the tract of country – six miles by five – which was known on Bindarra Station as the 'Yelkin Paddock', the largest paddock in the 'C Block'.

Multiply this area by six; divide and sub-divide the product by wire fences, such as those that enclose the Yelkin Paddock; water by means of excavations and wells and whims; stock with the pure merino and devastate with the accursed rabbit; and (without troubling about the homestead, which is some miles north of the Yelkin) you will have as good an idea of the Bindarra 'run', as a whole, as of its sixth part, the paddock under notice.

The conspicuous mark upon the distant belt of dingy low-sized forest – the object that glitters in the strong sunlight, so that it can be seen across miles and miles of plain – is merely the galvanised roof of a log-hut, the hut that has been the lodging of the boundary-rider of the Yelkin Paddock ever since the Yelkin Paddock was fenced.

And for a close-up:

There was the usual galaxy of log huts ... [with] the inevitable roofs of galvanised iron; these roofs duly expanded in the heat, and made the little tin thunder that dwellers beneath them grow weary of hearing, the warm world over. There were a few pine-trees between the buildings, and the white palings of a well among the pines, and in the upper spaces a broken but persistent horizon of salt-bush plains burning into the blinding blue. In the Riverina you cannot escape these features: you may have got more pine-trees and less salt-bush; you may even get blue-bush and cotton-bush, and an occasional mallee forest; but the plains will recur, and the pines will mitigate the plains, and the dazzle and the scent of them shall haunt you evermore, with that sound of the hot complaining roofs, and the taste of tea from a pannikin and water from a water-bag.

If you want to know what a whim might be, stand by for the explanation:

[Jim] lived by himself at the Seven-mile whim. Most of his time was spent under a great wooden drum, round which coiled a rope with its two ends down two shafts, raising a bucketful of water from one while lowering an empty bucket down the other. The buckets filled a tank; the tank fed the sheep troughs, and what Jim did was to drive a horse round and round to turn the drum.... In times of plenty, when there was water in the paddocks and great life in the salt-bush, the whim was not wanted, and other work was found for the whim-driver.

Tarhoudin, a brand-new arrival in the Riverina, has been hired as a 'jackeroo' – an untranslatable word says Hornung in 1900, apparently admitting defeat for once, but two years later the privileged readers of *At Large* (unavailable, alas, in the United Kingdom) would be supplied with an explanation by Jack Flint:

> "[He is] a young gentleman – for choice, the newest chum to be found – who goes to a station to get Colonial experience. He has to work like a nigger, and revels in it, for a bit. If he is a black sheep, amd has the antique ideas of the Colonies held by those who sent him out to whiten him, his illusions may last a couple of days; if he has read up Australia on the voyage, they will probably hold out a little longer, while he keeps looking for what his book told him he would find; the fact being that modern bush life hasn't yet been done into English. Meanwhile he runs up the horses, rides round boundaries, mends fences, drives sheep to water – if it is a drought – and skins the dead ones, weighs out flour and sugar, cleans harness, camps anywhere, and lives on mutton and damper, and tea."
>
> "But what does he get for all that?" asked Maurice, with visions of money-bags.
>
> "Rations and experience," replied Flint promptly. "When he's admitted to be worth his salt he will be asked to make other arrangements. Then some still newer chum will be selected for the post, through the introductions he has brought to the stock and station agents, and in his turn will drive his teeth into the dirty work of the station, which the ordinary pound-a-week hands refuse, and so get his Colonial experience."

Edmonstone, Flint's friend, suggests that this is a rather jaundiced account and asserts that jackeroos "are treated all right, and paid too, so long as they're smart and willing – the two things needful". But they are speaking, in any case, in 1886 and jackeroos may already be a vanishing breed. A few

years later Naomi, the Boss of Taroomba, introduces her guest
to the intricacies of sheep-shearing:

They drove down the length of the shed, which had small
pens attached on either side, with a kind of port-hole opening
into each. Out of these port-holes there kept issuing shorn
sheep, which ran down little sloping boards, and thus filled
up the pens ... [which] were all numbered.... "Each man has
his pen," she said, "and shears his sheep just inside those
holes. Then the boss of the shed comes round with his note-
book, counts out the pens, and enters the number of sheep to
the number of each pen. If a shearer cuts his sheep about
much, or leaves a lot of wool on, he just runs that man's pen –
[the boss] doesn't count 'em at all."

ଓଞ୍ଜ

They alighted from the buggy at the further end of the shed,
where huge doors stood open, showing a confused stack of
wool-bales within.... Beyond the bales was the machine
which turned them out. Here the two wool-pressers were
hard at work and streaming with perspiration. Naomi
paused to see a bale pressed down and sewn up. Then she
led her companion on to where the wool-pickers were busy
at side tables, and the wool-sorter at another table which
stood across the shed in a commanding position, with a long
line of shearers at work to right and left, and an equally long
pen full of unshorn sheep between them. The wool-sorter's
seemed the softest job in the shed. Boys brought him fleeces –
perhaps a dozen a minute – flung them out upon the table,
and rolled them up again into neat bundles swiftly tied with
string. These bundles the wool-sorter merely tossed over his
shoulder into one or other of the five or six bins at his back....
The air was heavy with the smell of fleeces, and not
unmusical with the constant swish and chink of forty pairs of
shears.

In *The Unbidden Guest* a 'possum shooting party, accompanied
by two dogs, goes into the moonlit paddocks:

Here the hunting-ground began without preliminary, for on
this side of the farm there were trees and to spare, the land
dipping in a gully full of timber before it rose to the high

ploughed levels known as the Cultivation. The gully was well grassed for all its trees, which were divers and manifold. There were gum-trees blue and red, and stringy-barks and she-oaks, each and all of them a haunt of the opossum and the native cat. The party promptly surrounded a blue gum at the base of which the dogs stood barking, and Missy found herself doing what the others did – getting the moon behind the branches and searching for what she was told would look more like the stump of a bough or a tangle of leaves than any known animal.

It is feared, for a time, that the dogs have been telling a lie – which is what is meant by barking up the wrong tree – but "a little bit of a knot in the bough" is spotted which proves to be a native cat, or little leopard, much given to tearing the farm fowls to pieces. Missy shoots it, and the corpse turns out to be a spotted little horror with a sharp snout and devilish fangs. John William then shoots a bush-tailed opossum, which looks "very big and soft and gray, lying dead in the moonlight".

Missy, out from England for only a year, also encounters – in the daylight – cherry peckers and mobs of chattering parrots, with their "red beaks and redder heads and tartan wings and emerald breasts", plus the odd brown snake "with darting tongue and eyes like holes in a head full of fire" which darts "back into its hole like a streak of live seaweed".

Anyone wishing to experience virtual reality in the 1890s, as distinct from the 1990s, need do no more than immerse himself in one of Hornung's Australian novels. For he had a positive genius for conjuring up, in a few deftly chosen words, a scene or an activity of astonishing complexity. And he did so in such a way as to make the reader feel only one stage removed from being an active participant.

5

STRICTLY PERSONAL

IN 1963 Mrs F.S. Collin presented the London Library with a collection of Hornung's novels. Most, but not all of them, bear a very brief inscription from the author, usually to a person whose initials are B.H. Thus the Library's copy of his very first book, *A Bride from the Bush*, bears the words "B.H. from E.W.H., October 23 1890" while *The Belle of Toorak* (1900) is inscribed, even more laconically, "B.H. from E.W.H., 1900". But so far as his third book is concerned he was positively garrulous, for it bears the words "Bertha Holden, with loving thoughts of her now and always, from E.W.H., April, 1893."

For Hornung's biographer this seems, at first glance, an exciting find. Bertha Holden was, clearly, a close friend; perhaps she had been his very first love? Was she, one wonders, a striking but rather large girl, as Gladys the Bride had been in 1890 and as Fanny Lowndes would be in 1898? And was there any particular reason why his inscription in 1893 should have been so fulsome?

Alas for speculation! Further investigation reveals that Bertha Holden was simply his elder sister, who had married George Holden, a London solicitor, in 1879 and been widowed almost instantly. Curiosity as regards first loves must remain unsatisfied. Just possibly, however, the emotional salutation in *Tiny Luttrell* bears witness to the fact that Hornung was now thinking in terms of matters matrimonial, for the book is formally dedicated "To C.A.M.D. from E.W.H.". The dedicatee in question was Constance Aimée Monica Doyle, the daughter of Charles Altamont Doyle and the sister of Dr Arthur Conan Doyle.

It is also just possible, perhaps, that Hornung's heart had been won when he glimpsed her pirouetting in a ballroom. "Would you see a graceful maiden at her best?" he would ask in 1901, in uncharacteristic teasing vein. "Then watch her dancing. Would you behold her most sweet? Then catch her unawares – if you can. Most graceful and most sweet, then – I admit that the combination is a rare one, but she should be dancing all alone; for, alas! the ballroom has its mask, and the dual dance its trammels."

At any rate, it was Constance whom Hornung married at St Edward's, a Roman Catholic Church in the District of St George's, Hanover Square, London on Wednesday, 27 September 1893. The groom was twenty-seven and the bride twenty-five.

Since the autumn of 1892, or possibly earlier, Hornung had been living at No. 17 Abingdon Mansions – a newly-constructed block of flats in Abingdon Road, near Kensington High Street. (Intriguingly, the *Post Office Directory* indicates that the occupant of No. 29 was a Miss Doyle.) Immediately prior to his marriage he moved into the Grosvenor Hotel in Belgravia, but the newly-weds would thereafter take up residence in another flat – No.14 Rossetti Garden Mansions in Flood Street, South Chelsea.

The witnesses to the ceremony were Gilbert Parker, Mary Doyle (the bride's mother), Theodore Hornung (the groom's brother) and H.H. Hornung (the groom's mother, presumably, despite that mysterious second H). Rather conspicuously lacking, however, is the name of the bride's well-known brother, which suggests that he was unable, or unwilling, to attend the proceedings. Also missing from St Edward's on that day was the bride's father, formally described in the marriage register as a "retired civil servant", but this was scarcely surprising: troubled by both alcoholism and epilepsy, Charles Altamont Doyle was institutionalised in Dumfries and would die there a fortnight later, on 10 October. If Conan Doyle *had* been present at the wedding, then he would obviously have been required (in the absence of his father) to give the bride away and it is almost inconceivable that he would not have signed the register. One can only assume that it was Parker who gave the bride away, with Theodore Hornung acting as his brother's best man. (But if Conan Doyle *did* give the bride away, without signing the register, then Parker would presumably have been the best man.)

Did Conan Doyle disapprove of the wedding taking place while the health of the bride's father was in such a critical state? Or did he disapprove, at this time, of Hornung's admission to their family? There had certainly been no reservations in 1892. "I like young Willie Hornung very much," he wrote to his mother in that year. "He is one of the sweetest natured and most delicate-minded men I ever knew. He is 26, and an author standing certainly much higher than I did at his age." In December 1892, together with Jerome K. Jerome, they had visited Scotland Yard's Black Museum.

We gather from John Dickson Carr that Conan Doyle "was a little dubious as to how the newly-weds would fare, since Willie's income was not very satisfactory" but this can scarcely be construed as out-and-out opposition to the marriage. But after 1892 his relations with Hornung were always rather strained: in a moment of intense exasperation in 1900, he would declare that he was unsettled "by contemplating the fact that William is half-Mongol, half-Slav, or whatever the mixture is".

Interviewed in the October 1895 issue of *The Idler* about the up-and-coming novelists of the day ('A Chat with Conan Doyle') the creator of Sherlock Holmes said:

> "There are at least a dozen men and women who have made a deep mark and are still young. No one can say how far they may go. Some of them are sure to develop."

Pressed by his excited interviewer to name names, he added:

> "There are more than a dozen. Barrie, Kipling, Mrs Olive Schreiner, Sarah Grand, Miss Harraden, Gilbert Parker, Quiller-Couch, Hall Caine, Stanley Weyman, Anthony Hope, Rider Haggard, Crockett, Jerome, Zangwill, Clark Russell, George Moore – many of them under thirty, and a few of

them much over it. There are others, of course. These names just happen to occur to me."

There was, clearly, one particular name that did *not* happen to occur to him.

Yet, however fragile the relationship between the two authors may have become, Hornung was very keen to strengthen the ties between them. Constance gave birth to a son on 24 March 1895, after the anxious father had spent a feverish hour or so pacing up and˜ down Flood Street, to King's Road and back, in the company of Whyte. But the new arrival was not named after his father nor even after his paternal grandfather (for Pitt's third son, born three months earlier, was already the third John Peter). He was named, instead, after his uncle, for his first name was Arthur, and Conan Doyle was called upon, soon after, to act as godparent to the child.

What is truly remarkable, however, especially in that particular year of 1895, is the *second* name which was conferred upon Willie's child.

For the name in question was Oscar.

6

WILDE ABOUT THE BOY

IT MUST be emphasised from the outset that, in the absence of information of a more tangible nature, what follows in the present chapter can be regarded, for the moment, as no more than conjecture. On the other hand, the circumstantial evidence for most of these suppositions is so startlingly strong that it is impossible for the biographer of E.W. Hornung to disregard it. To reject one coincidence is permissable, but to reject half-a-dozen comes perilously close to blatant dereliction of duty.

It is assumed, for present purposes, that Hornung came to London as a fledgling journalist in the late 1880s, that his circle of literary connections gradually widened and that, possibly through the good offices of Richard Dowling, he became acquainted with Oscar Wilde and obtained words of advice and friendly criticism from this quarter. We must remind ourselves of what was almost certainly Hornung's own upwards ascent by that account given of Bertram Adeane's worldly progress:

> He was enticed from his lodgings – which now consisted of two rooms – into certain drawing rooms further west. There his eyes were opened to many things – first of all to himself. He simply amazed himself by taking rather kindly to society, for all his life he had spoken of it with the loftiest scorn. His ignorant poet's prejudices died a violent death. He had his eyes opened, which did him good.

Oscar Wilde, born in 1854, was at this time approaching the very peak of his eminence – or, as some would prefer, his notoriety. From Trinity College, Dublin, he had won a scholarship to Magdalen College, Oxford, in 1874 and it was there that he came heavily under the influence of John Ruskin and, less happily, that of Walter Pater. Prolonged travels in northern Italy and Greece inflamed his imagination and so, in particular, did Greek ideas on beauty. Awarded a 'double First' in 1878, and winner of the Newdigate Prize, he left Oxford resolved to be a poet or a dramatist or, failing all else, simply to be well-known for being well-known. Flamboyant in dress, witty in speech, this warm-hearted, blue-eyed giant of a man had developed, by 1880, into the virtual head of the aesthetic movement in England, proclaiming the glories of beauty as an ideal in its own right, wherever it might be found. Mercilessly lampooned in *Punch*, mocked by Gilbert and Sullivan's *Patience*, his poetry derided, he nevertheless smiled amiably and went placidly on his way, oblivious to all criticism. He wrote an unsuccessful play, lectured in America, and collected blue china and peacock feathers. He cheerfully declared his aversion to all forms of sport and continued to be a brilliant conversationalist. In 1884 he married Constance Lloyd, who presented him with two sons, and it was the stories he wrote for their offspring which finally propelled him into successful authorship. *The Happy Prince and other tales* was immensely popular, but his subsequent fiction (of which *The Picture of Dorian Gray* was the most famous) was most definitely *not* for children. Suddenly, in the early 1890s, he found his feet as a dramatist. Three plays in succession – *Lady Windermere's Fan*, *A Woman of No Importance* and *An Ideal Husband* – proved wonderfully successful, but the best was yet to come: in August 1894 he began work on *The Importance of Being Earnest*. For the first time, he was well off – for there had been occasions, during the 1880s, when his fortunes had been very low indeed, and tradesmen had been held at bay by a variety of stratagems. His private life, however, was gradually ceasing to be private, for his predilection for sexual relationships with young men was destined to become a horrendous scandal – resulting, first and foremost, from his infatuation with Lord Alfred Douglas ('Bosie') and the almost insane desire of Douglas's father, the

Marquess of Queensberry, to wreak vengeance on the loathsome character who had captured his son's affections. Father and son were unbalanced to an almost equal degree, and family hatreds of a terrible intensity would soon transform the playwright's life into a hideous nightmare.

Wilde was twelve years older than Hornung and too young, therefore, to fill the role of substitute father-figure. But it may well be, for reasons to be clarified later, that (the presence of Theodore and John notwithstanding) Hornung came to regard him as someone almost equivalent to an additional elder brother.

In 1890, as we have seen, Hornung published his first novel and this was followed by a collection of short stories in 1892. Most of these tales featured either an Australian background or Australian characters. They were written with a light touch and, bearing in mind his youth, were marvellously accomplished productions. The title pages of these two books bore his full name – Ernest William Hornung – while their spines carried the contracted name of E.W. Hornung. To his intimates, moreover, Hornung was known as 'Willie' and the copy of *The Boss of Taroomba* which Hornung presented to his mother in 1894 was inscribed "from your loving son W". The new *Strand Magazine*, in publishing its first contribution from him (April 1891), had inadvertently described him as 'S. W. Hornung'. It may just be that Wilde solemnly admonished the young author on the desirability of his first Christian name being emphasised – on the importance, in fact, of being Ernest – as a means of ensuring that his utterances were packaged with sufficient *gravatus* to attract the attention of a public ever willing to be impressed. This admonition, delivered playfully on two or three occasions, could well have been the inspiration for what would prove to be one of the most brilliantly funny plays ever written.

It is conceivable that (with an author's irrepressible desire to insert cryptic private allusions into his literary productions, a practice prevailing since Shakespearian times) the first positive clue we have as to Wilde's influence on Hornung will be found in *Tiny Luttrell*, published in 1893. The plot has already been summarised, but it needs to be mentioned that Tiny's brother-in-law, Erskine Holland, takes it upon himself to act as guide in her choice of reading material. He is "a big, fair, genial fellow, fond of laughter and chaff and ... fonder of books than of the newspapers": someone, in short, whom she regards as a close friend and mentor. She reads whatever he puts into her hands, becoming acquainted first with *The Newcomes* and then with Ruskin's *Sesame and Lilies* and Stevenson's *Virginibus Puerisque*. "It was Erskine Holland's privilege to put each into her hands for the first time, and perhaps she never pleased him quite so much as when she said [after perusing *Sesame and Lilies*]: 'It makes me think less of myself; it has made me horribly unhappy; but if they were going to hang me in the morning I would sit up all night to read it again!'"

It should be noted that Tiny's brother-in-law is some twelve years older than herself, just as Wilde (a brother-figure) was twelve years older than Hornung. Even more tantalising, however, is the fact that her guardian angel should bear the surname *Holland*. For what instantly comes to mind, of course, is the fact that 'Holland' was the surname that Constance Wilde would adopt for herself and for their two sons, Cyril and Vyvyan, two years later in a desperate attempt to conceal their identity.

Yet how, unless he was psychic, could Hornung possibly have associated Wilde with this name as early as 1893? The answer lies in the fact that Constance's brother, Otho Lloyd, had been divorced in 1886 and that the event had attracted some publicity. Otho's second name was Holland and he had therefore decided to drop the 'Lloyd' and to be known simply as 'Otho Holland'. (It was the Christian name of his and Constance's great-grandfather, Holland Watson.) Oscar, presumably, would have been amused at his brother-in-law's seeking to achieve obscurity by discarding 'Lloyd' while retaining the distinctive name of 'Otho'.

While on the subject of names, one wonders whether, in response to jocular references about the importance of always being Ernest, the victim could have retorted that 'Erskine', with its judicial overtones, was an even *more* impressive name.✳(And, phonetically, 'Ersk' is not so very far removed from 'Osc'.) It should also be remembered that Hornung was small in stature and it is just possible that Wilde would have referred to him as 'Tiny'.

Later, Erskine Holland and his wife take Tiny to a garden party given by Lady Dromard. Passing a refreshment stall, they overhear the elegant small boy in charge of it being asked by a large lady customer which of the Dromard boys *he* is and his answer: "My name's Douglas." The lady tries to pursue their conversation, but he hands her an ice and remains silent. "Even the boy snubs her", whispers Holland. "Yet mark him. The mixture of politeness and contempt was worth noticing in a small boy like that. There's a little nobleman for you!" A little while later they pass "a shabby-looking person with a slouching walk and a fair beard". Tiny assumes that he is the gardener, but Erskine explains that he is actually the Earl – "old clothes are his special fancy in the country". Is it altogether beyond the bounds of possibility that the people referred to, in these incidents, are Lord Alfred Douglas and the Marquess of Queensberry?

For at least four years, after their marriage in 1893, Ernest and Constance Hornung lived in Rossetti Garden Mansions, a block of flats in Flood Street, South Chelsea: this was, almost literally, a stone's throw away from the house in Tite Street, where Oscar and Constance Wilde had lived since January 1885. Tite Street is the shorter road of the two but it does, in fact, run parallel with Flood Street. It takes less than five minutes to walk from one residence to the other.

The Importance of Being Earnest had its première on 14 February 1895. It was acclaimed by everyone, with the noticeable exception of Bernard Shaw, as a comic masterpiece. Hornung's son was born six weeks later, on 24 March. Already, however, the shadows were closing in around the dramatist, as a result of his dreadful involvement in the horrendous feud between Bosie and his father. Denied access to the theatre on the first night of *Earnest*, where he had intended to create a disturbance by delivering an unpleasant

✳ Erskine also features in Wilde's 'The Portrait of Mr W.H.' (1889), which conjectured that Shakespeare's sonnets were inspired by a youth called Willie Hughes.

'bouquet' of vegetables (which he left, instead, at the stage door), Queensberry now accused Wilde of posing as a Sodomite. Wilde felt obliged to sue for libel: preliminary hearings in March were followed by full-scale proceedings early in April. Queensberry was acquitted and Wilde was thereupon arrested and charged with having committed an act of gross indecency in private with another male person (a youth called Taylor). The jury failed to reach a verdict and a new trial was ordered. On 25 May the second trial resulted in Wilde being found guilty and sentenced to two years' hard labour. His places of residence, during the next two years, would be Pentonville, Wandsworth and Reading.

It was a scandal of the first magnitude: the only event with which it could have any parallel was the fall of Satan from Heaven into Hell during the first book of Milton's *Paradise Lost*. Wilde became, as it were, Public Enemy No. 1, an outcast from a shocked and decent society, and the performances of *Earnest* and his other plays were brought to an abrupt end.

The purpose of reciting, however briefly, this well-known sequence of events is to emphasise that, even in March 1895, it was clear that Wilde was becoming involved in some very murky legal proceedings indeed and that it would be virtually impossible for him to emerge unsullied. Hornung may be forgiven for not immediately appreciating the sheer enormity of what was about to happen, but on 3 May, when the irrevocable step of registering the name of his son as Arthur Oscar Hornung was taken, Wilde was in Holloway Prison, following the jury's inability to reach a decision at the end of his first trial, and would not be allowed out on bail until 7 May. To bestow the name of Oscar upon one's son, at such a time as this, was to display courage – or foolhardiness – of the very highest order. The nearest parallel, perhaps, would be a father who chose to name his son Adolf in the spring of 1945. As a vote of confidence, it was magnificent: as an act of prudence, it was questionable. But the child's first name was, of course, Arthur, and it was Conan Doyle who would act as his godparent. If we look, however, twelve years into the future we will find that 'Arthur' has been discarded: the boy would be known as Oscar, to relations and friends alike, and it was as Oscar that he would sign his letters.

All this having been said, however, honesty compels us to admit that there *was* a legitimate reason why the new arrival should have borne such a name. In 1849, it will be recalled, Harriet Hornung gave birth to a son who lived for only a few months. The name of that child was Oscar George Peter Hornung. Forty-six years had passed since the death of this unfortunate mite and it could be argued that Hornung was simply trying to gratify his mother by reviving the memory of her very first offspring. The gap of almost half a century between the two Oscars is, however, a substantial one, and it might equally well be contended that the 'family connection' provided Hornung with a very useful, respectable justification – or smokescreen – for selecting this particular name for his own first-born. This may be too cynical by half, and it is doubtless kinder to assume that Hornung's acquaintance with Wilde reminded him of the fact that his parents' very first son (born five years earlier than Wilde) had borne the same Christian name. In this sense, Hornung might have chosen to regard Wilde as a substitute for the brother whom neither he nor any of his siblings had ever known.

The name of Ernest would be, for a time, almost as notorious as the name of Oscar, and it may be that Hornung was privately relieved that the run of the play had come to a premature end. One must beware, of course, of clutching at straws, but it should be noted that there is a slight similarity (in spelling, if not in pronunciation) between the names of Worthing and Hornung. Jack Worthing, moreover, owns a house in Belgrave Square and Hornung had been living at the Grosvenor Hotel in Belgravia at the time of his marriage.

The central character of Hornung's *next* book, *The Rogue's March*, published in 1896, was a convict – or, to be more precise, someone unjustly imprisoned for a crime he did not commit, despite damning circumstantial evidence. Hornung narrates the course of the trial, then concentrates upon the humiliations and indignities heaped upon the prisoner – the thoughtless words of the judge, the jeers of the populace, and the donning of prison garb and leg-irons. The hero of the book has nothing whatsoever in common with Wilde, except that both undergo terms of imprisonment and suffer terribly in the process. Another important character, however, is a melancholy poet, the unstable son and heir of a baronet. Between father and son there is a dreadful state of war, most readily exemplified by the fact that a parcel of flowers (Hornung carefully avoids using the word 'bouquet') which the son had placed on his mother's grave is sent back by the father, a couple of days later, to the house where the son is staying. This drives the latter "almost crazy with rage and grief" and the heroine of the book decides that his father is "the most abominable old man alive". But we find out, long before reaching the end of this tale, that the strain of madness is not confined to the preceding generation. Without labouring the point unduly, there would seen to be something oddly familiar about these two characters.

In Hornung's thinly-veiled autobiography, *Young Blood* published in 1898, there is a company promoter called Gordon Lowndes, a high-spirited but rather curious individual whose fortunes oscillate between abject poverty and dazzling prosperity. He is a likeable rogue, but the real villain of the piece is someone called Scrafton, whom Hornung describes in blood-chilling terms. Harry meets him as he comes

> downstairs in his creaking shoes, with his snuff-box open in his hand, and his extraordinary head thrown back to take a pinch. There are some faces which one has to see many times before one knows them, as it were, by heart; there are others which one passes in the street with a shudder, and can never afterwards forget; and here was a face that would have haunted Harry Ringrose even though he had never seen it but this once.
>
> A magnificent forehead was its one fine feature; the light blue eyes beneath were spoilt by their fiery rims, and yet they gleamed with a fierce humour and a keen intelligence which lent them distinction of a kind. These were the sole redeeming points. The rest was either cruel or unclean or

both. The creature's skin was very smooth and yellow, and it shone with an unwholesome gloss. Abundant hair, of a dirty iron-grey, was combed back from the forehead without a parting, and gathered in unspeakable curls on the nape of a happily invisible neck A long, lean nose, like a vulture's beak, overhung a grey moustache with a snuffy zone in the centre, and lost pinches of snuff lingered in a flowing beard of great length.

Scrafton hates Harry and eventually develops an equally strong hatred for Lowndes, enjoying an unaccustomed bout of prosperity, whom he tries to incriminate towards the end of the book. "You can prove nothing [against me]!" he snarls at Lowndes.

But if I can't hang you, I can tell enough to make you glad to go and hang yourself. It doesn't much matter what happens to me. I'm old and poor and about done for in any case, or I might think more of my own skin. But you're on the top of the wave – and I'll have you back in the trough! You're living on the fat of the land – you shall see how you like skilly!

Scrafton's hatred of Lowndes is curiously reminiscent of the vicious sentiments expressed about Oscar Wilde by the Marquess of Queensberry. Wilde would describe him, in *De Profundis*, as "waving his hands in the air... uttering every foul word his foul mind could think of, and screaming the loathsome threats he afterwards with such cunning carried out".

If Scrafton is Queensberry, then it is tempting to argue that the amiable, skittish but untrustworthy Lowndes – a temporary substitute father-figure for Harry, until his defects became grossly apparent – is Oscar Wilde. For, after all, there is much that is good in the man and his irrepressible high spirits, showmanship and general panache make him congenial company.

The words "much that is good in the man" remind us, moreover, of Deedes Major, created contemporaneously with Lowndes and referred to at the very outset of the present volume. The thought planted in our head, when we meet him for the first time, is that of Major Deeds – although, if we remember that he had been expelled from school, and is now engaged in robbing inoffensive Australian banks, "Major Misdeeds" might seem more appropriate.

We must follow the logic of this a little further. If it is accepted that the characters of Gordon Lowndes and Deedes Major are based upon that of Oscar Wilde to some extent, and if it is agreed that A.J. Raffles is a more polished version of Deedes Major (although he also owes something to Edward Nettleship), then it follows that Raffles – pursuing a distinguished career by day and a wildly different career by night (no pun intended) – must owe something, on however modest a scale, to the character of Oscar Fingal O'Flahertie Wills Wilde. He lives, it should be noted, at chambers in The Albany, and it was at B.4, The Albany, that Algernon Moncrieff, in his own incarnation as Mr Ernest Worthing, claimed to reside.

And since Wilde was regarded, by his contemporaries, as having led young Lord Alfred Douglas astray (although, in reality, the exact opposite was the case), and since Raffles certainly leads young Manders astray, is there not a case for suggesting that, in name if nothing else, Bunny owes something to Bosie?

There is, moreover, a further connection between the man-about-town playwright who led a secret life and the man-about-town cricketer who led a secret life. To appreciate the connection, it must be explained that in 1820 Wilde's great-uncle, an author called Charles Maturin (1782-1824), published a famous book called *Melmoth the Wanderer*. When Wilde went into hiding as a semi-invalid after coming out of prison in 1897 – fated, thereafter, to endure a shadowy existence – he called himself 'Sebastian Melmoth'. When Raffles went into hiding as a semi-invalid after coming back to England in 1897 – fated, thereafter, to endure a shadowy existence – he called himself 'Mr Maturin'.

Turning to *Young Blood* for the very last time, it can be contended that Wilde comes very close to making a personal appearance, in his own right, in its pages. For Harry suddenly acquires a very relaxed, accomplished manner of writing, and we are told that he had looked again at the raw material at his disposal and found a new way of presenting it.

> It was not his own way. It was the way of the greatest humorist then living. Harry took the whole of his two years abroad, and eyed them afresh from the humorist's point of view, as he apprehended it. He saw the things the great man would have seized upon, and the way it seemed to Harry he would have treated them. The result was a comic lion in the moonlight, and a more or less amusing murderer. He had treated these things tragically hitherto.

Harry is at pains to emphasise, of course, that he had no direct connection with "the greatest humorist then living", but such a disclaimer would have been, in 1898, a standard precautionary measure to distance himself from the disgraced ex-prisoner. As it was, Hornung had come as close to naming him as he could. In 1890, when *A Bride from the Bush* was published, there were only two men who could contend for the title "greatest humorist then living". One was Mark Twain, while the other was Oscar Wilde. But whereas Twain was still active in 1898, Wilde had ceased to be a humorist by that date. In 'Lord Arthur Savile's Crime', however, he had demonstrated that murder was indeed a subject that could be treated with a certain degree of levity. (And A.J. Raffles may, of course, be indebted to Lord Arthur Savile, rather than to Hornung's brother-in-law, for the first of his Christian names.)

By 1898 the name of the "greatest humorist" whom he had so much revered eight or nine years earlier was one that Hornung dared not speak. It is noticeable, moreover, that the title pages of his books, from *The Unbidden Guest* onwards, bear the name E.W. Hornung – almost as though he were doing all he could to draw a veil over his first name, in public as well as in private. It might be contended, indeed, that he had now realised, for the first time in his life, the vital importance of *not* being Ernest.

7

AN ESTABLISHED PRACTITIONER

IT WILL have been observed, perhaps, that thus far in his career Hornung had not stayed with one publisher for more than one book. Smith, Elder & Co. in 1890 had been followed by A. & C. Black in 1892, by Cassells in 1893, by Bliss, Sands and Foster in 1894 and then by Longmans, Green & Co. For he was a popular novelist, and much sought after by publishers.

The term "popular novelist" merits a few moments' consideration. In no way is it intended as disparagement to say that popular novelists, in the mid-1890s, were almost literally ten-a-penny. The market was crowded with well-known writers, to a rather greater extent, perhaps, than either before or since. This was a phenomenon which may have been a reflection of the greater degree of literacy in the nation at large brought about by the Education Act of 1870. With the demise of the circulating libraries, and the virtual disappearance of novels running to two or three volumes (of which *Tiny Luttrell* had been one of the last), there was a far greater market for books and magazines than ever before. Publishers were falling over themselves to acquire the truly proficient practitioners of the art. Short books were now a viable proposition and early 'paperbacks' were appearing. Cheap editions of established favourites were plentiful. Magazines were purchased at station bookstalls, moreover, for long train journeys, as well as for domestic consumption, and particularly extensive tales could be assured of a double career – first as a serial, then as a novel. Writers, not to mention illustrators, had never had it so good – and there were some, such as George du Maurier, who managed to have a foot in both camps. Newspapers also featured fiction, sometimes in the form of a short story and sometimes in the form of a long-running serial, but it was the magazines – *The Cornhill*, *The Strand*, *Cassell's Family Magazine*, *The Fortnightly Review*, *Longman's Magazine* and *Temple Bar*, to name just a few, which flourished as never before during the final years of the nineteenth century.

Invidious though it is, if we are to see Hornung in his proper context – and to appreciate the progress that he had made in only five years – then it is necessary to present the reader with some kind of league table of the writers of this time . Among those at the very top, in the mid-'nineties (and in the year following Stevenson's death), were Henry James, Thomas Hardy and the three Georges – Meredith, Gissing and Moore. There were others who had certainly made a name for themselves, such as Kipling, Conan Doyle, Jerome K. Jerome, J.M. Barrie, M.E. Braddon, E. Nesbit, Quiller Couch, du Maurier and (a more occasional practitioner) Max Beerbohm. (Oscar Wilde had also achieved some notoriety, as we have seen, but his fiction had currently disappeared from the bookshops, while Shaw had wisely abandoned novel-writing for play-writing.) There were also the more run-of-the-mill practitioners, such as Hall Caine, Anthony Hope, Max Pemberton, Grant Allen, Morley Roberts, A.E.W. Mason, Stanley J. Weyman, S. Baring-Gould, L.T. Meade, Rhoda Broughton and Headon Hill. They would go on meticulously turning out book after book and, just occasionally, find themselves with a best-seller on their hands. And among the up and coming young writers just entering the lists were H.G. Wells, Joseph Conrad, W.W. Jacobs and Somerset Maugham.

Hornung was certainly not in the top league, but nor did he rank with the run-of-the-mill brigade. He was, in effect, a relatively recent (and junior) arrival in the second league headed by Kipling and Conan Doyle. The fact that *Cassell's Family Magazine* should have featured and advertised *Irralie's Bushranger* as a special supplement to their December 1895 issue speaks volumes for the position which he had now attained and occupied. He was included, as a matter of course, in the first edition of the revived *Who's Who*, published in 1897. He was known as somebody who could tell a good story in a relaxed and competent manner, normally with a twist in the tale, which would give pleasure and satisfaction and leave the audience wanting more. He was, in short, an established practitioner.

Irralie's Bushranger, a cheerful piece of nonsense, is basically a re-run of *The Unbidden Guest* – but with one crucial variation. The new English owner of Arren Downs sheep station, the Hon. Greville Fullarton (the younger son of a lord), arrives to take charge. He is an engaging young man with a devil-may-care attitude, known to be "a ne'er-do-well, and a chronic grief to good grey hairs" – principally those of his father . The station manager's daughter, Irralie Villiers – young, slim, fearless and frank – finds him extremely pleasant but is puzzled that he should be wearing such poor quality clothes, should be riding an exhausted horse and (while bringing no luggage) should be carrying a revolver. He laughingly suggests that the revolver is to defend himself against the notorious bushranger, Stingaree, who is much given to holding up gold escorts. His portmanteaus arrive the following day, but he confesses that he has no keys to open them and is obliged to force the locks. Irralie, convinced until that time that he was Stingaree himself, is reluctantly won over when he produces a tennis racket he has previously mentioned to her. Nearly everyone else takes him at face value, but in the midst of much jollity at a great dance at the station, when the new owner is casting a thoughtful eye over the famous Quandong diamonds worn by a stately guest, the real Greville Fullarton turns up. The new arrival, smartly dressed and wearing a monocle, denounces the impostor who is speedily pounced upon by a mob of men and placed under lock and key. But the new owner proves far less agreeable than his bogus predecessor (complaining, among other things, that the piano is out of tune) and Irralie realises that she is in love with a bushranger. She aids him to escape and away he rides into the darkness – *but it then transpires that the new arrival is really Stingaree, intent on grabbing the diamonds (which he does), and that the original arrival (suspicious circumstances notwithstanding) really was the Hon. Greville Fullarton all the time.* All gets sorted out in the end, after an exciting *finale* with bags of action. Greville and Irralie are united while Stingaree (a brilliant pianist and a cultivated man, but a double-dyed villain of the deepest hue, since he had been plotting to murder them both) is consigned to Darlinghurst Gaol, in Sydney, for the rest of his life. His true identity is never ascertained. (These points are worth noting, for reasons which will become apparent later on.) And, as an added bonus, it transpires that Irralie's father is an off-shoot of *the* Villiers family, so the Hon. Greville is in no way marrying beneath himself.

An engaging *soufflé*, running to no more than 30,000 words, *Irralie's Bushranger* was reprinted towards the end of 1896 in the New Vagabond Library launched by Neville Beatman Ltd and was thus, technically, Hornung's seventh novel. ("A capital little story of Australian love and adventure", proclaimed *The Nation*.) It had been preceded by his sixth book, *The Rogue's March*, published by Cassells.

A century on, the reader opens this substantial tome (running to well over 100,000 words) with dire forebodings. All too evidently, someone (Richard Dowling, perhaps) had persuaded Hornung to write a historical novel, on the grounds that these were nowadays all the fashion and the thing to go for. With sinking heart, one notes the characteristic trappings – the division of the tale into three sections (Parts I, II and III, imposingly proclaimed in Gothic print), and a short Preface which hints, modestly, at all the research that has gone into the tale in order to ensure authenticity. The opening chapter of Part I, set in London, announces that the action is taking place in 1837 and there follows, alas, much stilted dialogue and a plot that is not far removed from melodrama. The characters talk like characters in a book, whereas up till now Hornung's characters have talked like people in real life. They gasp, whisper, cry and exclaim, there is much flashing of eyes and gnashing of teeth, and a brutal murder has been committed ere we reach page 53. An innocent young man is arrested for the crime, with lots of circumstantial evidence (not least his own flight) deployed against him, and he spends a harrowing time in Newgate – an impending victim of the hangman – until a reprieve at the eleventh hour results in his being transported to Australia instead. In the background, of course, is a damsel in distress, wringing her hands in lamentation.

But the book has been sub-titled *A Romance* – warning us, at the very outset, that we are about to be plunged into a plot of inherent improbability – and Hornung puts the complexities of the creaking mechanism and conventions to good use. When the action switches to Australia (which it does in Parts II and III) he is, very evidently, on happier ground, and the interest of the tale gradually wins the reader over until, despite himself, he becomes absorbed. There are encounters with villainous characters galore, of every shape and hue, and Hornung keeps a few surprises up his sleeve until the very last moment. His hero, moreover (whose Germanic name on this occasion is Erichsen), falls some way short of perfection and so too does his heroine.

It must be acknowledged that the scenes in Newgate are indeed pretty harrowing, as are the details of prison life in Australia. A "horrible gauntlet" of a chain gang is memorably described as "a long line of heavily-ironed men, some eighty in all, strung together like beads on a rosary, and at work with pick and shovel beneath the burning sun and the eyes and muskets of the military". "[The Newgate chapters] are as near the truth as I have been able to make them", wrote Hornung in September 1896, "with the aid of sundry Parliamentary papers, supplemented by the very kindly assistance of (I believe) the first living authority on the subject [Dowling, to whom the book was dedicated].... As to the Transportation details, they have been gleaned partly from the blue-book published in 1837, partly from the New South Wales Calendar and the Sydney newspapers of those days, and partly from an admirable work by Mr Charles White, of Bathurst, N.S.W."

The hero (like Wilde) is the victim of unscrupulous enemies and has every conceivable degradation thrust upon him in the name of justice. An excessively harsh summing up by his original judge, and inept reflections by the prison chaplain verging upon impertinence, are followed by a period of unrelenting grimness:

All day they laboured in chains beneath the barrels and bayonets of the military. In the evening, when they returned to the stockade, loaded muskets and fixed bayonets showed them the way. Even in the stockade itself, fixed bayonets and loaded muskets gave them their supper. Thereafter they were locked up for the night in so many small boxes, lined with ledges something more spacious than book-shelves; on these ledges they lay down, as close as mummies in catacombs, until it should be five o'clock once more; and perhaps after a time, the only sound would be the clank of his fetters as this man or that turned over, in the magnificent space of eighteen inches that was allotted to each....

First they took his name and made an inventory of his marks, scars, and the colour of his eyes and hair; then they cropped the latter.... [Next, they put him in branded clothes.] And now they clasped round his body a green-hide belt, from which depended, in front, a heavy chain that became two heavy chains at about the level of the knees; and the two chains ended in still heavier rings round either ankle; and the whole made a capital Y upside down. In this harness it was impossible to walk, though with practice you might waddle; and it was never struck off, for a single instant, on any pretext whatever.

They now presented him with a spoon all to himself; his knife and fork, his pannikin and his mess-kit, he was to share with five other felons.

This was, admittedly, prison Australian-style and set in the late 1830s. Had he wanted to present his readers with an accurate picture of prison English-style in the mid-1890s the author would have had to take into account such features as the treadmill, while constant diarrhoea might only have been hinted at in the most delicate, cautious of tones. But the plank bed was common to both regimes and so, oddly enough, was cold Australian meat.

Simply as a study of the brutality of prolonged incarceration on even the most resilient of characters, *The Rogue's March* would have justified itself. Given that it becomes, in the event, its initial staginess notwithstanding, an exciting tale with a number of twists, so that we are kept guessing until the very end, it is something of a triumph. Having come to scoff, we stay to cheer. "The book is aggravatingly interesting", the critic of the *Daily Chronicle* conceded. "It was with the greatest possible difficulty that we refrained from scampering through the pages of each chapter to see what happened in the end of it. Mr Hornung keeps us in a state of palpitating wonder all through, and then surprises us at the last." Both the *Illustrated London News* and the *Sketch* hailed him as a natural successor to Charles Reade (author of *The Cloister and the Hearth* and *It Is Never too Late to Mend*). The *Morning Post* thought it "one of the most exciting tales that has appeared during many seasons" and the *Daily News* proclaimed it to be "a tragic, fascinating, extraordinarily vivid story, which it is difficult to put down when we begin to read it, and the impression of which it is impossible for a while to shake off". The *Saturday Review* found the Australian scenes "a veritable nightmare" and confessed, in similar vein, that it would "be some little time before we get ... the clank of the chains and the hero's degradation off our mind".

With his next book, *My Lord Duke* (1897), Hornung returned in light-hearted vein to themes he had explored in *A Bride from the Bush* and *The Unbidden Guest* – and explicitly stirred in, on this occasion, a strong dash of the real-life saga of the Tichborne claimant. The title has given a strong indication, immediately confirmed by the very first sentence ("The Home Secretary leant his golf-clubs against the chair") that we are back in the realms of high society. There follows a splendid piece of nonsense.

The eighth Duke of St Osmund's (a distant relative, perhaps, of the Duke of Omnium) is dead. In an ideal world, he would have been succeeded by his grandson Claude Lafont, an agreeable dilettante poet, but Claude's father had an elder brother – "the unmentionable Marquis of Maske" –

who had disappeared to Australia thirty years earlier and was reported to have "died horribly, from thirst in the wilderness" soon after his arrival. But had the unmentionable Marquis spawned a son and heir while he was over there? Indeed, it transpires that he has, for belated word has come from the family lawyer – sent out to scour the length and breadth of Australia by Claude – that the unmentionable Marquis had married and that, after much searching, his offspring has been discovered. Even now, his boat is about to dock at Southampton and Claude is soon hotfooting it to Victoria to greet his cousin and the lawyer. The ninth Duke turns out to be a burly, bearded, rough-looking, weather-beaten giant of a man, immensely cheerful, who insists on carrying his own bundle of luggage (which includes a cage housing three cats). And why the blazes don't they call him Jack, he demands? "Happy Jack's my name, that's what they used to call me up the bush. I'm not going to stop being Jack, or happy either, 'cause I'm a Dook."

His initial mood of ebullience is soon succeeded by one of distress, however, when he realises that he is embarrassing his well-meaning hosts. "I've pained you," he exclaims; "and you bet I'll go on paining you all the time! How can I help it? I'm not what us back-blockers call a parlour-man, though I may be a Dook; but neither the one nor the other is my fault. You should have let me be in the bush [as a boundary rider]. I was all right there – all right with my hut and my cats." London society is astonished, of course, by the eruption of this uncouth giant in their midst, but he is soon hustled off by Claude to Maske Towers, the family seat near Devenholme, where, under the latter's tuition, he acquires a spot of polish. He also acquires Claude's potential fiancée in the form of the Home Secretary's daughter, Miss Olivia Sellwood, whose mother (Lady Caroline) is determined that Olivia will marry the new Duke of St Osmund's, whoever he may be.

Lots of comedy follows, with the new arrival finding as much difficulty in adjusting to his new station in life as society find in adjusting to him. He builds himself a hut on the estate, an exact replica of the one where he had lived in Australia, as a means of assuaging his home-sickness. But the comedy is also interspersed with lots of drama and blackmail. Is the new arrival really the ninth Duke? Did the unmentionable Marquis have an earlier wife and son back in England? Who is the mysterious sardonic stranger – Jack's former boss – who appears on the scene towards the end of the tale? Which of the two heroes will Olivia marry? And will the Home Secretary ever be able to enjoy an uninterrupted round of golf?

For the answers to these, and other questions, it is still worth dipping into *My Lord Duke*. Published by Cassells, and running to about 72,000 words, it was greeted warmly by the critics. "Full of boisterous mirth", proclaimed the *Scotsman*, "and leaves the pleasantest of impressions." "With this tale", asserted its junior stable-mate, the *Glasgow Herald*, "Mr Hornung has made a distinct step forward as a novelist. A capital story." The *Morning Post* hailed its "undeniable freshness and originality"; the *Pall Mall Gazette* declared it "fascinating and powerful" and the *Academy* found it "one of the most agreeable novels that we can remember". "Worth any dozen of the novels which would compete with it for popular favour", thought the *Daily Mail*, while the *Daily Telegraph* and the *Athenæum* agreed that it was amusing and clever. "For many persons, no doubt", said the *Illustrated London News* rather sniffily, "the interest of the story will culminate in the discovery of 'the rightful heir', but life at 'The Towers' has incidents exciting and amusing enough, quite independent of its conclusion." The *Manchester Guardian* found it "skilfully constructed, and the final unravelling of its threads is likely to come as a surprise even to the most hardened of novel-readers." "It is pleasant", remarked *The Nation* in delight, "to turn to a real story by a real story-teller.... It is a capital little novel."

The critics were even more impressed the following year (1898) with the appearance of *Young Blood*, which was also published by Casssells and ran to about 100,000 words – although it is doubtful whether they would have realised the full extent to which the life of its hero was modelled on that of its author. It will be recalled that Harry Ringrose has for health reasons spent two years in Africa (doing service for Australia, which for once goes totally unmentioned) and has returned home on the eve of his twenty-first birthday. He discovers that, in his absence, dreadful things have been happening. His father, an ironmaster and an apparent pillar of the community, has absconded with ten thousand pounds, leaving irate creditors on every front. The family home has been sold up and Harry's mother is now living in very impoverished circumstances. They are befriended by a company promoter called Gordon Lowndes, a high-spirited but rather curious individual whose fortunes (as noted earlier) oscillate between abject poverty and dazzling prosperity. Lowndes has known Harry's father and it seems, at times, as though he is trying to ease his conscience by assisting them. In fact he is a rogue, albeit a likeable one, and Harry gradually becomes aware of his defects – while appreciating that there is, nevertheless, much good in the man. ("Whether Lowndes be entirely realised or not does not much matter," commented *The Bookman*; "the conception of him is already a distinction. He is an adventurer of genius, but not built on the usual lines.")

Harry finds it impossible to find a suitable job for himself, apart from spending a few weeks teaching at a Dame school, but by slow degrees his career as an author takes off and over a period of four years he becomes reasonably prosperous. He had fallen in love with Lowndes's daughter, Fanny, at an early stage of the proceedings, but his estrangement from her father curtails their courtship. Meanwhile, the real villain of the piece is a man called Scrafton, a long-established teacher at the Dame school, allegedly one of the creditors of Henry Ringrose, and so great is his hatred for Harry that he tries to have him dismissed from the school without further ado. It transpires that Scrafton is a brute, much given to the sadistic beating of his tiny pupils, and Harry finally intervenes to stop him – which results, after a fierce fight between them, in the headmistress dismissing Harry from the school for disgraceful behaviour. The book reaches its climax, four years later, when Scrafton tells Harry that Lowndes was responsible for murdering and robbing Harry's father when all three of them were in a steamer bound for France. The now-prosperous Lowndes turns up at this point, with a Scotland Yard detective (so he privately tells Harry) on call in the street outside, and says that, on the contrary, it was Scrafton who did these deeds. Scrafton refuses to retract, so Lowndes now summons the Scotland Yard detective. He turns out to be ("O frabjous day!") none other than Harry's long-last father – returned from his travels, and now able to pay off his long-suffering creditors. Henry Ringrose confirms that it was indeed Scrafton who had struck him a near-fatal blow and thrown him overboard, while it was Lowndes who was primarily responsible for landing him in his financial pickle in the first place. Scrafton faints away, then makes himself scarce, while Lowndes candidly confesses his own shortcomings. The tale ends with marriage between Harry and Fanny, a difference of six years in their ages notwithstanding.

There was, certainly, a strong element of mystery in the tale and (as usual) some surprises in the final chapters for those who simply appreciated a clever plot with unexpected twists and turns, but it was a serious piece of work (of the same degree of importance in Hornung's career as *Tiny Luttrell*) with totally believable characters, dialogue and developments. And there was published, in that same year of 1898, a book of eleven short stories, *Some Persons Unknown*, which served as a further display of his virtuosity. It opened with a pure tear-jerker of a cricketing yarn ('Kenyon's Innings'), with a small thin boy whose days are clearly numbered venerating a friend of his father (C.J. Forrester, one of the great players of the day), then came a couple of mildly entertaining stories about writers ('A Literary Coincidence' and '"Author! Author!"') to which we will return later. There were three romantic tales, two that were positively terrifying, two that were amusing in a sinister fashion and, finally, 'After the Fact', the action-packed thriller starring Deedes Major and his ex-fag, the Beetle. The great majority of them were set in Australia. "The dramatic and tragic aspects of Australian life", commented the *Spectator* judiciously, "are treated by Mr Hornung with that happy union of vigour and sympathy which has stood him in such good stead in his earlier novels."

It will be convenient, at this point, and for reasons which will soon become apparent, to depart from a strictly chronological sequence in considering the other books which Hornung wrote during the closing years of the nineteenth century. An author-turned-publisher had appeared on the scene in the form of Grant Richards, an exceedingly ambitious young man and self-proclaimed 'author-hunter'. He was anxious to build up a repertoire of best-selling authors as rapidly as he could – which meant, of course, poaching from other people – and Hornung found his financial inducements too enticing to resist. It was for Richards, therefore, that he produced two novels which the latter published in 1900 – *The Belle of Toorak* and *Peccavi*.

The Belle of Toorak, running to 45,000 words, was the sort of thing which, by this time, Hornung could write in his sleep. The setting is the Eureka Station in the Riverina. Moya Bethune, a young lady from a wealthy Melbourne family, has just become engaged to Rigden, its boss, and ventured out to sample the new life she is about to lead. But up rides a far-from-jolly swagman – he is, in fact, positively menacing – whom Rigden spirits away into a secret hiding-place. For a posse of mounted police is on the swagman's track and Rigden denies all knowledge of the man when they arrive. Moya gazes on in disbelief, her lip curling in contempt, and breaks their engagement at the first available opportunity. Rigden wishes he could explain, but doesn't, and when the posse returns to take up residence at the station for a night or two he misleads them as to the route their quarry has taken – while helping the mysterious swagman to disappear in the opposite direction. He eventually explains to Moya that the fugitive in question is his very own father, Captain Bovill, a famous bushranger in his day, who has escaped from gaol after thirty years' incarceration. Filial duty has compelled him to help the old man. But the posse now realise they have been duped by a false trail and Rigden is arrested. Moya tracks down the fugitive, appealing to him to come to his son's rescue, but her appeal falls on deaf ears – in fact, he turns positively shirty and tries to kill her. Moya then twigs that this man is not really Rigden's father at all, but a fellow-escapee who has murdered the genuine Captain Bovill and assumed his identity. "Ilis eyes were brown," she cries; "it was in the description; but yours are the blackest I ever saw." She lays him low and rushes off to tell the sergeant. The villain is arrested, Rigden is released, the engagement is resumed and back they go to the homestead.

Peccavi was a rather different type of book from *The Belle of Toorak* – neither light-hearted nor lightweight, but an extremely serious study of a man's sin, downfall and ultimate atonement. It merits a chapter to itself. But critics must have found it difficult to judge either book dispassionately in 1900, for Hornung's fame as a writer had suddenly veered off in a totally different, and rather astonishing, direction. Judged by the very lowliest of contemporary standards (and ignoring, for this purposes, the impressive range of reviews that have been cited), it could be said that, until 1898, Hornung had penned competent, agreeable yarns, but stories which were very much of their time and had nothing particularly electrifying about them. He was someone who could be depended upon to tell a good story which, more often than not, had an Australian angle to it. While his work (or most of it) retained an undoubted quality of freshness, and gave much pleasure, he did not possess the ability to actually shock his readers.

But all this was about to change. Fame would be transformed, for a time, into notoriety. For Max Pemberton, the editor of *Cassell's Magazine* (as it had now become) announced at the end of its May 1898 issue that it would be publishing a "series of exciting stories" by E.W. Hornung during the second half of the year. "Mr Hornung's work", he continued, "is familiar to most of us. He is an exceedingly picturesque and pleasant writer of short stories; but this time we find him in a new rôle. It is scarcely an exaggeration to say that these stories are, in their way, worthy to be compared with the famous 'Sherlock Holmes'. They are tales of the darker side of London life, and their interest is quite extraordinary."

Something rather momentous was evidently in the offing.

8

OUT AND ABOUT

BEYOND the fact that she was Conan Doyle's sister, we know very little about Constance Hornung. Born on 4 March 1868, she was (according to Dickson Carr) decorative, large-eyed and pretty – and able to type. "Suitors had pursued her all over Europe; more than once she thought she wanted to marry, but always backed out. 'Not for the world,' her brother several times declared, in almost the same words, 'would I interfere. If you love him, that's an end of it. But – he has no brains, my dear.'" Jerome K. Jerome would recall "a handsome girl" with curly hair and a fresh complexion who "might have posed as Brunhilda": he found her cheerful and lively, with a sympathetic nature.

Conan Doyle mentions Hornung only twice in his *Memories and Adventures*. "Connie, the younger sister," he writes, on the first of these occasions, "had come back from Portugal earlier, and had joined us at Norwood, where she had met and eventually married E.W. Hornung, the novelist, of whom I will speak later."

Hornung had been, of course, a guest at 12 Tennison Road, South Norwood, at the novelist's invitation. Doyle had purchased this large, gabled red-brick house, in June 1891, where it accommodated not only his growing family but also offered a potential roof to his brothers and sisters. It is possible that Connie, like some of her sisters, had been attending a finishing school in Portugal, and it will be recalled that Hornung had also visited Portugal in the early 1890s, but so far as Doyle was concerned Tennison Road was the venue for their first encounter and courtship. Clearly, he could not reject his sister's latest suitor for shortcomings in the brain department, for on this score Hornung was extremely eligible, and in 1892 (but before considering him as a prospective brother-in-law) Doyle had been positively singing his praises of "one of the sweetest natured and most delicate-minded men I ever knew". It was pleasant to watch Connie and Willie playing lawn tennis. The only cause for concern, from Doyle's viewpoint, was whether Connie's new husband would be able to keep her in the style to which she was accustomed.

A very strong hint as to the manner in which their courtship was allowed to develop is given by Hornung in an impish short story entitled 'A Literary Coincidence'. Conan Doyle is thinly disguised as a popular novelist and magazine editor called Wolff Mason. Thirty years are added to his age, and Connie (alias Ida) becomes his daughter rather than his sister. But in all other essentials the story that unfolds is as true to life as Hornung dared make it. Mason is reconciled to the fact that his two elder daughters are married, "but if Ida followed their example, what on earth was to become of her unfortunate father? Who was to typewrite his manuscript, and correct his proofs, and peel the stamps from the enclosed envelopes of the people who wrote for the novelist's autograph? No, he could not do without Ida at any price."

But he is puzzled, nonetheless, that Ida should look so pale and depressed. His wife (a fragile invalid, like Louise Doyle) explains that Ida is in love with Overman, a young man whom the family had recently met while on holiday at the seaside – and to whom Mason had been rather brusque. "You liked him well enough before he proposed to Ida," his wife points out, which Mason readily admits. "But his proposal", he adds, "was a piece of infernal impertinence, and I told him so."

Later, the two men are reconciled and Overman explains that, with regard to his literary career (on which Mason casts a benign eye), he prefers to be judged on his merits and retain his independence, because "you were the one man in England who could help me on". It is worth noting that Hornung contributed only occasional stories to the *Strand Magazine* during the 1890s, at a time when Doyle was its star performer – fearing, perhaps, that there would otherwise be talk of nepotism.

But clearly, and irrespective of whether or not he came to Constance's wedding, the relations between Conan Doyle and Hornung stopped some way short of close intimacy. "Tomorrow", wrote Doyle to his mother in May 1894, "I dine with the P[all] M[all] magazine staff. Willie will be there." There is perhaps a faint note of resignation in the final remark.

One has the strong impression that Conan Doyle and Hornung were consciously endeavouring, in the mid-1890s, to improve their relationship. In 1894 Hornung was invited by Doyle to assist him in writing a four-act play intended as a vehicle for Henry Irving and Ellen Terry. It was set in Regency times and entitled *The House of Temperley*. In the event, however, the collaboration proved short-lived and Doyle finished it by himself. In 1895, as we have seen, he accepted the invitation to be godfather to the Hornung's son (their only child, as it transpired).

There was perhaps, even at this stage, an element of rivalry in their relationship. Conan Doyle was far better known than Hornung, on the strength of his Sherlock Holmes stories, but he may have had a sneaking suspicion that his brother-in-law's works were rather better than his own – for he virtually admitted as much in 1892 – and was keen to keep this potential upstart firmly in his place. Hornung's own unswerving loyalty to Doyle (as exemplified on the dedicatory page of his first Raffles book) may even have served as a minor irritant. It was a case of the hale and hearty Britisher, pledged to support the Union Jack, the decencies of life and the cause of law and order, versus the seemingly inoffensive, but insidiously subversive, "half-Mongol, half-Slav, or whatever the mixture is".

In another of his short stories of the 1890s, '"Author! Author!"', Hornung gives us what is almost certainly a further glimpse of his relationship at this time with Conan Doyle (now dubbed Pharazyn):

In a manner we were rivals, for we were writing the same sort of thing for the same sort of publications, and that was how we had come together; but never was rivalry friendlier, or mutually more helpful. Our parts were strangely complementary: if I could understand for the life of me the secret of collaboration, I should say that I might have collaborated with Pharazyn almost ideally.... When he had a story to tell he told it with a swing and impetus which I coveted him, as well I might to this day....

[One evening he had an idea which] was as new, and simple, and dramatic as any that ever intoxicated the soul of a story-teller or made a brother author green with envy. I can see him now, as I watched him that night, flinging to and fro with his quick nervous stride, while he sketched the new story.... But when he told me, quite suddenly, as though on an afterthought, that he meant to make a play of it and not a story, I had the solid satisfaction at that moment of calling him a fool.... I [eventually] became as enthusiastic about it as though the work were mine (which it never, never would or could have been), yet I was unable to suggest a single improvement, or have so much as a finger-tip in the pie.

Doyle may also have resented, albeit only half-consciously, the fact that Constance had deserted the protection of his imposing roof at South Norwood to go and live in somewhat reduced circumstances with the rival novelist of the family, for Doyle's own domestic life had begun to pass through a very unhappy phase. He would have welcomed (apart from the never-ending advice of his mother, who lived in Yorkshire) the presence of another woman in the household to assist him in coping with his wife Louise, whose health now became extremely bad. She had never been particularly robust at the best of times, but in the autumn of 1893 a troublesome pain in her side resulted in a diagnosis of galloping consumption and the news that she had only a few months to live. In fact, Louise (or Touie, as she was known within the family) managed to hold out until 1906, but these were thirteen years that took a heavy toll of Conan Doyle. There were trips to the Alps, in search of a kinder climate, periodic recoveries and periodic dashing of hopes. While remaining true to his wife, Conan Doyle eventually sought solace and companionship elsewhere – and this, as we shall see, triggered off an almighty row with Hornung. With nurses and his sister Lottie in attendance on his wife, he nevertheless endeavoured to undertake his usual amount of foreign travel and pursue a relatively normal public career. In 1896, having been advised that the air for invalids was better in that part of Surrey than it was in South Norwood, he bought a site at Hindhead, near the Devil's Punchbowl, and commissioned the building of a new country house for himself and his family.

The Conan Doyles took up formal residence in their new home in the autumn of 1897, and Hornung would make use of that locality, some thirteen years later, for a short story entitled 'The Man in the Driving Seat'. It told the tale of a dastardly attempt by some Indian plotters to assassinate Lord Amtyl, a shrewd and popular pillar of the Empire and the owner of a large country house at Hindhead – a gentleman, in short, not totally dissimilar from his brother-in-law.

Hornung's mother Harriet, who had returned to Middlesbrough after her husband's death, died at No. 7 Southfield Villas on 4 June 1896 at the age of seventy-two and in the presence of her son Charles. The novelist would dedicate a book of short stories to her memory in 1898 and a tribute forthcoming from another quarter was a poem written by Dr Bryan Charles Waller, a rather mysterious figure who was a close associate of both Conan Doyle and *his* mother, Mary Josephine Elizabeth Doyle. Harriet had evidently been a very positive character in her own right.

Just possibly, the memories of his childhood which would have been evoked by his mother's death were responsible for Hornung's taking, from this time onwards, an interest in his old schools – beginning with the one at which he had been a boarder in 1879 and 1880. "Hornung and I", wrote Shane R. Chichester in 1941,

> first met at my private school – St Ninian's, Moffat – in the summer term of 1896. From that time for a quarter of a

century he was to me a big brother and a father, all rolled into one. He had come on a visit to St Ninian's as an Old Boy, and as a budding author he regaled us with his tales.

His great interest in boys and young men and school life generally, had the natural result of drawing the best out of them. He had close associations with many schools, and on the occasion of the little addresses in chapel, which he gave on some of his visits... he held his audience from start to finish: not a cough, not a movement – a pin could have been heard to drop.

Conan Doyle accompanied the Hornungs on a trip to Rome in March 1898. Here the two writers encountered two other writers, namely H.G. Wells and George Gissing. Wells (Hornung's exact contemporary) had made his mark with *The Time Machine*, published in 1895, and had followed it up with *The Invisible Man* and *The War of the Worlds*. Gissing was nine years older than Hornung and Wells and a well-established writer by this time, *New Grub Street* and *The Old Women* being his most recent productions. A strange, solitary, parsimonious man, with two broken marriages behind him (and, before that, a short spell in prison for theft), capable of sudden but short-lived moods of vivacity, his only close literary friend up till now (apart from Morley Roberts) had been Wells himself. "After dinner", noted Gissing in his diary on 12 March, "a card was sent in to me, with the name Hornung. It was the novelist (of whom I have read nothing). A man of 30, suffering much from asthma; married to sister of Conan Doyle. Invited us all to call to-morrow evening." The following evening, a Sunday, they (i.e., Gissing plus Mr and Mrs Wells) duly presented themselves at the Hornung's apartment (38 Gregoriana). They found their hosts agreeable company and stayed until eleven o'clock. "Mrs Hornung", noted Gissing, "a large, healthy, good-humoured woman, with wonderfully bright eyes." They called again on 18 March and were once more the Hornungs' guests on the following Sunday evening.

"We have seen quite a lot of Gissing and Wells during the last fortnight," Hornung wrote to Frederick Whyte on 22

March. "Wells has joined Gissing here for two or three weeks. We like them both quite immensely. Wells is a very good little chap when you know him, humorous, modest, unaffected. As for Gissing, he is a really sweet fellow – Connie says so and it is the only word.... He has charm and sympathy, humour too and a louder laugh than Oscar's. That man is not wilfully a pessimist. But he is lonely – there has been some great sorrow and ill-health too. I took him the *Academy* this forenoon ... and found him writing a short story in his insect's hand – 1,000 words on each (quarto) page. I spoilt his morning's work but left him merry. I could have stopped there jawing all day." Gissing himself (somewhat less exuberant than this letter suggests), making his diary entry for that day, records that he had written almost one page and was "then interrupted by visit by Hornung. Bad attack of lumbago. Had to go to bed dinnerless. Then a night of diarrhoea."

Gissing's initial enthusiasm for the company of his new friend was, perhaps, beginning to wane. The diary entry four days' later, on 26 March, reads: "After dinner to a musical party at Hornung's. Only interesting new acquaintance, Mrs Mallet – who recited a thing of Edward Lear's. Mrs Hornung amazes me by her robust and beautiful health. Her sister, Mrs Foley (who lives on a little island beyond Posillipo) also a fine physical type; a little less robust, and more handsome." And on 28 March: "Ceaseless rain.... In afternoon came Hornung, and talked ad infinitum, as usual."

Separations would come on 12 April, with the Wellses moving on to Naples and Gissing to Berlin, and final farewells were said on the 8th. "Dinner with Conan Doyle, the Wells's and the Hornungs, at Trattoria Colonna," Gissing recorded in his diary. "Then all together to see moon on Colosseum, and ended evening at Hornungs." (Somebody else who apparently visited Rome in 1898 was Oscar Wilde, although the dates of his visit are not clear.)

Momentary irritations notwithstanding, Gissing thought it would be useful to maintain contact with Hornung. "When you write again (not specially)", he told Wells on 26 August, "will you let me know Hornung's address. I want to ask him something about Australia – a point for use in fiction." Hornung and his wife had, in fact, been greatly attracted by Italy and – with his literary activities proving more profitable than ever before – had resolved to stay there throughout the winter. They had returned to England for a short time, after the trip to Rome, but then set off for six months' stay in the south of Italy, where they had rented a historic villa at Capo Posillipo. "Give my love to dear old Gissy when you see or write to him," wrote Hornung to Wells on 3 July, "and tell him that he too ought to come and quaff the juice of Gaiola grapes."

Gissing resisted the temptation to visit them at their intriguing retreat, but he did get in touch with them again that summer. Hornung had evidently sustained an injury of some kind (from swimming, perhaps?), for on 28 September Gissing tells Wells: "I have heard from Hornung. He says that nothing more than a week's discomfort resulted from his accident. They stay thro' the winter at Posillipo."

Posillipo was a place of enchantment. (It was also, incidentally, the place where Wilde and Douglas, although appallingly short of funds, had lived together for several weeks in the autumn of 1897.) That August Hornung wrote a long account of his holiday to an unknown correspondent (Whyte, perhaps) and the letter found its way into *The Cornhill Magazine* in May 1899, appearing under the title 'A Villa in a Vineyard'. His account still reads vividly and agreeably and provides an interesting insight into the pattern of their life at this time. "This early morning", he begins,

> I could sleep no more: a mosquito had won through the curtains and either it or I must go. The ignominious remedy was much simpler, and I came through my bedroom window, out upon the drawing-room roof. It was just after five; the sun sat flaring on the spurs of Vesuvius, turning the mountain from grey to angry purple, even as I watched; in the still air his crest of smoke stood straight on end. Every night a crimson gash glows and grows in the mountain side, to heal at dawn. And every night (while we have no moon) the bay is a blackness spangled with the lights of the fishing-

boats; but this morning it was the boats that lay black upon a golden sheen.

Someone asked me exactly where we are, but the man was a cricketer. I said that Naples was long-leg, Vesuvius long-on (well-round), Nisida point, Procida cover-point, Ischia extra cover, and Capri 'in the deep', with a vengeance, some twenty miles over the bowler's head. Capo Posillipo is our square-leg umpire, but the bowler is a mere buoy.

In point of fact, the place is a vineyard, and the homestead in the middle of it we have taken for six months. It hangs on an angle of the cliffs, at their very edge, and from below looks a dizzier height than we find it. It is a house with a history. Lucullus built it, no less. It was his very own villa. And yet we are deeply ignorant about Lucullus! He was, "of course", a Roman general of the Empire, but I cannot conquer the impression that he fought his battles with the dactyl and the spondee, and scanned his own lines oftener than those of the enemy. Catullus and Tibullus are my snare. A patron of the arts we know Lucullus to have been, and here are evidences. I look out of my study window into the green basin that was the general's private theatre. My landlord has unearthed a marble plinth, with Leda and the swan in still bold relief, clearly the property of his more illustrious predecessor. We have two ways down to the sea; and by one we pass the still standing walls of a villa of Virgil himself. There are other ruins, relics, associations, if one was learned enough to write about them. Perhaps the learning will come. Meanwhile I have a vague recollection of Lucullus at school, as a man of war. But I am beginning to know him by a repute which I may say that I can check.

We have two ways down to the sea: the Virgilian way is for the most part a gradual descent by a dusty pathway through the vines; the other is precipitous and even more romantic. It is a secret stair to the water's edge, three-parts subterranean, two hundred and fifteen steps in all. It has not yet been used in a novel, to my knowledge, but its time may come. Ending, as it begins, in honest daylight, these steps land you at the mouth of a cavern containing every facility for a bloody dénouement; meanwhile you can undress there in luxury, and but for the rocks there would be no better bathing-place in the bay. This morning the water was as warm as milk, as invigorating as dry champagne. But the sunk rocks barked my nakedness, and either the weed that grows upon the rocks, or the marine mosquito which infests the weed, stung considerably. What matter? The faithful Fiorentina was astir when I clomb the two hundred and fifteenth step, and even her coffee was good to drink this morning.

Fiorentina is a poor cook, yet the best that we can get to come so far out of Naples, the only one who would tackle our lane and the daily journey to Posillipo for the *spesa*; and Fiorentina, we discover, had her reasons. She turns out to be a fortune-teller as well as a cook – it is to be hoped a better one. We understand that she practises her secondary (or primary) profession in the intervals of the *spesa*, or marketing. We know that she robs us in her good-natured, light-hearted way; but we are beginning to like Fiorentina in spite of her idiosyncrasies, which include a rooted objection to stays and shoes, and an open fondness for the wine of the vineyard. What we dislike, our one and only grievance, is the system of *spesa* which Fiorentina illustrates, and which is forced upon us by our distance from the shops. Not one of them will send. We might stew in the juice of our own grapes, but every crumb of our daily bread has to be fetched from afar.

One must not scamp Fiorentina. She is a woman of more than character; the charm of mystery is instinct in her untidy person and wild eyes. She has weekly interviews with her solicitor, on the head of some legacy, as far as we can make out. I have heard the jingle of money in her room. Yet the most valuable current coin of Italy is worth less then twopence. Is she such a wise virgin as all that? Coin in Italy! She is not free from education, Fiorentina. Only last night I found her writing with my pen and ink, at this very desk. On the other hand, there is no quicker worker than Fiorentina; she polishes everything of in the morning, and retires to bed for the afternoon. She can boil an egg in ten seconds. You say ten minutes if you want her to give it three.

To me the crowning merit of our villa is its villino, three little rooms by themselves, the best of the three my den. It is remote from the house, and Fiorentina; never had man a fairer chance in fairer workshop. Vines look in at one window, and through the other smokes old Vesuvius, as though butter wouldn't melt in his crater. Both windows have the light-tight shutters of the country, and face east and west respectively, so that in summer I can have as little sun as I like, in winter as much. The mere morning is worth a long day in London; there are no interruptions; you can work in flannels, or your pyjamas, without fear of friend or enemy; and not before luncheon can you get your letters.

I said the *spesa* was our only grievance, but, with one of us at any rate, the letters are a worse. They may arrive any time between the middle of the day and the middle of next week. The postman is as bad as the shopkeepers, without their right; nothing will entice him to our door. Sometimes he leaves the letters with friends of ours on the shore, and we get them when we call, or our friends bring them when they call on us. Sometimes he has consigned them to a decrepit crone at the top of our lane, but never when we send up to see. Last Saturday he seems to have dealt our letters round like a pack of cards, and to-day (Monday) they are still creeping in, like stricken soldiers. Heaven knows how many have fallen by the way! Yet I am blamed for not correcting proofs. I have tried correcting the postman, but it is little use, and rather disagreeable. He is a splendid fellow, handsome, stalwart, but he weeps outright if you bully him, and his one excuse is subtle if not complete:

"Excellency! I have eight daughters...."

There is no more to be said.

These hot afternoons one may do worse than follow the example of the seasoned Fiorentina and the couch in my study (when she does not borrow the cushions) affords a satisfying siesta; but one fly in the room on such occasions is worse than any number in the ointment, to say nothing of my enemies the mosquitoes. There is no remedy against the latter.

Tea between three and four is indispensable in Italy, even more so than elsewhere, as it seems to us. And after tea, if there is still no sign of your letters and the three-days-old paper with the latest cricket, you can always scribble for another hour or two, as I am doing now. But the serious delight of the day is close at hand, and from five to six o'clock you go down to the sea once more for the incomparable swim before dinner. Not this time by the subterranean stair, but through the vineyard and past Virgil's villa, without a thought of the poet or of his pious hero, though I fancy there is a passage of which one ought to think. I wish I could think of it at this moment, or knew where to borrow an *Aeneid*....

It is over, the great *bagno*, the exquisite evening bathe. We were in three-quarters of an hour; we swam a quarter-of-a-mile at least. Can nobody invent a cyclometer for the swimmer, a natatometer, or patent log? It is our only exercise out here in August. I am curious to know how much we 'do'. This bathing place is to the other what Lord's cricket ground is to a pitch in Regent's Park: you are not for ever in danger of an unmerited bruise. Instead of the ubiquitous rock, you have the well-marked foundations of a Roman house, as easy to avoid as they are grateful to rest upon. It was glorious to-night! The sun was setting redder than he rose this morning, setting through rich grey clouds the colour of Ischia, but much farther north, even north of Nisida. Not since I came have I known it calmer; and the ripples ran rosy to your chin, as you swam against them, into that gorgeous dying light upon shore and sea! And there is neither cold nor heaviness in these summer waters; the body seems as light as the heart, gliding through them. Ah! hard to feel the burden of the flesh once more, even as you drag it, dripping silver, back to dull dry land!

But how good to climb home through the dusty vineyard, clean of body and soul, with such an appetite, and a mind at peace! Giuseppe is finishing among the vines; he has deep-set, twinkling eyes, and, since he missed his last month's shave, a chin that would scrub a floor. A Neapolitan of the Neapolitans, than whom no citizens have a less enviable name. In Naples, one gathers that you never know when a man 'has his knife in you', until you see its point sticking out of your waistcoat. I don't believe it of Giuseppe, for one. With nothing to gain, he treats the humble tenant as though he were full lord of the vineyard, and off comes his hat as usual:

"Buona sera, eccellenza!"

"Buona sera, Giuseppe!"

The Hornungs came back to London early in 1899, but instead of returning to a flat in Chelsea they took up residence at 9 Pitt Street, a house in West Kensington, which would be their home for the next six years. Gissing, anxious to avoid "too much fatigue" while on a brief business trip to London from his modest home at Dorking, was their guest on 7 April: writing to his mistress, Gabrielle Fleury, he described his host as "a very good fellow who has for a long time begged me to come & stay with him". (Conan Doyle evidently dropped in, for he reported the event to H.G. Wells in an undated note: "Saw Gissing last week at Hornung's.")

A change of address coincided with a change of direction in Hornung's literary career. He was aware, by this time, that he had gone just about as far as he could in capitalising on his Australian experiences and was in danger of becoming rather too hackneyed, not to say stereotyped, if he continued to make use of his recollections of life on the Riverina thirteen years earlier. Already, he had come very close to sending himself up, for a character in a short story entitled 'The Magic Cigar' – Hell-fire Jim, a foul-mouthed, drunken sheep-shearer – suddenly lapses into impeccable English, as he relaxes with a decent cigar and recalls his days at Eton and Oxford, but hastens to reassure his listener that on this occasion he's "not the wicked baronet or the disguised duke" and that his father is only a country squire.

He was evidently experiencing, moreover, pangs of guilt as he reflected on the extent to which he had exploited, on the slender basis of a visit lasting only two years, the characters and environment of the people he had met. It could be argued that he had shamelessly abused the trust of his ingenuous hosts by treating them as artist's models, and setting himself up as an expert on all things Australian. But perhaps he could, however belatedly, make amends? At any rate, in a story entitled 'The Poet of Jumping Sandhills' he provided himself with a fictionalised younger sister, sent out to recuperate at Meringul Station, New South Wales, where her brother had been before her.

It was many years ago, in Olive's childhood, but Philip Armitage had been writing bush stories ever since, with the station and its mighty paddocks for the unmistakable background of the often impudent pictures. In the silly Old Country he was said to be taken quite seriously as a representative Australian writer. If so, as Mr Pochin [his former host] averred, "it was about time those colonies paddled their own canoe"; but he and his at any rate knew the fellow for what he had been as a beardless boy in their midst.

Olive, blissfully ignorant of the extent to which her brother's impertinent book-writing activities are resented, delights in finding that the scenery and the station with its corrugated roof are just as Philip had depicted them in his stories, but where were the people he had described – "his little army of lost angels in the shape of gentlemanly whim-drivers, boundary-riders, and bushrangers"? Her host is obliged to tell her that his own whim-drivers and boundary-riders don't answer to that description – "And as for bushrangers, Miss Armitage, the Kellys were the last authentic gang, and that was some years before your brother was here."

"But surely you have the stockman and the tramp who have seen better days?"

"I've no doubt we have, but they don't always give it away for our benefit."

A retort that is greeted with roars of laughter, much to the discomfiture of Miss Armitage.

In short, the creator of some of the standard figures of what was allegedly contemporary Australia – aped by a squad of industrious imitators, who zealously reproduced them on far too generous a scale – was now anxious to distance himself from his earlier work. And it was, in any case, time to move on. In *The Shadow of the Rope*, written in 1902 and set in England, a novelist remarks that tales involving swagmen from Australia were "the sort of thing [that] has been done to death in books". To be the Australian counterpart of Bret Harte was enjoyable, but it was not quite enough. A retailer of popular fiction needed to replenish his stock from time to time and have something absolutely fresh on the shelves to offer his customers – while not totally abandoning, of course, the lines that had served him so well in the past. By the turn of the century, Hornung was doing just that.

9

AN OSCAR FOR OSCAR

PECCAVI, the second of Hornung's books to be published by Grant Richards in 1900, was the most austere that he had yet penned. Set in a Suffolk village, and commencing in the summer of 1882, we find ourselves present at the tailend of a funeral. The deceased is a young girl, the unmarried daughter of Jasper Musk, and the service is conducted by the Rector, Robert Carlton. The girl had died in childbirth, and Musk suspects that she had, on her deathbed, told the Rector the name of the man who betrayed her. Carlton, in a mood of terrible misery, says that he does indeed know the name of the man – for it is his own. Musk recoils in horror, vowing vengeance, and within half-an-hour the news is all round the village. The residents, not surprisingly, are up in arms. The Rector's closest adherents and admirers turn against him. When darkness falls the rectory is stoned by an angry mob, and later that night somebody sets fire to the church. A little while later, Carlton's dog, the one creature that had remained faithful to him, will be clubbed to death.

It is a grim commencement to a haunting story. The Church authorities suspend Carlton from his duties for a period of five years and he is expected to leave the district. Instead, having some private means of his own, he stays put in the shattered rectory and endeavours to atone for the harm he has done by setting in hand the restoration of his ruined church. But the squire, Sir Wilton Gleed, M.P., is determined to drive him out and gives strict instructions that none of the local builders are to respond to his request for their services. Nor will any of the local shops supply him with food. In the end,

Carlton resolves to rebuild the church single-handed and the greater part of the book is devoted to a rivetting account of precisely how he sets about doing this and how he obtains his sustenance. It is in similar vein to the shipwrecked mariner chapters of *Robinson Crusoe* and was the sort of story that C.S. Forester would excel in producing – *Brown on Resolution*, say – thirty-five years later. Hornung was keenly aware of the fact that he was treading in Defoe's footsteps on this occasion. "Unparalleled position for an endowed clergyman of the Church of England," he exclaims,

> the incumbent of an enviable living, an Oxford man, a man of family, an enlightened and alluring preacher, towards the latter end of the nineteenth century! Scandalous priest though he had proved himself, his case was as pitiable as unique; a pariah in his own parish; the outcast of his own people; an inland Crusoe, driven to the traditional expedients of the castaway, and living the very life of such within sight and hail of a silent and unceasing world. It was a position which few men would have faced for an instant. This man maintained it throughout the winter. And throughout the winter his work went on. And the spring found him technically sane.
>
> But his brain bore it better than his heart. Some vital part of him was certain to suffer. His brain escaped altogether, his body for a time; but his heart was hard within him; all his prayers could not suffer it; and presently he lost the power even to pray.... [His face became] the face of one in the coils of malignant despair. But the more gradual and substantial change, in such a man, was terrible beyond deduction from its mere outward shadow.
>
> Here was no sudden and sweeping infidelity; no plucking of loose roots from a shallow soil. Shallow this man was not, nor easily shaken in the least of his convictions. His general tenets stood intact. He still believed in the efficacy, under God, of earnest and worthy prayer. But he could no longer believe in the efficacy of his own prayers. They were not worthy: that was the whole truth. They were earnest enough, but utterly unworthy, and it was better not to pray at all.
>
> His most passionate prayers had been for his own forgiveness, for the restoration of his own peace of mind, for

the blessing of God upon his own little labours; selfish prayers, one and all; and he saw the selfishness at last. It shocked him. He tried to stamp it out, this new and obtrusive egoism; but he failed. Denied all contact with his fellow-creatures, with only his own wishes to consult, his own work to do, his own heart to probe, his own life to discipline, the man was an egoist before he knew it; and it was only through his prayers that he ever discovered it at all. They were not only unanswered; they no longer brought their own momentary comfort, as heretofore. Of old it had been much more than momentary; now it was no comfort at all. There must be some reason for this; he asked himself what reason; and the answer was this revelation of the true character of his prayers. They were poisoned at the fount. He tried to purify them, but all in vain. Self would creep in. So then he prayed only for a renewal of the faculty of pure and unselfish prayer. And this was the most passionate of all his prayers. But it also was unanswered. So he prayed no more.

He was unforgiven: so Carlton explained it to himself. And a little brooding convinced him of his idea. If God had forgiven him, He would have shown some sign of His clemency through men. But what had men done? They had broken his windows; they had burnt his church; they had closed up every avenue to such poor atonement as was in his power; they had forced him into a position which he had never sought, though for a little it had consoled him; then tried, by false accusation, to force him out of it; and now they had cut him off from themselves, had set him apart as a thing eternally unclean, had even stooped to destroy the one dumb being that clung to him in his exile!

The murder of the dog was no little thing in itself; coming at the foot of such a list, at the bitter end of a night of bitterness, it was the last drop that petrified a truly humble and a strenuously contrite heart.

But it did not petrify his hand; and the work of that hand went on without ceasing.... While five fingers could control the chisel, and the other hand strike true, no weather could have deterred him. And no weather did.

But it was necessary, alas, for a sub-plot to be developed. Sir Wilton actually has Carlton charged in court with setting fire to his own church, but Carlton defends himself so effectively that he is declared not guilty, even though many of the local residents continue to harbour their doubts. The squire then abandons his attempt to drive Carlton out of the area, and simply endeavours to ignore him, but his niece Gwynneth takes a close interest in this solitary toiler. Then, of course, there is Carlton's illegitimate son, living close at hand and being brought up by his grandparents, and so we have to be introduced to young Georgie (a rather nauseating child, to modern eyes, and far less winsome than he is evidently intended to be).

Eventually, however, the five years come to an end, the Rector is suspended from his clerical duties no more and he holds his first open-air services in the largely restored church – a gaunt, prematurely-aged, white-haired figure by this time, but still a fine preacher and a better, gentler person than in the days of his original fame. Public opinion has, by now, been largely won over: Carlton has redeemed himself and his old adherents, knowing a true man when they see one, return to the fold. (And Gwynneth, studying a photograph of Georgie's mother, feels that there is something rather unpleasant about her mouth.) But the roof of the church has still to be provided, and Sir Wilton (with an eye on the Press) decides to come to the rescue and let bygones be bygones. But Carlton is aware that public opinion, ever fickle, is now tending to make him a hero, which he never wanted to be. He resolves to leave the village the moment the church has been reconsecrated and to take himself off to Australia – away from the temptation posed by Gwynneth – for there is, so he tells his bishop, "need of clergy in the far corners of our empire, greater need than here" and he has offered his services to the Bishop of Riverina.

On the very eve of the reconsecration, however, the church is set on fire for a second time. The culprit, on this occasion, is soon identified as Jasper Musk, for he is trapped in the roof, and it transpires that Carlton has been aware, all along, that Musk was responsible for igniting it on the first occasion as well. The grim old man has never relented in his hatred of Carlton, but the Rector nevertheless tries to save him from the conflagration – and, in the event, both of them perish in the flames. The story ends with Gwynneth, having visited Carlton's grave, taking Georgie away with her to London, where she and her friend, Nurse Ella, will bring him up.

It was a fine, impressive piece of work, the obnoxiousness of Georgie notwithstanding, and showed that Hornung had reached a new level of maturity in his development as a novelist. It was totally unlike anything that he had done before. It can be bracketed, perhaps, with *The Scarlet Letter*, while the opening chapter, with its vivid depiction of village life, almost leads us into the realm of Thomas Hardy. The *Spectator* found this "striking and admirable story" to be "at once the most serious and the strongest novel that has issued from Mr Hornung's engaging pen". "Mr Hornung", commented the *Academy*, "rivets our attention on a spectacle of grandiose simplicity.... The realism of the story is commendable.... One suspects exaggeration, but surrenders to the charm of a simple, direct story.... To say that *Peccavi* is far better than the author's last story is scarcely to place it. It is, in a sense, outside his art."

There was one word, however, quoted in the book on two occasions, which may have stirred the memory of some of its readers. The malevolent Sir Wilton accuses Carlton of not really intending to rebuild the church with his own hands. "You mean to pretend to try", he says. "You mean to pose." Sir Wilton repeats the accusation several chapters later and declares that Carlton is "posing as a martyr – really laughing in his sleeve and crowing over all right-minded men." The word that catches the eye is, of course, "pose", for we are reminded of that famous card which accompanied the bouquet delivered by the Marquess of Queensberry – "To Oscar Wilde posing [as a] Somdomite [sic]."

And at this point it becomes overwhelmingly clear that the author is thinking, once again, of the stricken playwright. Just as he had written a book about imprisonment, and the indignities endured by a convict, while Wilde was in prison, so now he wrote a book about the aftermath of a great sin – when forgiveness may, or may not, be forthcoming – at a time when Wilde had been released from prison, having discharged his formal debt to society and having suffered terribly in the process. Is this talented man to be shunned, and treated as a leper, for evermore? "Whatever he has done," declares Gwynneth, "he has paid very bitterly for it, and made such amends as were never made by anybody I ever heard of.... We shall honour ourselves in future by honouring him, and dishonour ourselves by continuing to dishonour him. He has had his punishment, and look how he has borne it! Why, he has done what was never done in the world before by one solitary man."

A little later on the issue is spelt out even more explicitly. "Are you sure that it matters how people behave," Gwynneth inquires of her companion, Nurse Ella, "if you really love them?"

"How they behave?" echoed her friend. "Why, Gwynneth, of course! Nothing does matter except behaviour."

"It wouldn't to me," Gwynneth exclaimed, almost through her teeth.

"But surely what one does is everything!"

"Not in love," averred Gwynneth, whose convictions were few but firm.... "No, you love people for what they are, not for what they do."

Nurse Ella laughed outright.

"That may be good metaphysics," said she, "but it's shocking common-sense! Our actions are the only possible test of our character, as its fruit is the only test of a tree."

In Gwynneth's eyes burnt wondrous fires, and on her cheeks; and her breath was coming very quickly. But most persons look straight ahead as they walk and talk, and between these two fell the kindly fog besides.

"Suppose you loved somebody," the young girl cried at last; "and suppose you suddenly discovered he had once done something dreadful – unspeakable. Would that alter your feeling towards him?"

"It could not fail to do, Gwynneth."

"It would not alter mine!" ...

116

"Well Gwynneth," said Nurse Ella, with a laugh, "we were evidently born to differ. In my view that would be the one sort of excuse for changing one's mind about a man – whereas you see others!"

"But I am not talking about one's mind," said Gwynneth; "the feeling I mean ... lies infinitely deeper than the mind."

"And no crime could alter it?"

"Not if he atoned – not if the rest of his life were one long atonement."

"But, Gwynneth, that would make all the difference."

Gwynneth walked on in silence. She was reconsidering her own last words.

"Atonement or no atonement," she exclaimed at length, "it would make no difference – if I loved the man. Atonement or no atonement!" repeated Gwynneth defiantly.

It will be clear from this, of course, that Gwynneth is leading Nurse Ella into very deep waters – or, if the simile be preferred, in a direction that comes very close to having the Albany apartment of A.J. Raffles as its ultimate destination. If someone whom one loves commits what is overwhelmingly regarded, by the standards of the day, as an evil act, can one – or should one – continue to love that person? Is loyalty of greater importance than morality?

Life, for once, imitated art. *Peccavi*, published in 1900, ended with the death of Robert Carlton, while final oblivion overcame Oscar Wilde on 30 November 1900. Prolonged suffering, in both cases, was followed by merciful release and so the nightmare and tensions came to an end. Yet the aftermath, so far as the real life episode was concerned, brought some uneasy awakenings. "It is among the offices of suspense to make word and deed mechanical," Hornung reflected in 1901, "and life a dream. The senses are dulled; nothing is released – not even death itself, when death comes. Afterwards you remember with horror your callousness: when all the time your senses have been dulled by the most merciful of Nature's laws. Afterwards you find that you received many an impression without knowing it."

If the surmises of this present study are accepted as proven, then *Peccavi* must be regarded as Hornung's final tribute to his old mentor. And Wilde had, moreover, provided him with a further burst of inspiration – or, at any rate, intellectual justification, if such were needed – for a series of stories that were to be totally without precedent. "An artist", Wilde had asserted, "has no ethical sympathies at all. Virtue or wickedness are to him simply what the colours on his palette are to the painter. They are no more and they are no less. He sees that by their means a certain artistic effect can be produced and he produces it. Iago may be morally horrible and Imogen stainlessly pure. Shakespeare, it has been said, had as much delight in creating the one as he had in creating the other." Here, once again, was a signpost pointing directly towards the Albany.

10

CRIMES AND PUNISHMENTS

IN JUNE 1898, with a marked degree of trepidation, *Cassell's Magazine* published the very first Raffles story – 'The Ides of March'. Or, to be more precise, it published this story as the very first in a new series entitled 'In the Chains of Crime' – "Being the Confessions of a late Prisoner of the Crown, and sometime accomplice of the more notorious A.J. Raffles, Cricketer and Criminal, whose fate is uncertain." The accompanying illustration at the head of the story, which would be reproduced in like position in each of the five subsequent issues, showed a wretched Bunny Manders on his knees with a chain around his neck being pulled ever closer to his doom by a skeleton wearing a cloak and hood.

For Cassell's were half excited at their own audacity, and half ashamed of themselves, for publishing the Raffles stories. They were anxious to make it clear, from the very outset, that they were intended as Cautionary Tales which would be A Warning to Others and that in no way did the leading performers carry their seal of approval. Only when these trappings and disclaimers were firmly in place did they draw a breath and, with fingers tightly crossed, allow the author to proceed. But they published no more than six stories (and would never publish any more) so that when Methuen's edition of *The Amateur Cracksman* arrived in the bookshops in April 1899 delighted readers found that the full quota amounted to eight.

The narrator of the stories is Harold Manders, although his Christian name would not be revealed until 1905: Raffles calls him Bunny, and this is the name by which he has come down to posterity. (An appalling Hollywood film of the 'thirties, starring Ronald Colman, provides Raffles with a manservant who actually greets Manders with the words "Good morning, Mr Bunny.") Bunny, a young man desperately short of money, appeals to his old idol, A.J. Raffles, for advice. He had fagged for him at school and their acquaintance has recently been renewed. Raffles had then been captain of the eleven and we will learn, very shortly, that he is now "a dangerous bat, a brilliant field, and perhaps the very finest slow bowler of his decade". In an unguarded moment Bunny confesses that he will do anything to save himself from imminent ruin, and is even willing to break the law – "Name your crime, and I'm your man." Raffles thereupon tells him he too is equally skint but that he has a good friend in New Bond Street who will lend them some money, even at two o'clock in the morning, and they sally forth from the Albany to find this remarkable Samaritan. It eventually dawns on Bunny, after they have gained access to the friend's flat and it proves to be empty, that Raffles has conned him into assisting in a raid on the jeweller's shop located underneath this flat. Horrified but resolved, he mounts guard for Raffles and they come away with a choice hoard of jewellery. Raffles welcomes Bunny to the burglary profession, and explains that he too had once been horrified at the notion – but, having slipped from the straight and narrow while on a visit to Australia, he'd "tasted blood, and it was all over with me. Why should I work when I could steal? Why settle down to some humdrum uncongenial billet, when excitement, romance, danger, and a decent living were all going begging together? Of course, it's very wrong, but we can't all be moralists, and the distribution of wealth is very wrong to begin with. Besides, you're not at it all the time. I'm sick of quoting Gilbert's lines to myself, but they're profoundly true."

The stories that follow narrate the subsequent adventures of our two villains. In their *next* escapade they fail to capture Reuben Rosenthall's purple diamonds, but Raffles saves Bunny from the wrath of the brute. In 'Gentlemen and

Players', in which cricket looms large, Raffles explains that while cricket is much less exciting than crime it is necessary to have a parallel ostensible career as a means of allaying suspicion. "Fill the bill in some prominent part, and you'll never be suspected of doubling it with another of equal prominence." Lady Melrose's fabulous necklace is stolen by professional burglars, but Raffles manages to intercept it and thereafter explains to Bunny how he first fell from grace during his visit to Australia (as the member of a touring team). Already, however, nemesis is at hand, for Inspector Mackenzie of Scotland Yard has appeared on the scene – initially, under the alias of Clephane – and will soon be taking a very close interest in their activities. (Hornung evidently felt that the Inspector's alias was too good to waste, for he used the name again in *No Hero*.) Finding himself followed home by the old fence to whom he sells their loot, Raffles contemplates murdering the man – but finds that someone else (a young blood of their acquaintance) has beaten him to it. He and Bunny then accept a commission from a solicitor to recover some stolen goods. One of the burglars whom he had foiled earlier, who had been sent to Dartmoor for his part in the Melrose affair, makes his escape and come to Raffles for help. With Inspector Mackenzie hot on the scent, this takes some doing – but the trick is eventually pulled off. Finally, on a cruiser bound for Naples, Raffles succeeds in stealing a famous pearl from its German custodian – but Mackenzie gets on at Genoa, and wastes no time in arresting them. The pearl is surrendered. They are ten miles from the shore. Raffles manages to dive over the side of the vessel and is assumed to have drowned, but Bunny – having been thrust in irons and imprisoned in a second-class cabin – spies through his port-hole a tiny speck on the horizon. "Now it rose, now sank, and now I gave it up utterly. Yet anon it would rise again, a mere mote dancing in the dim grey distance, drifting towards a purple island, beneath a fading western sky, streaked with dead gold and cerise. And night fell before I knew whether it was a human head or not."

So ends *The Amateur Cracksman*, which covers the period from March 1891 to July 1893. Legitimate morality has triumphed, and the career of our two villains has been short indeed. Clearly, Crime Does Not Pay. Raffles is thought to be dead, while Bunny is now about to serve an eighteen-month prison term. Yet, even so, the great reading public fell upon the book with immense delight and the author found himself positively notorious. Detectives, with the great Sherlock at their head and an army of Watsons to chronicle their adventures, had become boringly commonplace in recent years. There were some who simply admired Hornung for the breathtaking audacity with which he had dared to turn the tables and present things from the criminal's point of view. And there were others who found the stories immensely fresh and enjoyable in their own right. Throughout the English-speaking world the tales proved an immense success. "For sheer excitement and inventive genius", proclaimed *The Bookman*, "the burglarious exploits ... carry off the palm. Raffles is as distinct and convincing a creation as Sherlock Holmes." *Punch* was equally enthusiastic. "Mr E. W. Hornung's hero in *The Amateur Cracksman*", it informed its readers,

> is a certain A.J. Raffles, man about town, slow bowler of surpassing merit, fascinating companion, prince of criminals.... We live in an atmosphere as unmoral as any atmosphere can possibly be. Nothing stops Raffles. He scales walls, picks locks, abstracts jewels, baffles not merely the detectives but also the professional gentlemen with whom burglary is a trade, and holds us captivated by his rollicking high spirits, his unfailing originality of resource, and his convincing aptitude for every undertaking. Not even when he decides on a murder do our sympathies desert him, for the intended victim is one of the meanest and wickedest of mankind.... The careless reader who rises from the absorbing perusal of this book is as likely as not to call for his dark lantern, his skeleton keys and his jemmy, and to sally forth on an errand of crime, fully convinced, as he must have been by Mr Hornung's art, that the presiding genius of Raffles will bring him unscathed and much wealthier

through his adventures. Raffles has a foil ... who fulfils this purpose by being as fatuous as such foils (e.g. Sherlock Holmes's Watson) usually are. In the end, of course, Bunny suffers while A.J. Raffles escapes. Anyway, well done Mr E.W. Hornung.

The *Spectator* agreed that it was well done, but had its doubts as to whether the deed ought to have been done at all. Stern moralists, it remarked, would hardly fail to condemn the book "as a new, ingenious, artistic but most reprehensible application of the crude principles involved in the old-fashioned hero-worship of Jack Sheppard and Dick Turpin.... It is only fair to add that in the long-term dire disaster befalls Raffles and his comrade. Still we cannot refrain from expressing our satisfaction that this audaciously entertaining volume is not issued in a cheap form. It is emphatically a feat of virtuosity rather than a tribute to virtue."

Clearly, the door had been left ajar for a sequel and in *The Black Mask*, published by Grant Richards in 1901, the miscreants have a second innings. It is now 1897 and the shabby and near-penniless Bunny is delighted to find himself prodded into applying for the post of male nurse – for Mr Maturin, the patient in question, turns out to be none other than his old friend. "But O, how changed thou art!" For Raffles is now white-haired and prematurely aged, leading a wretched, furtive existence under the watchful eye of his doctor – confined to his bed by day, unable to show his face in public, and slipping out (literally) over the tiles when darkness falls. He can no longer smoke his beloved Sullivans, in case they give him away, and dare not even look out of his window. He is almost as hard up as his hireling. "Altogether", laments Bunny, "it was a very different story from the old festive, unsuspected club and cricket days, with their *noctes ambroisianæ* at the Albany." The alias adopted by his patron, as noted earlier, is the name of the celebrated creator of *Melmoth the Wanderer* – i.e., Charles Maturin – but the invalid's stock of commonplace cigarettes are concealed behind "a steel engraving of the great Raffealle".

One suspects, in passing, that Hornung's eldest brother had remonstrated with him for creating so attractive a villain, for the doctor who seeks to keep an eye on Mr Maturin is named Theobald. Yet, even so, the old gentleman and his nurse manage to have a few adventures: within hours of being re-united, they are cheerfully swindling a jeweller out of some of his wares. Later, while Theobald is away, they venture out in daylight and steal a priceless gold cup from the British Museum (concealed under Mr Maturin's top-hat) which Raffles subsequently sends to Queen Victoria as a Jubilee present in a Huntley & Palmer's biscuit tin – "My dear Bunny," he explains, in mitigation of his behaviour, "we have been reigned over for sixty years by infinitely the finest monarch the world has ever seen" – the criminal fraternity, like every other in the land, should pay tribute to her. By this time, Raffles is no longer quite so gaunt and the author begins referring to his hair as grey rather than white.

What turned his hair white in the first place is explained in 'The Fate of Faustina', in which Raffles tells Bunny of his adventures in Italy after diving overboard from that German cruiser. Hornung put his 'own backyard' to good use in this story, for the villa and vineyard where he had lived two years earlier is now pressed into service – with Raffles treading the grape as a humble labourer and falling in love with Faustina, intending to settle down to the simple life for ever more. But in so doing he falls foul of Count Corbucci, the wicked owner of the villa and a leading light of the Camorra society: Faustina is murdered and a heartbroken Raffles slays her assassin and comes close to murdering the Count himself. It then turns out that the Count is not dead after all and that the tentacles of the Camorra society have reached as far as the Earls Court Road, where Raffles now lives. The Count tries to wreak his fiendish revenge, and Bunny comes to his friend's rescue just in time. (And this time, as the result of a delayed-action googly bowled by Raffles, the Count *is* polished off.)

Bunny is at great pains to emphasise to the reader, yet again, that Crime Does Not Pay. The great majority of their unrecorded exploits, he insists, are sordid and unprofitable, not glamorous at all, and he himself is the first to agree with the strictures passed "by more than one wielder of a virtuous pen" about their despicable character. "I maintain", he declares,

> that it is the liveliest warning that I am giving to the world. Raffles was a genius, and he could not make it pay! Raffles had invention, resource, incomparable audacity, and a nerve in ten thousand. He was both strategian and tactician... Yet for months he had been hiding like a rat in a hole, unable to show his altered face by night or day without risk, unless another risk were courted by three inches of conspicuous crape.

A little while later, shortly after encountering "an old flame" who recognises him and becomes rather too possessive, Mr Maturin dies – and Bunny suddenly acquires a brother Ralph, who joins him in his cottage on the edge of Ham Common. They equip themselves with bicycles and more adventures follow, but the South African War is suddenly upon us and Raffles dyes his hair ginger and goes off to fight for Queen and Country. Bunny goes with him, of course, and we find our two heroes lying together on the veldt under the blazing sun, exchanging fire with the enemy. Bunny is wounded in the thigh (leaving him "more or less lame for life") but Raffles, thoroughly enjoying himself, continues to shoot away, maintaining a running commentary all the time. "Got him – got the hat!" he cries at one point. "No, I'm hanged if I have; at least he wasn't in it. The crafty cuss, he must have stuck it up on purpose. Another over ... scoring's slow ... I wonder if he's sportsman enough to take a hint? His hat-trick's foolish. Will he show his face if I show mine?" And a moment later, in a slightly higher voice, he exclaims: "It's not only been the best time I ever had, old Bunny, but I'm not half sure –" But the rest is silence. "The sentence was not finished," concludes Bunny, "and never would be in this world."

There could scarcely have been a dry eye among the great majority of his readers, by the time this final page was reached, and while Hornung was still accused of glamorising a detestable trade the sales of this sequel proved as great as its predecessor. "Raffles", declared the *New York Herald Tribune*, "is amazing; his resource is perfect; he talks like a gentleman and acts like one, except when occupied with pressing business in another man's house, at midnight." "Sheer yearning", commented *The Academy*, rather more drily, "of the most unmoral kind... Perhaps not a book for an unbalanced juvenile, but all right for a politician or J.P." The *Spectator* remained distinctly unhappy about the whole venture – and, in retrospect, was even harsher about the original book than it had been at the time. "It is impossible", it declared,

> to avoid repeating the sentiments expressed in these columns on the appearance of the earlier chronicles of these two worthies – that this sort of book presents crime in a form too entertaining and attractive to be moral; but we must acknowledge that the sequel is not so dangerous as the first book. In *The Amateur Cracksman* Raffles and his friend live like gentlemen among other gentlemen, and add a very unpleasant kind of treachery to their other misdemeanours. Now the worthy pair are frankly criminals, and live a hand-to-mouth existence not particularly attractive to contemplate. But at the end of the book the war gives them an opportunity to atone for their misdeeds, and so that we may know that it is a veritable end the graceless Raffles earns for his grave the inscription, which atones for many sins, beginning 'Dulce et decorum'.

Grant Richards published a cheap edition of *The Amateur Cracksman* in 1901, as Methuen had also done, and *The Black Mask* also went through a number of different editions. But the two books were combined into *Raffles, The Amateur Cracksman* by Eveleigh Nash in 1906 and this collection of sixteen stories would be printed and reprinted over and over again during the thirty years that followed. A sixpenny version brought out by Newnes in 1907, and an edition published by Thomas Nelson in 1909, were among the earliest.

The impact of the Raffles stories was indeed, as *Cassell's Magazine* had cautiously opined in 1898, "quite extraordinary". Not only had Hornung blithely upset, in the twinkling of an eye, the established standard values of contemporary English fiction, but he had conjured into existence a wonderful series of tales which have endured throughout the twentieth century and are likely to survive well into the twenty-first. As fresh on their tenth reading as they are on the first, they poke fun at respectable notions of right and wrong and appeal to the wayward element in all of us. The sheer excitement of being on the wrong side of the fence, and of being able (however vicariously) to challenge authority in all its pomp and pomposity, is a heady adrenaline to the most respectable of citizens. Raffles takes outrageous chances and runs risks which none of his readers, however longingly they might contemplate the possibility, would themselves dare attempt. The drama of fiction compensates for the dullness of real life. He acts as a safety-valve – someone with whom, in moments of boredom, it is possible to kick over the traces. He is a whipping-boy, enabling a medieval monarch (the reader) to enjoy all the pleasures of misbehaving, and savour the fun of sheer naughtiness, without having to endure retribution. In this sense, Raffles fulfilled – and still does, to some extent – a very real psychological need.

He is, of course, physically good-looking, for we are told of "his indolent, athletic figure; his pale, sharp, clean-shaven features; his curly black hair; his strong unscrupulous mouth". But he is also an immensely attractive personality – a dare-devil, mocking character, quick-thinking and cool in moments of crisis, but a realist and a romantic at one and the same time. He was an Edwardian version of Robin Hood, the James Bond or John Steed of his age. We can savour the excitement as he sets out on yet another midnight expedition, equipped with his mask and his bag of tools, and there is the sheer professionalism of the man to marvel at – the patient lengths to which he will go in surveying the lie of the land, the infinite precautions he takes and the way in which he can improvise, without turning a hair, when it comes to getting out of tight corners. Moreover, he is (like the gentleman in Baker Street) a master of disguise. Admittedly, he is outwitted on several occasions and eventually obliged to assume the character of a reclusive invalid, hiding away from society, but his spirit remains undimmed. He is an incorrigible daredevil to the very last and dies, romantically, fighting for his country.

But it must be borne in mind, of course, that Raffles is not really evil at all. To appreciate this point it is necessary to compare him with Deedes Major, his prototype, who has many of the Raffles attributes and speaks in much the same fashion. On meeting his ex-fag Bower, known as the Beetle, he suggests they emulate the robber who has just held up the local bank (himself, of course) and recalls that the Beetle was "well enough plucked at school".

"Deedes," said I, "what the devil do you mean?"

"Mean? What I say, my dear Beetle – every word of it! What's the use of being honest? Look at me. Look at my shirt-cuffs, that I've got to trim every morning like my nails; look at my trousers, as I saw you looking at 'em just now. Those bags at the knees are honesty; and honesty's rapidly wearing them through on an office stool. I'm as poor as a rat in a drain: it's all honesty, and I've had about enough of it. Think of the fellow who walked off with his fortune this morning, and then think of me. Wouldn't you like to be in his shoes? No? My stars, you don't know what it is to live, Beetle; honest idiots like us never do. But I'm going to turn it up. If one can play at that game, two can; why not three? Come on, Beetle; make a third, and we'll rob another bank tomorrow!"

"You're joking," said I, and this time I returned his smile....

"All right, old Beetle!" said he. "I won't chaff any more – not that it was all chaff by any means. I sometimes feel like that, and so would you in my place. Bunked from school! In disgrace at home! Sent out here to be got rid of, sent to blazes in cold blood! The things I've done for a living during these ten years – this is the most respectable, I can tell you that. It's the respectability that drives me mad."

His bitter voice, the lines upon his face, his grey hairs at twenty-eight (they were not confined to his moustache), all appealed to me with equal and irresistible force; my hand went out to him, and with it my heart.

Deedes is genuinely fond of the Beetle. In hiding, he tames a mouse. For, as Miss I'Anson declares, he has "fine qualities" and could yet redeem himself. But his countenance, although handsome, is dissipated, and when Bower (basically a law-abiding chap, but disinclined to betray his old friend) endeavours to bring him back to the straight-and-narrow Deedes turns very nasty indeed. By this time he has shaved off his moustache (as Raffles would do after his Australian adventure) and Bower thinks that he has "never seen so vile a mouth. It had degenerated dreadfully since his boyhood." There are by this time very few redeeming features about Deedes, whatever Miss I'Anson might think, and we breathe a sigh of relief when he is eventually shot dead. For Hornung (having passed the midway point of his story) had realised that he was on very dangerous ground and had speedily de-glamorised Deedes. Morality had been asserted at the eleventh hour, and justice had to be administered without further ado.

Clearly, a character who smacks of undiluted evil and whines about his lot in life is not the stuff of which a string of successful stories are made. The punters would wrinkle their noses in distaste and turn away. (Even Stingaree would have to be tidied up a bit, as we shall find very shortly.) After experimenting with his new concept in 'After the Fact', Hornung was aware that his amateur cracksman would have to be a thoroughly decent chap even if he *is* a bit of a law-breaker. Economic necessity would drive Raffles, just as it had driven Deedes, and retribution (as ever) would have to be meted out without too much delay, but the Raffles we meet is debonair – most decidedly, he is *not* in rags – and he makes it plain that he pursues burglary as a sort of sporting challenge. ("Art for art's sake is a vile catchword, but I confess it appeals to me.") Moreover, he is not a social outcast, as Deedes had just about become, nor had he been expelled from school, but is a Varsity man (Oxford, in fact) and has acquired an enviable status in London society from his prowess on the cricket field. Despite what Bunny says, there is nothing sordid about A.J. Raffles in the eyes of the reader. He is potentially just as ruthless as Deedes, and contemplates cold-blooded murder on two or three occasions, but – as good fortune will have it (and setting aside the justifiable execution of Faustina's murderer) – will never be called upon to demonstrate that ruthlessness. He is a man-about-town whereas Deedes had become a slinker-about-a-township.

Raffles maintains, indeed, ultra high standards. "My dear fellow," he exclaims, "I would rob St Paul's Cathedral if I could, but I could no more scoop a till when the shopwalker wasn't looking than I could bag apples out of an old woman's basket.... There's some credit, and more sport, in going where they boast they're on their guard against you. The Bank of England, for example, is the ideal crib; but that would need half-a-dozen of us with years to give to the job.... A man's reach must exceed his grasp, dear boy, or what the dickens is a heaven for?" And there, leaning back in one of the luxurious chairs with which his bachelor flat in the Albany is furnished, a cynical smile on his face and a Sullivan between his finger tips, he rests his case.

With the merest twirl of his skeleton key, A.J. Raffles had opened up the magic door to Elysium's fictional mansion and sauntered through (with Bunny in tow) to join the rest of the great immortals. But some observers, not the least of them Hornung's own brother-in-law, were distinctly uneasy about the way in which he had gained admission. For he was, in every sense, a rank outsider.

11

RAFFLES v. SHERLOCK

"Well, Watson, what do you make of it?"
[*The Hound of the Baskervilles, Strand Magazine*, August 1901]
"Well," said Raffles, "what do you make of it?"
['Nine Points of the Law', *Cassell's Magazine*, September 1898]
"I am afraid, Watson, that I shall have to go," said Holmes, as we sat down together to our breakfast one morning.
['Silver Blaze', *Strand Magazine*, December 1892]
"Bunny," said Raffles, "I'm awfully sorry, old chap, but you've got to go."
['An Old Flame', *The Black Mask*, 1901]
"You see, but you do not observe."
['A Scandal in Bohemia', *Strand Magazine*, July 1891]
"You've neither observation nor imagination, Bunny."
['To Catch a Thief', *The Black Mask*, 1901]

THE 1899 EDITION of *The Amateur Cracksman* was inscribed "TO A.C.D. This Form of Flattery" but Arthur Conan Doyle was not altogether happy about this particular dedication. (It disappeared from all subsequent editions.) To a very obvious extent, as Doyle himself was one of the first to emphasise, Raffles and Bunny were inverted versions of Holmes and Watson – the latter pledged to uphold the law, the former concerned with flouting it – but they had the disconcerting effect of transforming Holmes and his associate into a pair of old fuddie-duddies and respectable pillars of the establishment. Raffles, one suspects, might well have been able to run rings around Sherlock had the two ever come to grips. At the very least, it would have been a close-run thing.

It might be argued that even the name of Hornung's hero was borrowed from Doyle. In fact, it was probably chosen to reflect the original meaning of 'raffle' – namely, a game of chance played with dice, which generated the word "raffish". There was also a renowned East Indies colonial governor called Sir Thomas Stamford Raffles, active in the early years of the nineteenth century, from whose respectable family A.J. (as well as a famous hotel in Singapore) might have stemmed. An unfortunate rogue called John Raffles – another distant relative of A.J.'s, perhaps – also looms large in the second half of George Eliot's *Middlemarch*. Trollope created Sir Raffle Buffle. (And Wilde was acquainted, to his cost, with a certain André Raffalovich.) But, even closer to home, Doyle was the author of a novel entitled *The Doings of Raffles Haw*, which had been published in 1891 – the year in which the Raffles saga begins, and the year in which Holmes made his début in the pages of the newly-established *Strand Magazine*.

Outwardly, of course, the format of the Sherlock Holmes stories was followed by Hornung. Bunny Manders relates episode after episode in the first person, just as Dr Watson does, and the length of the stories is much the same. But there is, nevertheless, a significant difference. In *A Study in Scarlet*, the reader's very first introduction to Sherlock Holmes (not a short story, admittedly, but a novelette), Watson feels obliged to tell us at some length about his early career, and how he was wounded in the second Afghan war and obliged to leave the Indian Army, and why he needed some relatively cheap lodgings after living in a hotel for several months, and how it was that he came to be introduced at Barts hospital to a strange young man carrying out some rather curious experiments in the chemical laboratory who is also in search of fresh lodgings and of how they agree to share a set of rooms at 221B Baker Street. We get there in the end, and our interest has been aroused, but it is all a bit long-winded and cumbersome. Now compare this to the opening of the very first Raffles story:

It was about half-past twelve when I returned to the Albany as a last desperate resort. The scene of my disaster was much as I had left it. The baccarat counters still strewed the table, with the empty glasses and the loaded ash-trays. A window had been opened to let the smoke out, and was letting in the fog instead. Raffles himself had merely discarded his dining-jacket for one of his innumerable blazers. Yet he arched his eyebrows as though I had dragged him from his bed.

"Forgotten something?" said he, when he saw me on the mat.

"No," said I, pushing past him without ceremony. And I led the way into his room with an impudence amazing to myself.

"Not come back for your revenge, have you? Because I'm afraid I can't give it you single-handed. I was sorry myself that the others –"

We were face to face by his bedside, and I cut him short.

"Raffles," said I, "you may well be surprised at my coming back in this way and at this hour. I hardly know you. I was never in your rooms before to-night. But I fagged for you at school, and you said you remembered me. Of course that's no excuse; but will you listen to me – for two minutes?"

In my emotion I had at first to struggle for every word; but his face reassured me as I went on, and I was not mistaken in its expression.

"Certainly, my dear man," said he, "as many minutes as you like. Have a Sullivan and sit down." And he handed me his silver cigarette-case.

"No," said I, finding a full voice as I shook my head; "no, I won't smoke, and I won't sit down, thank you. Nor will you ask me to do either when you've heard what I have to say."

"Really?" said he, lighting his own cigarette with one clear blue eye upon me. "How do you know?"

"Because you will probably show me the door," I cried bitterly; and you'll be justified in doing it!"

Our interest has been aroused immediately, by being plunged headlong into the narrative at a crucial point. We have been speedily alerted to the situation and to the relationship between the two men. What we *don't* have is Bunny explaining to us, as a necessary preliminary, that he was an only child, that he had gone to a public school and fagged for A.J. Raffles, the captain of the eleven, and assisted him in slipping away from the school when lights were out, that he had embarked none too successfully on a literary carccr, that he had inherited a legacy three years earlier but spent it all, that he had a flat in Mount Street but was deeply in debt, that he had recently met Raffles again and that, in a desperate attempt to regain his fortunes, had played baccarat with A.J. and some other people at those rooms at the Albany earlier that evening, had proved a hopeless loser and had issued dud cheques to the victors. All this information will, indeed, be imparted to us within a short space of time, but the reader is obliged to 'dig' for it – to actively participate, in short, rather than passively absorb – and to be on the alert for clues which will put him properly in the picture.

In fairness to Conan Doyle, of course, it should be acknowledged that the very first *short* story about his master-sleuth begins with the words "To Sherlock Holmes she is always *the* woman", which certainly commands our attention, but Watson is assuming that *A Study in Scarlet* and *The Sign of Four* will already have familiarised the great majority of his readers with the Baker Street setting and the relationship between Holmes and Watson. The groundwork, in short, has been done elsewhere.

A perceptive review of *The Amateur Cracksman* which appeared in the *Academy* on 22 April 1899 drew a direct contrast between the two authors:

> No one would deny that the Sherlock Holmes series, for example, has both vision and sincerity; Dr Conan Doyle 'realises' intensely, and his best work is obviously and thoroughly sincere. That his outlook is narrow, and his characters crudely conventionalised, is beside the point, for all art is narrow when compared to life.... [But] where Dr Doyle and his imitators fall short is in the quality of aesthetic beauty, of which most of them seem not to have the slightest perception. It must be said, however, for Mr E.W. Hornung

that his book does disclose a certain feeling for beauty. His search for the precise epithet is sometimes quite successful, and all his stories have a gracefulness of contour not often to be observed in this species of work. Mr Hornung is avowedly an imitator (or shall we say a 'flatterer'?) of Dr Doyle. Yet he has his originalities....

[Raffles has a code of honour and sticks to it. His gay banter continues] till all one's notions of right and wrong are turned topsy-turvey....

The book is distinctly a good one. It is perhaps inferior to its exemplar in that wealth of corroborative detail which convinces, and that ingenuity of weaving which enthrals, but, on the other hand, it has a lightness and brightness which Dr Doyle never attempted.

Hornung had scored, of course, a palpable hit with the Raffles stories, and Doyle cannot have been too pleased with the tone of this particular review. He might also have been unhappy, for that matter, about the extent to which Hornung, in borrowing a basic idea from himself, had perverted the Holmes-Watson relationship in an even more unpalatable sense. Holmes and Watson were very good friends, and shared lodgings for a time, but Watson deserts Baker Street for a wife at the earliest opportunity, leaving Holmes to derive what consolation he can from his injections of cocaine. Never, at any time, was there the slightest hint of impropriety in their relationship. With Raffles and Bunny, however, things were not quite the same.

In all his books, up until now, Hornung had dutifully introduced a 'love interest' and he would complain in 1903 that the exigencies of serial publication invariably necessitated the presence of a heroine. In Dead Men Tell No Tales, written at the same time as the first batch of Raffles stories, he supplied a young damsel in distress in the shape of Miss Eva Denison, an outspoken but very good-looking nineteen-year-old with whom the narrator falls madly in love. Eva's charms are described in the passionate tones of a Victorian novelist on several occasions and she obligingly swoons away from time to time, which provides an opportunity for her to be gathered up in the hero's arms and held tightly against his chest – rather hot stuff for Hornung. (In a later yarn, *The Camera Fiend*, he gets even more daring and at one particularly dramatic moment the heroine confronts the hero in a dressing gown "and almost bare feet".)

But the fair sex are hardly mentioned in *The Amateur Cracksman*. There is, admittedly, a Miss Melhuish who chats away to Bunny at the dinner-table in the third story, 'Gentlemen and Players', but her only function in the tale is to impart some valuable information. Not until the very last story, when Raffles and Bunny set sail for Naples, does "a slip of [an Australian] girl with a pale skin, dark hair and rather remarkable eyes" appear on the scene. Raffles pays court to her, much to Bunny's intense annoyance. "They were always together," he complains querulously to the reader. "It was too absurd. After breakfast they would begin, and go on until eleven or twelve at night.... I confess to some little prejudice against her. I resented her success with Raffles, of whom, in consequence, I saw less and less each day. It is a mean thing to have to confess, but there must have been something not unlike jealousy rankling within me."

One can scarcely imagine Watson talking in such a manner about Holmes! Bunny sounds, indeed, more like 'a woman scorned' than a partner in crime. He acknowledges, in the same passage, that Raffles has had much experience of women "(a side of his character upon which I have purposely never touched, for it deserves another volume)" but it is made abundantly clear that Bunny Manders is passionately attracted by the personality of Raffles and resents any potential rivals, be they male or female. And Raffles, of course, treats him with affection. When recalling our earlier supposition that Raffles and Bunny are, in a sense, fictionalised versions of Wilde and Bosie, then it is hardly surprising that there should be this hint of a homosexual relationship.

Once he finds out that the Australian girl is passing on confidential information about the location of a priceless pearl on the ship, Bunny is profoundly relieved. But Raffles, for his part, gets rather annoyed. "It doesn't occur to you", he says sharply, "that I might like to draw stumps, start clean, and live happily ever after – in the bush?" Bunny chortles at the idea, which annoys Raffles still further. In the same story, in the privacy of their cabin, Raffles snarls at his sidekick for stupidity and Manders spiritedly defends himself. Raffles is then apologetic and calls him Bunny again. "My nickname and his tone went far to mollify me," says the narrator; "other things went farther, but I had much to forgive him still." This reference to "other things" appears to have slipped unnoticed past editorial eyes.

The latent homosexuality, it should be added (and as Owen Dudley Edwards has pointed out), is played down in the two subsequent volumes of short stories. In *The Black Mask* Raffles tells Bunny about his romance with the ill-fated Faustina and later re-encounters an old flame in the shape of Jacques Saillard (a woman, despite her name), while in *A Thief in the Night* he posthumously re-unites Bunny with the beloved girl (name withheld, but a niece of Lady Melrose) whom he had once intended to marry. So both our heroes, it is now made emphatically clear, are definitely heterosexual. But clarification had come, admittedly, a little late in the day. (One is reminded of that final episode of *Round the Horne*, when Julian and Sandy suddenly introduce Kenneth Horne to their wives: we note the assertion, but we are not convinced.)

Finding his own creations superseded in popular favour by the decadent twosome of Raffles and Bunny, Conan Doyle evidently decided that it was time for decent wholesomeness to reassert itself. He had killed off Holmes in June 1892, when the *Strand Magazine* published 'The Adventure of the Final Problem', but the success of *The Amateur Cracksman* (1899) and *The Black Mask* (1901) could well have been among the crucial factors which encouraged him to narrate an 'earlier' Holmes adventure in *The Hound of the Baskervilles* (the first episode of which appeared in the *Strand* in August 1901). It is, certainly, generally acknowledged by his biographers that the decision to bring Holmes back to the land of the living, in *The Return of Sherlock Holmes* (beginning with 'The Adventure of the Empty House' in the *Strand* in October 1903) was prompted simply and solely by his jealousy of Hornung's success with A.J. Raffles. 'The Adventure of the Empty House' is the Holmesian equivalent of 'No Sinecure', with the elderly book-collector suddenly turning into Holmes just as Mr Maturin, the elderly invalid, had suddenly turned into Raffles.

This is an appropriate moment to consider the *second* occasion on which Doyle referred to Hornung in his *Memories and Adventures*, published in 1924. The passage in question runs as follows:

> Willie Hornung, my brother-in-law, is another of my vivid memories. He was a Dr Johnson without the learning but with a finer wit. No one could say a neater thing, and his writings, good as they are, never adequately represented the powers of the man, nor the quickness of his brain. These things depend upon the time and the fashion, and go flat in the telling, but I remember how, when I showed him the record of some one who claimed to have done 100 yards under ten seconds, he said: "It is a sprinter's error." Golf he could not abide, for he said it was "unsportsmanlike to hit a sitting ball". His criticism upon my Sherlock Holmes was: "Though he might be more humble, there is no police like Holmes." I think I may claim that his famous character Raffles was a kind of inversion of Sherlock Holmes, Bunny playing Watson. He admits as much in his kindly dedication. I think there are few finer examples of short-story writing in our language than these, though I confess I think they are rather dangerous in their suggestion. I told him so before he put pen to paper, and the result has, I fear, borne me out. You must not make the criminal the hero.

Looked at carefully, this amounts to a really splendid piece of patronising, pompous condescension. We are told that Willie had little learning, that his books did not adequately represent the sharpness of his brain and that he was extremely witty in private conversation – although the three examples Doyle quotes do indeed go a little flat in the telling. (They drew forth some characteristic sneers from Hesketh Pearson, twenty years later, who thought that the great man must have been easily amused.) Doyle claims, with some justification, that Raffles and Bunny owe much to Holmes and Watson – claiming the credit, as it were, for being their real creator – but instantly nullifies his tribute to the quality of the stories by describing them as "rather dangerous". He complacently concludes, with a sad shake of the head, that the result (what result?) has borne him out and that the criminal ought not to be a hero.

So Doyle had the last word on Hornung – and one which has been unhesitatingly accepted by a good many subsequent critics. But what seem, initially, to be hearty slaps on the back for the shade of the dear departed turn out to have been, on closer inspection, a few hearty stabs. Like the victors in war, who write the initial crop of history books, a triumphant Doyle was able to make his pronouncements simply because he had lived longer than his brother-in-law. The disturbing suspicion that must have haunted him over the years – that Willie was, perhaps, the better writer of the two – could now be safely laid to rest.

And yet, a combination of magnificent magnanimity and pernickety pettiness, Doyle was still generous in his praise. "I always admired you," he would tell Hornung. "Yes," came the pointed response, "I know you honestly admired parts of me." This puts one in mind of the curate's egg. (The fact that these remarks were exchanged on 21 July 1921, exactly four months after Willie's death, is an issue that will be dealt with later.)

12

SPILLS, CHILLS AND THRILLS

APART FROM the Raffles stories, and a book called *At Large*
which requires separate consideration, Hornung also
produced two other thrillers during these years – *Dead Men
Tell No Tales* (1899) and *The Shadow of the Rope* (1902). The
titles were the most lurid that he had yet employed –
designed, obviously, to tempt all and sundry (save for the
most fastidious) through his portals – but the two books were
markedly different in style. *Dead Men Tell No Tales*, published
by Methuen in the same slim, cheap format that they had
adopted for a new edition of *The Amateur Cracksman* – with
450 words per page rather than 220, and selling at six pence
(2.5p) rather than six shillings (30p) – was a made-to-measure
adventure yarn. Written in the first person, allegedly in 1897,
but looking back forty-four years to the gold-rush days of
1853, it tells how young Mr Cole (whose Christian name we
never learn) is the sole survivor of a disaster at sea. On the
Lady Jermyn, a clipper bound for Liverpool from Melbourne
under the captaincy of Captain Harris, he falls in love with
Eva Denison, the step-daughter of a sinister Portuguese
gentleman, Jacquin Santos. But the ship suddenly goes up in
flames – there is allegedly a secret cargo of gunpowder aboard
– and passengers and crew take to the sea in two boats. The
one carrying our hero sinks – he clings to a hen-coop and is
eventually rescued – while Eva, Senor Santos and Captain
Harris, on board the other boat, die of illness (or so the boat's
log records) and so too does everyone else.

Back in London, Cole is a celebrity but deeply depressed
and in rather an emotional state – and he becomes convinced

that mysterious persons are following him. He is befriended by cheerful young Frank Rattray, the squire of Kirby Hall, who makes available a cottage on his Lancashire estate, where he can have a good rest and plenty of fishing. But Cole is astonished to find, on peering in the window of Kirby Hall one dark night, that Rattray is deep in conversation with Senor Santos, Captain Harris and one or two others who had allegedly perished at sea – and that Eva is still alive and a prisoner in the house. Bags of action follow, with tables being turned and re-turned in every other chapter, and we gather that the reason for these strange happenings is that the gig bearing away these individuals from the stricken *Lady Jermyn* had 12,000 ounces of gold dust (valued at £48,000) hidden aboard it. About to take their ill-gotten gains to the bank, the conspirators had learnt that Cole was still alive and were anxious to ascertain whether he had suspected anything before they could proceed on their way to the cashdesk. Although most of the villains *are* killed in a final shoot-out with policemen from Scotland Yard, which has a strong element of *The Pirates of Penzance* about it, the title appears to have been tacked on as an afterthought. It transpires that Eva is actually in love with Rattray (a kindred spirit to Raffles), who escapes from Kirby Hall via a secret passage and eventually ends up in Argentina. Apparently he has taken Eva with him, but in the final line we discover that she has stayed with the narrator instead and has never had cause to look back. (Well, hardly ever.)

Leaving aside the characteristic last-minute twist in the story, it is difficult to identify this book as one of Hornung's. It is written in a fashion that is, perhaps, a deliberate pastiche of styles employed for such adventure yarns earlier in the century. Initially, there is a touch of Edgar Allen Poe, while later on there are echoes of Wilkie Collins (Santos being a latter-day Count Fosco) and Stevenson (*The Pavilion on the Links*). It was an adequate tale of mystery and adventure, but the author would have been the first to admit that it could not be regarded, by any stretch of the imagination, as great literature. It simply discharged a contractual commitment to Methuen. (But one wonders, in passing, what Hornung's sister-in-law made of the heroine's unpleasant Portuguese step-father.)

"Dead men tell no tales, and live men only those that suit them!" This was actually a sentence from Hornung's *subsequent* crime novel, *The Shadow of the Rope*, published by Chatto & Windus in 1902 and running to 75,000 words. Rachel Minchin, against all expectations, is acquitted by twelve good men and true of the murder of her husband. But the nation at large, so we gather, is convinced of her guilt. In desperation, she accepts a proposal of marriage – in name only, by mutual agreement – from a mysterious and immensely wealthy white-haired gentleman called Mr Steel, a spectator throughout the trial, who claims to be convinced of her innocence and conquered by her beauty. He whisks her away into riches and temporary obscurity. But can she trust him? And who is the real murderer of her husband? Fortunately, an enthusiastic young novelist – a writer of mystery yarns – is on hand to do a spot of sleuthing on her behalf and there are, as ever, some remarkable surprises in store for the reader. The two principal characters are Australian but the action is set in England, veering between Chelsea and a chilly mansion two hundred miles to the north in close proximity to a city suspiciously like Middlesbrough ("a world of smoke and rain, with furnaces flaring through the blurred windows, and the soot laid with the dust in one of the grimiest towns in the island").

Yet one is suddenly aware of Wildean overtones. The story is set, carefully but unobtrusively, in 1892 and 1893. One minor piece of action takes place at a house in Tite Street (where Wilde then lived) and another at the Cadogan Hotel (where Wilde would be arrested). A very famous criminal court looms large – "It was years since there had been a promise of such sensation at the Old Bailey, and never, perhaps, was competition keener for the very few seats available in that antique theatre of justice." So runs the opening sentence of the second chapter, although it is surprising, on reflection, that what would seem to be a relatively mundane murder trial should attract such nationwide attention. But the Old Bailey was where Wilde would be tried (twice) in 1895 and there is even a reference to "the most eminent of living playwrights" being present at the fictional 1892 proceedings (although he doesn't stay for the verdict).

Why Hornung should drop such increasingly blatant hints – almost to advertise, as it were, his connection with Wilde – must remain largely a matter for conjecture. Perhaps he enjoyed living dangerously. Or perhaps he simply did it for savage amusement – speculating, it may be, on whether it would ever occur to posterity to put two and two (or, more precisely, one and one) together. Most probably he now felt guilty, or even exasperated with himself, at not having spoken out more openly in defence of the man and for having escaped scot-free from any taint of association. Certainly, even though the hue and cry was now over, he would appear to have been troubled by recollections of things past. "There is nothing more confusing to the brain than memory," he had written in 1901. "Often there is nothing so agonising and unsparing in its torture, when memory preys upon the present, consuming all its peace and promise like some foul vampire."

But it was a cross he would have to bear.

13

FOR EXPORT ONLY

CURIOUSLY, one other book which Hornung wrote at this time remained a virtual secret so far as his fellow-countrymen were concerned. In New York, in February 1902, there was published under his name a substantial volume entitled *At Large* which ran to almost 370 pages and approximately 92,000 words. It was not published in the United Kingdom – even now there is, seemingly, not a single copy of it in either the British Isles or Ireland – and it went unmentioned in the author's entry in *Who's Who*. The reasons why a veil should have been drawn over this particular production are, to say the least, perplexing.

The book in question is best categorised as a low-key thriller. The curtain rises in 1882 on a scene in which our hero, Dick Edmonstone, and his Irish partner, Jack Flint, are driving their hooded wagon across a depressing desert in the middle of Australia. Dick, aged twenty-one, has been in Australia for no more than ten weeks (as opposed to the ten years spent by Flint) and is keen to make his fortune and return home without delay. They are a pair of hawkers, or travelling salesmen, and carry with them profits totalling £130, which Dick is anxious to bank as soon as possible. But, half an hour before sunset, they are ambushed by Sundance, a bushranger who has terrorised half of Australia in recent months, and the two members of his gang. One of them, a nasty fat villain called Jem Pound, throws himself upon Dick, who has heroically resisted the attack, and threatens to knife him. Sundance rescues Dick who says, passionately, that if Sundance is going to steal their profits then he might as well shoot him here and now and have done with it, since his life is ruined. Sundance, amused that the lad should be so passionately attached to his £130, ascertains that Dick sees it as the nucleus of his fortune: if the money is lost, then all is lost. Unmoved, however, he apparently takes the money, plus a few other things, and the two travellers are tied up. Only when Dick and Jack have managed to free themselves do they discover, to their amazement, that their money is intact and that Sundance (a mysterious masked figure clad from top to bottom in a black cloak) had evidently taken pity on Dick.

Four years later, in June 1886, our hero arrives home on a slow-moving cargo ship. We learn that the £130 was indeed responsible for making his fortune, for he and Jack had set up a trading store at what proved to be a gold-rush town and profits had been enormous. (The explanation blandly supplied is that they had opened the eyes of the squatters "to the iniquitous prices of the Jews, who had hitherto enjoyed a monopoly of their custom".) Jack, moreover, had come into an unexpected inheritance and returned to Ireland after a couple of years, leaving Dick to thrive by himself. So here's prosperous young Dick, on the point of disembarking in England, excited and optimistic. He reflects that it was thanks to the forbearance of Sundance that he managed to accumulate his fortune, and is positively sorry to recall that, just before leaving Australia, Sundance had been captured by the Queensland authorities. But he has come home to claim the hand of Alice, the girl he loves, who lives with her father, Colonel Bristo, in Graysbrooke, a splendid house in Teddington, a short distance away from the more modest abode of his own widowed mother, brother and sister.

Yet when he arrives at Graysbrooke to claim the hand of his potential bride, Dick is disconcerted to find that the beloved's response is cordial rather than rapturous. For there is a guest in the house, tall Mr Miles, also from Australia, who has a handsome beard and curly blonde hair and is on extremely good terms with both the Colonel and his daughter. He is, evidently, a splendid chap, for he has recently saved the

Colonel from drowning, owns a prosperous sheep-farm in New South Wales, has impeccable manners and displays a good sense of humour. Dick retires from the scene, hurt and vanquished, and his relations with Alice rapidly deteriorate. Mrs Parish, the housekeeper at Graysbrooke, meanwhile decides that Mr Miles would be the ideal husband for Alice and does all she can to encourage his suit. But Mr Miles, strange to relate, much dislikes having his photograph taken and has one or two other strange little foibles. He has no other friends in the country and there is never any post for him. (And why should he borrow money from the Colonel, we ask ourselves, on the strength of being temporarily short of funds?) Dick decides he is up to no good, much to Alice's contempt, and later has much pleasure in telling Miles, one dark night, that a stranger outside wishes to see him.

Dick assumes that the stranger is a detective from Australia, come to bring Miles to justice, and follows them into Bushey Park to eavesdrop on their conversation. He is astonished to discover, what the astute reader has long ago guessed, namely that Miles is really none other than the bushranger Sundance, alias Ned Ryan, who had escaped from custody and come to England on a much faster ship than the one Dick travelled on. The mysterious stranger, moreover, is villainous Jem Pound – sacked from the gang some while back, as a penalty for engaging in murder – who demands that Ryan give him some of the proceeds of his last big robbery, namely 500 ounces of gold taken from Mount Clarera Bank, as the price for going away. As his trump card, Pound then produces from the bushes (which must have been somewhat crowded by that time) a bedraggled lady who turns out to be Ryan's abandoned wife, Elizabeth. Miles/Ryan, coping with this disastrous situation as best he can, promises to meet this scruffy pair the following evening and hand over some money. As soon as Pound and Elizabeth have gone, however, Dick steps out from concealment, reveals his true identity as the young hawker to whom Sundance had done a good turn in 1882, and – instead of handing him over to the police – tells Miles to leave Graysbrooke instantly and never clap eyes on

Colonel Bristo or his daughter again. In this way, their accounts are squared. Miles obeys, and all seems well.

In the second half of the book, the attention switches to a shooting lodge in Yorkshire which Colonel Bristo has rented for the summer and to which four or five guests have been invited. Initially Dick had not been of their number, for relations between himself and Alice are now icy in the extreme, but learning that the vengeful Jem and Elizabeth are plodding northwards, on the assumption that Miles will be there, he changes his mind and accepts the Colonel's invitation. He arrives one summer evening, only to find that Miles has immediately preceded him. Later, there is another confrontation. A humbled Miles pleads that he is a changed man, that he has booked a passage to New York the following week for himself and his wife, and that he has simply come to Yorkshire to bid a fond farewell to Colonel Bristo and his daughter, who are really decent folk and the best people he has ever encountered in his life. With much reluctance, Dick promises to give Miles one last chance but declares that he will keep a close eye on him during the next few days. Evidently, Miles is indeed a reformed character – but so quiet, polite and subdued that his erstwhile hosts and Mrs Parish are very puzzled and disappointed by the change in his character.

But Miles is not really a reformed character at all. The two tickets on the liner to New York are simply a blind, for he has planned to abduct Alice and to disappear in another direction entirely. But when Jem and Elizabeth turn up yet again then he is obliged to speed up his plans. Once again, he asks the Colonel for money. The Colonel is suspicious and – when Miles, Alice and Mrs Parish have set out on a four-mile walk to church – asks Dick for advice. Dick, thunderstruck at learning that Miles is after the Colonel's money, thereupon reveals all. Miles and Alice come back, Alice going to her room in a distraught state, and there is another confrontation between Dick and Miles. This time, in the presence of the Colonel, Miles is revealed in his true colours as a dastardly villain. Harsh things are said on both sides. Alice, hearing all, comes down and in a dreadful state of hysteria berates both

Miles and Dick before collapsing – and it rapidly becomes apparent that this is something far worse than a mere swoon. Miles apparently makes his escape in the confusion, but in fact he is hurrying off to fetch medical aid from Melmerbridge, the nearest town – for his visit to its church that morning had truly redeemed him, and he had decided *not* to abduct Alice. The rain pours down, as he struggles up hill and down dale through the Yorkshire countryside. On the way he encounters a drunken Jem Pound, who fires his gun to fatal effect. But Miles/Ryan is not quite dead, for he manages to shoot Pound in return and then staggers a few more yards over the bridge into town, still desperately trying to bring aid to Alice. So he dies redeeming himself, with the blood gushing from his body and being washed down the empty street in the rain. Dick, driving pony and trap, arrives on the scene on the same mission, just in time to catch his dying words.

There are two postscripts to come, for the tale is far from over. Alice lies in the cottage in a critical condition, Dr Mowbray having pronounced that she is suffering from brain fever and requires a nurse. Meanwhile, Elizabeth learns with great distress that her husband is dead, finds a lock of Alice's hair clasped in his hand as she gazes at him in his coffin, and vows to avenge herself on our heroine. Night has fallen, but she gains access to the cottage – eluding Dick, who is pacing up and down outside, while Mrs Parish and the Colonel have fallen asleep from exhaustion – and reaches Alice's bedroom. But stay! The girl is dead already. Then Elizabeth notices a faint twitch of life – she realises that the girl's head has been shaven – and the fit of madness leaves her. Repentant, she creeps away from the cottage, but is arrested by Dick. "Are you the nurse?" he cries. "Yes," she replies, after a moment's pause, "I am the nurse", at which point Dick rushes her back to the bedside. Dr Mowbray, calling the following morning, declares that no finer nurse could be found and that the dangerous corner may well have been turned. Meanwhile, a genuine detective from Australia, hot on the trail of Sundance for reasons of his own, now turns up. What was thought to have been a suicide by Ryan is soon ascertained, with the discovery of Pound's body, to have been a murder, but the detective – despite all entreaties – is reluctant to agree to these revelations being hushed up. He wants it to be known, he insists, that he had only been a step or two behind Sundance. But then Elizabeth Ryan comes into the room and – sensation! – it turns out the detective is Elizabeth's brother and that he had abandoned hope of ever finding her again. Reunited with his sister, he readily agrees to draw a veil over these recent events and not to reveal the true identity of Mr Miles. By slow degrees Alice gets better, and the brother and sister book their passage back to Australia on the *SS Roma*.

It transpires that Dick is going to travel back to Australia on the same ship, for there is nothing to keep him in England now. His sister is going to marry jolly Jack Flint (a character perhaps based on Dowling) and his money has (we hope) helped to ease the lot of his widowed mother and pen-pushing brother. But, with a mood of prolonged bitterness and savage amusement finally behind him, he politely calls at Graysbrooke on the eve of his voyage to bid the Colonel and his daughter a calm farewell. Mrs Parish, now humbled and apologetic, regrets that the Colonel is out but perhaps Dick would like to see Alice? Certainly, if she has no objection, so he is ushered into the library and, by degrees, breaks his news to the young lady of the house. Is there nothing, she asks, still white-faced and fragile, that will keep him in England? No, there is not. But he wavers, as she repeats the question, and we learn that the *SS Roma* subsequently sailed without him.

This summary, it must be instantly acknowledged, is a brutal abridgement of what is really quite an intricate plot. Many scenes and a considerable number of secondary characters (including an innkeeper called Rutter, which is a name that Hornung had already used in a Raffles story, 'Wilful Murder', and would use again ten years later) have been passed over in silence. What seems undeniable, however, when reducing the tale to its bare bones in this fashion, is that it is an extremely *melodramatic* plot and one that might have been better suited to the stage of a theatre than to the pages of a novel. Throughout, there are dramatic scenes and confrontations which, even today, might well lend themselves to the medium of a rather lurid television serial. But this impression is perhaps misleading, for Hornung was far too skilled a craftsman to simply move from one sensational event to another. In fact, he endeavoured to tell his tale in as low a key as possible and to narrate the adventures and feelings of his hero and heroine, not to mention Edward Ryan himself (in the latter part of the book), as quietly as he dared. If a melodramatic plot was to be presented in an *un*melodramatic fashion, but with the tension being maintained, then this was a subtle technique in which he had long been a proven master.

For there are chapters in which, to all intents and purposes, nothing happens – or, at any rate, just enough to advance the development of the plot by the merest nudge and whisper. And, as always (or nearly always), there were the marvellous descriptive passages at which Hornung excelled – the matter-of-fact portrayal of complex scenes and scenery. The three main characters – Dick, Alice and Miles – are, admittedly, fairly standard ones. But it is indicated from the outset that Dick is not quite the wise, experienced man of the world that he thinks himself, while Alice also falls short, both in temperament and beauty, from being the ideal heroine:

> The lamplight, from under its crimson shade, fell upon her hair and face and neck with marvellous results, for it made her beautiful. She was not at all beautiful. She had a peerless complexion, a good nose, matchless teeth; otherwise her features were of no account. But she was exceedingly pretty; and as she sat there with the warm lamplight changing her ordinary light-coloured hair into a ruddy glow fit for any goddess, a much less prejudiced person than Dick Edmonstone might have been pardoned the notion that she was lovely, though she was not.

This is disconcerting, but interesting. Later, in a ploy borrowed from Wilkie Collins and others, Alice is allowed to speak directly for herself in a chapter composed of extracts from her diary.

Miles is something of a cross, perhaps, between Raffles and Stingaree, and we gather that what really appeals to him about Alice, above all else, is her marvellous singing voice. It is not until the book is almost into its final quarter that we get to grips with the "real" Miles and discover a tortured soul, torn between villainy and the desire to lead a better life. (Not keeping a diary he is obliged to speak his innermost thoughts out loud at one crucial point, another device reminiscent of the Lyceum Theatre.)   He is capable, until the very last, of strange fits of savagery and passion, veering between opposite extremes, and the vehemence of his moods almost succeeds in persuading us that such a character could genuinely exist. (He served, perhaps, as a useful vehicle for some of Hornung's own private anguish.)

But it is, as ever, Hornung's evocation of places that makes the deepest impact.   In the first half of the book, on that occasion when Jem reappears in the bushranger's life at dead of night, it is the images of Bushey Park that one remembers:

They had been standing between two noble trees of the main avenue. This avenue, as all the world knows, is composed of nothing but horse chestnuts; but behind the front rank on either side are four lines of limes, forming to right and left of the great artery four minor parallel avenues. Miles and his companion, turning inwards, crossed the soft swards of the minor avenues, and emerged on the more or less broken ground that expands southwards to Hampton Wick. This track is patched in places with low bracken, and dotted in others with young trees. It is streaked with converging paths – some worn by the heavy tread of men, others by the light feet of the deer, but all soft and grassy, and no more conspicuous than the delicate veins of a woman's hand.

Later, Miles leaves the Park in the company of Dick:

The night was at its darkest when they reached the avenue; so dark that they crossed into the middle of the broad straight road, where the way was clearest.   Straight in front of them burned the lamps of the gateway, like two yellow eyes glaring through a monstrous crape mask. They seemed to be walking in a valley between two long, regular ranges of black mountains with curved and undulating tops – only that the mountains wavered in outline, and murmured from their midst under the light touch of the sweet mild breeze.

In the second half of the book, when the action has shifted to Yorkshire, one of the Colonel's guests, a young journalist called Laurence Pinckney, borrows Alice's camera and sets off to take some artistic photographs:

> His destination was a certain ancient abbey, set in gorgeous scenery, eight long miles from Gateby. But long before he got there a hollow of the plain country road tempted him, and he fell.
>
> It was quite an ordinary bit of road; a tall hazel-hedge, and a pathway high above the road on the left; on the right, a fence with trees beyond it, one of them, an oak of perfect form, that stood in the foreground, being of far greater size than most of the trees in this distance, and in strong contrast to its neighbours. That was really all. It never would have been picturesque, nor have taken our artist's fancy, but for the sunlight on the wet road and the fleecy pallor of the sky where it met the sharp line of distant dark blue hills far away over the hazel-hedge, to the left. But the sunlight was the thing. It came, as though expressly ordered, from, so to say, the left wing. It rested lightly on the hedge-tops. It fell in a million golden specks on the shivering leaves of the old oak. But it cleared the deep-cut road at a bound, leaving it dark. Only a long way further on, where the bend to the right began, did his majesty deign to step down upon the road; and just there, because everything was wet from last night's rain, it was a road of silver.
>
> No sooner, however, was the picture focused than the sun, which made it what was, disappeared behind a cloud – a favourite and mischievous dodge of his for the mortification of the amateur photographer.

Middlesbrough, although unnamed, lurks in the background. Alice notes in her diary that "the great smoky town which we passed through the other day is within twenty miles of us" and Mr Oliver, one of her father's guests, is an ironmaster from the city. We glimpse it from afar further on, on that fateful Sunday (22 August 1886, identified with

peculiar meticulousness) when Miles escorted the two ladies
to church at Melmerbridge:

When they had threaded the soft, rutted track that girdles the
heather with a reddish-brown belt, when they had climbed
the very last knoll, they found themselves on the extreme
edge of that range of hills. Far below them, to the right,
stretched mile upon mile of table-land, studded with villages
and woods, divided by the hedge into countless squares. No
two neighbours, among these squares, were filled in with the
same colour; some were brown, some yellow, and the rest all
shades of green. Far ahead, where the squares were all lost
and their colours merged in one dirty neutral tint – at the
horizon, in fact – hung a low, perpetual cloud, like a sombre
pall of death. And death indeed lay under it: death to green
fields, sweet flowers, and human blue skies....

Old Mrs Parish pointed to the long black cloud on the
horizon, and explained that it was formed almost entirely of
the smoke of blast-furnaces, and was the constant canopy of a
great town that they could not see, because the town was
hidden in perpetual smoke. More than this she might have
said – about the mighty metals that were disgorged from
under their very feet – about the rich men of yonder town
(old Oliver, for one), not forgetting the poor men, beggar
men and thieves.

The morning had been, on the whole, a sunny one. But later
that day, when Miles hastens over the same route in his quest
for medical assistance, the sunshine has faded:

The afternoon was dull but not dusky. The clouds were so
high and motionless that it seemed as if there were no clouds,
but one wide vault of tarnished silver. To point to that part of
the canopy that hid the sun would have been guesswork.

Between the tall hedges the air was heavier than in the
morning: the flies and midges swarmed in myriads. Even on
the moor there was now no breath of wind. The heather
looked lifeless, colourless; the green fronds peeping between
had lost their sparkle; the red-brown of the undulating belt of
road was the brightest tint in the landscape up there.

Quite apart from anything else, *At Large* is worth reading
for the pleasure of encountering descriptive passages such as

these. But the book as a whole manages to hold the reader's attention from start to finish, for its component elements are assembled with a sure hand and the author even manages to keep a few surprises up his sleeve. Hornung was seeking primarily to entertain, not to write great literature (although the harrowing chapters narrating how Elizabeth Ryan fared, both before and after she learned that her husband was dead, have an almost Dickensian intensity about them). Purely as an adventure yarn, *At Large* is adequate. One would not rank it among the very best of Hornung's books, but it is far from being the worst – and it was immeasurably superior to such ventures as *Dead Men Tell No Tales* (1899) and *Dennis Dent* (1903). The problem arises, therefore, as to why it should not have been published in the United Kingdom, especially since all of the action (after the two opening chapters) takes place in England.

There are two possible explanations.

First, the book was published by Charles Scribner's Sons, one of the most prestigious publishing houses in the United States at this time. They were also one of the most generous, and Stevenson, seventeen years earlier, had been staggered by the terms which they offered for *A Child's Garden of Verses*. "For the future", he told one of their representatives in March 1885, "you and the sons of the deified Scribner are the men for me. Really they have behaved most handsomely." And to the firm itself: "I think it only right that I should thank you in person for so liberal an offer. A man were more than human, if he did not sometimes complain of the way in which things go in the States; but I have the greater pleasure in recognising conduct so handsome as yours." Scribner's Sons had published American editions of most of Hornung's books, but it may be that, rather than play perpetual second fiddle, they invited him to write a book exclusively for the American market – and had made it extremely well worth his while to do so. Yet one would have thought, even so, that they would have consented to the finished product being republished in England a year or two later – providing that due acknowledgment was made to themselves.

The second possibility is that Hornung was, quite simply, ashamed of the book and wanted it to remain undiscovered by United Kingdom readers. He had remarked several times, of late, that Australian stories were becoming rather a drag on the market and acknowledged that the vein which he had himself had exploited with such brilliant success, some ten years earlier, was now virtually exhausted. Bushrangers, after all (as he had frequently made clear in recent years) had become an extinct breed by the early 1880s, after Ned Kelly and his gang had been rounded up, and it was only silly romantic novelists who sought to perpetuate their existence in the story-books. It will be recalled that Tahourdin, the naïve young Englishman who arrived in Melbourne with lots of exciting preconceptions, had been relishing the prospect of being held up by bushrangers, providing that he had very little about his person at the time, because "with their well-known magnanimity they would probably hand him that little back again". It had to be explained to Tahourdin that bushrangers were a thing of the past. And now here was Sundance, in the year 1882 and in a book written by Hornung, magnanimously handing back to Dick Edmonstone the sum of £130 which meant so much to the lad.

At Large did not, admittedly, stay any longer in Australia than it needed, but Hornung may also have been uneasy about the sheer absurdity of a tale in which an anachronistic Australian bushranger escapes to England for refuge – and is pursued, moreover, not only by a disgruntled member of his gang but also by his wife and also by his wife's brother. At this rate, can his sisters and his cousins and his aunts be far behind? And there were, too, those ultra-melodramatic scenes (not to mention some astonishing coincidences) which might have raised a few eyebrows among Hornung's readers in the United Kingdom. Such things might suffice very nicely for the American market, where the temperature could be hotted up without fear of protest, but something rather less blatantly sensational was needed for domestic consumption.

But this is simply speculation. All that one can be reasonably sure of is that Charles Scribner's Sons would have paid Hornung very well indeed for this particular production and that, seemingly, he was content for *At Large* to remain at large, and well beyond the knowledge, let alone the reach, of his admirers in the United Kingdom.

14

CRICKET – AND NOT QUITE

"THERE ARE eminent men of action", wrote Hornung in 1902, "who can acquit themselves with equal credit upon the little field of letters, as some of the very best books of late years go to prove. The man of letters, on the other hand, capable of cutting a respectable figure in action, is, one fears, a much rarer type."

He spoke from personal experience. In the spring of 1899, soon after the Hornungs returned from their prolonged stay at Capo Posillipo and had moved into their new home at 9 Pitt Street, Kensington, he was invited by James Barrie to participate in a game of cricket between the Artists and the Allahakberries. The Artists were captained by Barrie and the match was played at Denmark Hill, in south London, on 19 May. Hornung (in common with Bernard Partridge, the well-known *Punch* cartoonist) scored four runs, while Barrie himself chalked up a total of three. The following year he took part in another cricket match, this time under the captaincy of Conan Doyle. "He was the best read man in cricket lore", wrote Doyle in 1923, "that I have ever met, and would I am sure have excelled in the game himself if he had not been hampered by short sight and villainous asthma. To see him stand up behind the sticks with his big pebble glasses to a fast bowler was an object lesson in pluck if not in wicket-keeping."

Simply to survive at the wicket, in a strictly passive sense, was something of an achievement for Hornung. "The worst player in the world," he wrote in 1903, "with his eye in, may resist indefinitely the attack of the best bowler; after all, a ball is a ball and a bat is a bat, and if you once begin getting the one continually in the middle of the other, and keeping it out of harm's way, there is no more to be said and but little to be done."

Cricket features in many of the Raffles tales, of course, but in the early 1900s Hornung also wrote a handful of short stories devoted exclusively to the subject. The best remembered of these are 'Chrystal's Century', 'The Power of the Game' and 'A Bowler's Innings'. In 1907, much to his delight, he was elected a member of the M.C.C.

Writing in 1909, he looked back ten years to a day when a

tropical shower-bath had left the London air as cleanly and as clear as crystal; the neutral tints of every day were splashes of vivid colour, the waiting umpires animated snow-men, the heap of sawdust at either end a pyramid of powdered gold upon an emerald ground. And in the expectant hush before the appearance of the fielding side, I still recall the Yorkshire accent of the Surrey Poet, hawking his latest lyric on some 'Great Stand by Mr Webbe and Mr Stoddart', and incidentally assuring the crowd that Cambridge was going to win because everybody said Oxford would.

We must return, however, to that early summer of 1900, when he had been playing under the captaincy of Doyle. It will be remembered that Doyle's wife Louise, known as Touie in the family circle, had been an invalid since 1893 and had, in a sense, been living on borrowed time. Doyle had done all that he could, in summoning the best medical advice to her aid and taking her on trips abroad to recuperate, to prolong her life, but the toll on himself (in his own eyes, at any rate) had been heavy. "I have lived for six years in a sick room", he lamented to his mother in a letter dated 30 December 1899, "and, oh, how weary of it I am; Dear Touie: It has tried me more than her – and she never dreams of it and I am very glad." He had sought solace elsewhere, while not neglecting Touie, and found it in the companionship of an attractive woman called Jean Leckie, who was twenty-seven at the turn of the century.

Coming into the pavilion at Lords, on a Tuesday in June or July 1900, Hornung was startled to find his brother-in-law and Jean in what was evidently regarded, in that day and age, as a compromising position. It may be that Conan Doyle had his arm around the girl, or that they were simply holding hands. Whatever the ins and outs of the situation, Hornung was embarrassed at having surprised them and presumably withdrew as soon as he could. "In fear of his thinking evil", Doyle reported to his mother, "I told Connie the facts that evening, and gave her leave to say what she liked to Willie about it, afterwards, speaking a little to him myself, when I went downstairs and referring him to her for the details. She was very nice and promised to lunch with us at Lords next day. Willie also seemed nice and said 'that he was prepared to back my dealings with any woman at sight and without question'. Next day however I had a wire of excuse from Connie both for lunch and dinner (tooth-ache, dentist). I went down about 11, found she had gone to bed, and Willie highly critical and argumentative. I suppose their hearts spoke first and then they were foolish enough to allow their heads to intervene. Willie's tone was that of an attorney dissecting a case, instead of a brother standing by a brother in need. Among other remarks he said that I attached too much importance to whether the relations were platonic or not – he could not see that 'that made much difference'. I said 'the difference between guilt and innocence'. But could you conceive such nonsense? Of course when I saw this carping tone I refused to speak further upon so sacred a matter, and I left the house not angrily but in a serious frame of mind which is more formidable. When have I failed in loyalty to any member of my family? And when before have I appealed to them?"

Conan Doyle had, it must be acknowledged, an unexampled gift for feeling sorry for himself. But he did have some justification for taking umbrage at the next turn of events, for Hornung now took it upon himself, either in person or via Constance, to make strong representations to his mother-in-law on the subject – on the assumption, presumably, that Mary Doyle was the only person capable of bringing her son to his senses. Doyle responded to his mother in a blustering letter of self-justification. "I have nothing but affection and respect for Touie", he declared. "I have never in my whole married life had one cross word with her, nor will I ever cause her any pain. I cannot think how I came to give you the impression that her presence was painful to me. It is not so. William's argument re. Connie, himself and you, is most unsound. He is not Touie's mother. If he were, I should have expected him to see it with a mother's eyes. I should be unreasonable if I expected sympathy from Mrs Hawkins. But I expected the attitude of a friend, and a brother, from William and I got neither."

Not surprisingly, Doyle was furious at his brother-in-law for this grossly uncalled-for intervention in his private affairs and a breach opened between them that was not truly repaired (formalities apart) for several years. "I have written a polite note to Connie", he told his mother a little while later, "which, between ourselves, is more than she deserves. And I don't feel better for contemplating the fact that William is half-Mongol, half-Slav, or whatever the mixture is." Obviously, only some one with foreign blood coursing through their veins could have acted in so insidious a fashion. Doyle would have felt particularly upset at the fact that he, the famous patriot of the British Empire and staunch upholder of decency and traditional family values, should have been lectured by this little upstart from eastern Europe on where his duty lay.

Louise died in July 1906, after thirteen years of illness. Doyle was devastated by her death. "Though he had not been in love with Touie," commented his biographer, John Dickson Carr, in 1949, "he was as fond of her as he had ever been of any person; and to say this is to say much." For a time, at any rate, he would be singing her praises. It was perhaps in anticipation of this event that Hornung had dryly reflected, in 1903, that the unlikeliest tongues ran away with themselves "under strong emotional strain: so we prattle of our newly dead, magnifying the good that we belittled in our lives".

Ten years later, in the autumn of 1911, it was Hornung's turn to feel aggrieved. Conan Doyle had created the irascible Professor George Challenger, *The Lost World* being scheduled for publication the following year, and had great fun dressing up as that gentleman so that some faked photographs might accompany the *Strand*'s serialisation. This entailed donning a bushy beard and false eyebrows. In gleeful mood, he decided to play a joke on the Hornungs and presented himself on their doorstep. "Announcing that he was der Herr Doktor von Somebody," writes Carr (an author prone to jovial exaggeration), "this hirsute apparition towered in the doorway. He said he was a friend of Herr Doktor Conan Doyle, who was from home, and would Herr Hornung receive him? Hornung, fortunately or unfortunately, was short-sighted. Moreover, he was used to the fact that a friend of his brother-in-law might be anybody from some broken-down tramp to the Prime Minister. His welcome was effusive. The visitor, rattling off long strings of German, really did get away with it for several minutes. Then Hornung was furious. Showing his guest to the door, he swore he would never forgive this. The silk-hatted Herr Doktor, his shoulders heaving with chuckles, departed in disgrace."

The story reappeared fifteen years later in Pierre Nordon's biography of Conan Doyle. "One day", he writes, "he greeted Hornung wearing a false beard. When he discerned the trick, his brother-in-law flew into a violent rage. Conan Doyle's roars of laughter did not mend matters, and the recollection of the incident always provoked him to noisy delight."

It is a rum little tale. Hornung's biographer can only conclude, on the evidence to hand, that his subject over-reacted in an extreme fashion. The rage seems strangely out of character, particularly when one remembers that (in the words of his nephew, Brigadier Foley) Hornung "had great charm and a subtle and delightful sense of humour". Clearly, he failed to see the joke – not, admittedly, one of the most subtle – and his charm deserted him on this occasion. Perhaps it may indeed have been the case that he felt that Conan Doyle was taking cruel advantage of his being short-sighted and that, one way and another, it simply wasn't cricket. (But there are times, certainly, when the creator of Raffles does appear to have been rather priggish.)

15

CONFESSIONS OF A NOVELIST

THE SHADOW OF THE ROPE, published in 1902, enjoyed the same degree of success as most of its predecessors. "From the opening chapter until the concluding one", declared *The Times*, "the author does not loose his grip of the reader.... The book is a notable one." "One of the best books of its kind that we have read," commented the *Morning Post*, "and the character-drawing lifts it far above the average of this particular class of fiction." The *Daily Mail* thought that Mr Hornung had "woven a most subtle mystery" and the *Morning Leader* and the *World* both compared him to Wilkie Collins, his skill at devising ingenious, baffling and (ultimately) satisfying plots having now win him an almost unique position among the ranks of contemporary authors. But, as *Truth* acknowledged, "you are interested in the characters of the story almost as deeply as in its mysteries, and are relieved to find that your sympathies have been from the first rightly ranged". Once again, in short, unstinted praise flowed in from every direction.

Hornung was now a master of his art. Yet although, as we have seen, he had displayed some remarkable talents from the very outset of his career, the skills at which the critics marvelled had not been acquired overnight. They had developed over some fifteen years as the result of hard work, constant practice and a willingness to learn from his mistakes. One wonders, in passing, how much attention the critics of *The Shadow of the Rope* paid to remarks made by, and about, the young novelist in the book, Charles Langholm. Rachel notes that his name "is not very common" and reversing its two syllables gives us 'Holmlang', which is sufficiently close to that of his creator to confirm (if confirmation is still needed, and even without the additional information that his wrists are thin and his sleeves only half-filled) that we are in the presence of a younger Mr Hornung – although the older Mr Hornung self-deprecatingly assures us that Langholm was not a particularly popular writer. "The novels of Charles Langholm", he adds, "were chiefly remarkable for their intricate plots, and for the hope of better things that breathed through the cheap sensation of the best of them. But it was a hope that had been deferred a good many years. His manner was better than his matter; indeed, an incongruous polish was said by the literary to prevent Langholm from being a first favourite either with the great public or the little critics."

Langholm (a misogynist, following an unhappy love affair) complains to Rachel about "the heroine whom the exigencies of 'serial rights' demanded in his books". When asked how he thinks of his plots, he explains that they sometimes come out of his head and occasionally from real life but are more often a blend of the two combined. "You don't often get a present from the newspaper that you can lift into a magazine as it stands. Facts are stubborn things; they won't serialise."

Later, we encounter Langholm when he has been "writing all day, and for many days past, and was filled with the curious exhilaration which accompanies an output too rapid and too continuous to permit a running sense of the defects". But he has "no illusion as to the present product of his teeming pen", which he describes as "nonsense" churned out solely to meet a deadline – "but it is not such nonsense as to seem nothing else when one's in the act of perpetrating it". This frank admission counters, in effect, a criticism that would be levelled against him by Oliver Edwards (alias Sir William Haley) in *The Times* in June 1966 – "The truth is that Hornung was always a hit or miss author, and when writing never seemed to know whether he had a winner or a non-starter on his desk."

A lady acquaintance declares that, if she were to write a book, then she would need to travel in mysterious foreign parts in search of inspiration. Langholm dismisses this idea. "I had exactly the same notion when I first began," he declares, "and I remember what a much older hand said to me when I told him I was going down to Cornwall for romantic background. 'Young man,' said he, 'have you placed a romance in your mother's backyard yet?' I had not, but I did so at once instead of going to Cornwall, and sounder advice I never had in my life. Material, like charity, begins at home; nor need you suppose that nothing ever happens [there]. That is the universal idea of the native about his or her own heath, but I can assure you it isn't the case at all."

There is also a reference to "the detachment and mild surprise with which he occasionally dipped into his own earlier volumes", evidently being gratified at finding them rather better than he had expected.

Such, in short, were the confessions of a jobbing novelist with no illusions about his handiwork, and two more novels which Hornung jobbed in 1903 need to be taken into account before this chapter comes to an end.

The first was *No Hero*, published by Smith, Elder & Co (the publishers of *A Bride from the Bush*) and running to 44,000 words. An elegant production narrated in the first person, with occasional echoes of Henry James, it tells how Catherine Elers seeks the assistance of the man who had wooed her, unsuccessfully, some twenty years earlier, on a mission of some delicacy. Her ex-suitor is Captain Duncan Clephane, invalided out of the army after being wounded in both legs at Spion Kop and heavily dependent on two sticks. Mrs Elers, now an attractive widow, has a son of nineteen called Robin, but known as Bob, in his first year at Cambridge. She has learnt that Bob, on holiday in a Swiss hotel near the Matterhorn, has apparently fallen into the clutches of a designing widow, Mrs Lascelles. Will Captain Clephane venture out there on her behalf, please, and put an end to the liaison? Still attracted by Catherine's charms, and encouraged by the faint hope that she will one day wish to remarry, Clephane does just this – but the further he gets from

Catherine, the more he becomes aware of the odious nature of his task.

At the hotel, where he has allegedly gone to convalesce, open-hearted Bob makes him very welcome and introduces him to Mrs Lascelles – "We are absolutely pals and nothing else." Clephane realises he had met her in India, when she was then Mrs Heymann. The guilty party in a divorce case, but her second husband now deceased, she too is extremely attractive – but a notorious woman of the world, it seems, and not at all a suitable partner for a young lad fresh out from Eton. Clephane eventually decides to disrupt their relationship (the talk of the hotel) by paying court to her himself – a not disagreeable task, it transpires. Bob becomes very jealous, and (thanks to Clephane) is precipitated into proposing to her before disappearing to climb the Matterhorn by night (and risking his life in the process) while awaiting her reply. The title of the book, it should be mentioned at this point, is taken from a verse in 'A Light Woman' by Browning, a poet whom Mrs Lascelles tells Clephane she has never read –

> And I, – what I seem to my friend, you see –
> What I soon shall seem to his love, you guess.
> What I seem to myself, do you ask of me?
> No hero, I confess.

Clephane urges Mrs Lascelles to reject Bob's proposal and leave the hotel and she realises, for the first time, that he is there on Catherine's behalf. She is scornful of his role and his interference, points out that she herself is only twenty-six, and gives every indication of intending to marry Bob. In fact, she *does* leave at dawn the following morning – and we subsequently learn that she had planned to do so all along. For the truth of the matter is that she had never intended to accept Bob's proposal, although Clephane's urgings had very nearly goaded her into doing so. Bob ruefully accepts his rejection, becoming more mature in the process, and Clephane pursues Mrs Lascelles from hotel to hotel, eventually finding her at Baden-Baden, to thank her for surrendering the lad. She makes, understandably, some sharp rejoinders. He meekly accepts the well-merited rebukes but notices that the book she had laid down is a volume of Browning's poems.... Back in England, he reports on the success of his mission to Catherine Elers but emphasises that Mrs Lascelles was not at all the designing woman that they had originally assumed. Catherine eventually accepts his word for this, carefully makes clear in passing that she herself has definitely decided *not* to remarry, and laughs at the idea that Robin might have become "Number 3" in the lady's list of husbands. Clephane assures her there is no likelihood of this, for he himself has married the lady. (This does not rule out the possibility, of course, that Robin may one day become "Number 4".)

No Hero is a gripping novelette, clean-cut, beautifully told and with some excellent descriptions of people and places. One of the guests at the hotel is the famous actor, Belgrave Teale – a very thinly-disguised Beerbohm Tree. "He comes down in one of his parts every day," vouchsafes a fellow-guest; "today it's the genial squire, yesterday it was the haw-haw officer of the Crimean school." At one point, gammy legs and sticks notwithstanding, Clephane accompanies Mrs Lascelles along

> the zig zags to the right of the Riffelberg and followed the footpath overlooking the glacier, in the silence enjoined by single file; but at last we were seated on the hillside, a trifle beyond that emerald pass that some humorist has christened the Cricket-ground. Beneath us were the seracs of the Gorner Glacier, teasled and tousled like a fringe of frozen breakers. Beyond the seracs was the mainstream of comparatively smooth ice, with its mourning band of moraine, and beyond that the mammoth sweep and curve of the Théodule where these glaciers join. Peak after peak of dazzling snow dwindled away to the left. Only the gaunt Riffelhorn reared a brown head against the blue.

"Rarely", remarked the *Daily Express*, "has Mr Hornung written a novel more felicitous and workmanlike than *No Hero*. The situations are unhackneyed, and the treatment not only interesting, but fresh and amusing." *Outlook* thought that "each of the half-dozen characters is a clear-cut cameo" and that "the handling of the inherently risky theme is admirable". "Considered purely as a work of art," concluded *Public Opinion*, "it has the freshness and charm of a well-executed miniature."

Alas! If only one could have said the same for his *second* 1903 production, *Dennis Dent*, which was published by Isbister & Co. Once again, this time egged on by somebody called P.M. Martineau (the brother or father, perhaps, of his solicitor, Charles Martineau) Hornung had succumbed to the temptation to write a historical novel. A great monstrosity of a book (80,000 words), set primarily in the gold fields of Australia in the mid-1850s but with another shipwreck and the Crimean War thrown in for good measure, it comes across to modern-day readers as an unhappy version of *Martin Chuzzlewit* rewritten by G.A. Henty in partnership with Georgette Heyer.

So far as the plot is concerned, suffice to say that poor but honest Dennis Dent spends many months in the diggings at Ballarat, so that he can amass a small fortune and return to England to claim, on equal terms, the wealthy girl he loves. He does so, but finds that his rival and devilish arch-enemy, Captain Ralph Devenish, has got there first by means of sundry underhand tricks. Fortunately, she discovers Ralph's treachery immediately after the wedding, so the marriage is never consummated. Ralph has the decency to be killed in battle – but not before, on his deathbed, he has been reconciled with Dennis (who has joined the Grenadier Guards as a corporal). Dennis returns to England to claim his bride and we learn, in the last sentence, that a tall prospector who had materially assisted him in Australia was none other than the recently-deceased Marquis of Salisbury, Queen Victoria's last Prime Minister (although Hornung is too coy to actually name him).

Some detailed descriptions of the canvas encampments at Melbourne and Ballarat, and the battles of the Crimea, bear witness to the fact that Hornung had done a conscientious amount of research. But it is all heavy-going – a dull plod rather than a brisk canter – for his lightness of touch totally deserted him on this occasion. With a stock hero and a stage villain, the action is lifeless and, ultimately, a great waste of time. He was himself aware, it seems, that the finished product fell short of original expectations. While dedicating the work to Martineau, a brief note dated 27 October 1903, with the Reform Club as its address, ran as follows: "The little picture of the past attempted in this tale owes more than one touch to your kindness. I only wish that the whole were nearer the mark aimed at, and so worthier to bear your name upon this page."

It was tired old stuff written by a tired author. It was time, perhaps, to take a rest from writing novels. Pausing, in fact, only to churn out the Stingaree yarns and the final batch of short stories about Raffles, which were a relaxation rather than a chore, this was precisely what he would now do.

16

ROBBERS – AND SOMETIMES A COP

IT HAS BEEN ARGUED, earlier, that Raffles is not really an evil character at all and that the widespread fear of serious harm being caused to the nation's moral fibre if fictional criminals escape justice was perhaps ill-founded. But in the June 1900 issue of the *Strand Magazine* there appeared a short story entitled 'The Saloon Passenger' about somebody most certainly of an evil disposition who succeeds in doing just that. The man in question has committed a murder – not a perfect one, necessarily, but a reasonably good one – and boards a ship to Australia without delay. He has banked on getting to the other end of the world undetected, but when an urgent message comes through on the ship's radio, and the hitherto affable captain speaks abruptly to him for a time thereafter, then he guesses that his plot has been foiled and that there will be a reception committee waiting for him at Melbourne. There follows a tense battle of wits, in which he succeeds in allaying the captain's suspicions that he might have realised the situation and adroitly escapes capture at the very last moment. It is a chilling but brilliantly effective tale – written, it should be noted, ten years before the capture of Dr Crippen by means of a ship's radio.

This was one of several stories that Hornung contributed to the *Strand Magazine* at the turn of the century. Each of them was a polished little gem, and following the success of *The Amateur Cracksman* and its successor the editor evidently invited Hornung to provide him with a serial or, failing that, with a series of stories about a colourful character – somebody not totally dissimilar from A.J. Raffles, say – as a means of holding readers' interest and pushing up the *Strand*'s circulation figures still further. For inspiration, Hornung went back nearly ten years.

It will be recalled that a villain called Stingaree had played a leading role in *Irralie's Bushranger*, first published in 1895 as a magazine supplement, and at the end of that book had been consigned to Darlinghurst Gaol, in Sydney, for the rest of his life. A brilliant pianist and cultivated man, elegantly dressed with a single eye-glass and martial moustache, he was nevertheless a potential cold-blooded murderer – his attempt to kill both Irralie and the Hon. Greville Fullarton being foiled only in the nick of time. *Irralie's Bushranger* had apparently never been republished since 1896, however, and Hornung may have assumed that his readers had only a very sketchy recollection of this particular desperado.

What Hornung now did was to wave a magic wand, as though the distressing events at Arren Downs sheep station had never taken place, and produce a whiter-than-white version of Stingaree. He still holds up banks and stage coaches, but only occasionally fires his gun and has never been known to kill anyone. He is still notorious, but he is also much loved – "Good old Stingaree!" being the cry of the average man in the Australian street, when news of his latest derring-do becomes common knowledge. The average man in the Australian street might even be, for that matter, Stingaree himself, for it now becomes clear that he is a master of disguise, notwithstanding his remarkable height: all he has to do is to remove his eye-glass, and perhaps shave off his moustache occasionally, to transform himself into anyone he chooses – whether it be a young trooper, a hunch-backed detective, a drunken slob, a bishop's chaplain or an erudite Irish author. And all he *then* has to do is to screw the glass back in his eye to produce astonished cries of "Good heavens, it was Stingaree all the time!" (One is reminded, in this context, of the dastardly penguin in Nick Park's immortal *The Wrong Trousers*, who cunningly and impenetrably disguises himself as a chicken by putting a red rubber glove on his head.) Riding a white horse, and sometimes accompanied by a side-kick called Howie, Stingaree scours every part of Australia, partly in search of loot but also to do good deeds and right wrongs. He is very much a Robin Hood figure and almost a national hero – except, of course, to the police, whose primary function is to gnash their teeth at being frustrated yet again. (His true name is never revealed, although he encounters at least one visitor to Australia who knows it, and we gather that he is an ex-Oxford man who, for reasons unclear, was once expelled from a London club – evidently, the first step on his downward descent.)

So Hornung obliging churned out a batch of ten stories, which Chatto and Windus would publish in 1905. They take place over a period of nine years – from 1882 until 1891. Stingaree is still a lover of fine music, although rarely able to visit concert-halls, and the very first story ('A Voice in the Wilderness') tells how he publicises the magnificent singing voice of Hilda Bouverie, a humble lady's-companion, who goes on to fame and fortune and becomes another Nellie Melba. In 'The Black Hole of Glenrald' he turns the tables on those who had designed an ingenious plot to trap him and is magnanimous towards a young lad who captured him for a short time. In '"To the Vile Dust"' he exacts poetic retribution on someone who had sought to take advantage of his good nature, in 'The Honour of the Road' he pretends to be a policeman and unmasks the true killer of old Hard Cash Duncan (to clear his own name, admittedly) and so it goes on. One person who does catch him, most emphatically, is our old friend Bishop Methuen, the Lord Bishop of the Back-Blocks – repaying one assault with another, and justifiably, since Stingaree had stolen his clothes and left him miles away in the outback clad only in his silk pyjamas and without any shoes. But Stingaree and Howie had not reckoned on muscular Christianity when they summoned the residents of Mulfera station to an evening service and then stuck them up:

> A strange and stealthy figure, the cynosure of all eyes but the
> bushrangers' for a long minute, reached the open end of the

veranda; and with a final spring, a tall man in silk pyjamas, his grey beard flying over either shoulder, hurled himself upon both bushrangers at once. With outspread fingers he clutched the scruff of each neck at the self-same second, crash came the two heads together, and over went the table with the three men over it.

Stingaree and chum are taken into police custody, but escape within two days. But the Bishop, of course, is the real hero of this episode and the uncouth residents of Mulfera station experience an almost instant conversion after noting the appalling state of his feet. In a later tale ('The Villain Worshipper'), after Stingaree has come back to the scene of a crime to exonerate a silly young lad who has claimed the credit for it, there is a further encounter between himself and the Bishop. On *this* occasion it is the strong-minded *Miss Methuen* (another old acquaintance of ours) who is responsible for his apprehension and imprisonment. Stingaree soon escapes from prison, of course, and goes off to hear his protégé, Miss Bouverie, perform at the local town hall. He then turns up in her boudoir, requesting money to help him on his way. He finds that immense fame and riches have changed her for the worse – but she takes pity on this old and haggard man, after an initial burst of contempt, for tears have filled her eyes: "the simplicity of her girlhood had come back to the seasoned woman of the world, at once spoiled and satiated with success". She willingly parts with a bundle of notes and a rope of pearls, pops down to the hotel foyer (at Stingaree's bidding) to reassure the Governor that she is quite safe, and returns a few moments later to find her visitor gone. And then, "with wet eyes and a face white between anger and admiration", she finds that the notes and pearls are still there.

There are no more tales of Stingaree [Hornung concludes]; tongue never answered to the name again, nor was face ever recognised as his. He may have died that night; it is not very likely, since the young married man in the well-appointed bungalow, which had been broken into earlier in the day, missed a suit of clothes indeed, but not his evening clothes, which were found hung up neatly where he had left them;

and it is regrettable to add that his opera-glasses were not the only article of marketable character which could never be found on his return. There is none the less reason to believe that this was the last professional incident in one of the most incredible criminal careers of which there is any record in Australia. Whether he be dead or alive, back in the old country or still in the new, or, what is less likely, in prison under some other name, the gratifying fact remains that neither in Australia nor elsewhere has there been a second series of crimes bearing the stamp of Stingaree.

They are dreamlike, almost surreal stories. The characters are puppets and the scenery against which they perform does not claim to be anything more than a painted backdrop. (For it was almost twenty years since Hornung had left Australia.) One is reminded, at times, of Chesterton's Father Brown stories; at others, of Kipling's tales of life in barracks – and all three men were, of course, poets. But the yarns are enjoyable, certainly, and with a seeming briskness which carries us along in its sweep. Thus, the opening paragraph of 'The Taking of Stingaree':

> Stingaree had crossed the Murray, and all Victoria was agog with the news. It was not his first descent upon that Colony, nor likely to be his last unless Sub-Inspector Kilbride and his mounted myrmidons did much better than they had done before. There is no stimulus, however, like a trembling reputation. Within four-and-twenty hours Kilbride himself was on the track of the invader, whose heels he had never seen, much less his face. And he rode alone.

And here is the opening paragraph of 'A Duel in the Desert' (originally entitled 'The Real Simon Pure'), which would be deleted when the tale appeared in book-form:

> The disastrous episode of the sticking-up of Mulfera Station, N.S.W., is on all grounds ineligible for inclusion in these little memoirs. Of the telling of Stingaree stories, round the camp-fire or in the men's hut, there is, indeed, no end to this day; but in print, at least, a certain precedence is due to those which reflect least discredit upon Stingaree. His villainies were often brutal, seldom inexpert; at Mulfera, however, they were both. And yet, even here, the trouble began in one of

those grim jokes which were a continual temptation to this masterless mind. But all the back-block world knows how a bishop and a bushranger met twice on one summer's day, and how the bushranger laughed first, but the bishop last and longest.

And the conclusion of 'The Purification of Mulƒera', when the manager of the station (foul-mouthed these days, but an ex-public school chappy) brings his reluctant overseer and book-keeper into line is pure Kipling:

> "I told you just now I didn't care twopence what either of you thought of me," he roared, "though there wasn't the least necessity to tell you, because you knew! So I needn't repeat myself.... Now, it isn't in human nature to fly from one extreme to the other; but we are going to have a try to keep up our Sunday end with the other stations; at least I am, and you two are going to back me up."

> He paused. Not a syllable from the pair.

> "Do you hear me?" thundered Carmichael, as he had thundered in the dormitory at school, now after twenty years in the same good cause once more. "Whether you like it or not, you fellows are going to back me up!"

> And Carmichael was a mighty man, whose influence was not to be withstood.

To the modern eye, the construction of the Stingaree tales may seem rather mechanical. Many contemporary critics, however, evidently found them as satisfying as the Raffles stories. "Mr Hornung", said the *Morning Leader*, "has more than a touch of the literary artist, and the tales are rendered doubly fascinating by his virile style." The *Daily Mail* thought it "a very deft piece of work" which held the interest to the end: "[his] invention is brisk and his spirit unflagging". "His mature art is seen at its best", commented the *Scotsman*. Several critics hailed Stingaree as the natural successor to Boldrewood's Captain Starlight.

Eight of the Stingaree tales had featured in the *Strand Magazine* from September 1904 to April 1905 – a supporting item on the bill, on two occasions, to a couple of the short stories forming part of *The Return of Sherlock Holmes*. At long last, therefore, Hornung was performing regularly on what was, at that time, the most illustrious platform of all, and contentedly playing second fiddle to Conan Doyle – albeit with productions rather different from those penned by Bunny Manders.

But it was the fame of Raffles that overshadowed all else at this time. Hornung had produced an instant modern classic and (quite apart from collaborating in the production of a stage-version of his hero's adventures) was pressurised, not surprisingly, for yet further tales to add to the collection. He obliged in 1905, with the publication by Chatto & Windus of ten more stories under the title *A Thief in the Night*.

"If I must tell more tales of Raffles," Bunny explains at the outset of this new collection, "I can but go back to our earliest days together, and fill in the blanks left by discretion in existing annals. In so doing I may indeed fill some small part of an infinitely greater blank, across which you may conceive me to have stretched my canvas for a first frank portrait of my friend. The whole truth cannot harm him now. I shall paint in every wart. Raffles was a villain, when all is written; it is no service to his memory to gloze the fact; yet I have done so myself before today. I have omitted whole heinous episodes. I have dwelt unduly on the redeeming side. And this I may do again, blinded even as I write by the gallant glamour that made my villain more to me than any hero. But at least there shall be no more reservations, and as an earnest I shall make no further secret of the greatest wrong that even Raffles ever did me."

We learn, for the first time, that Bunny had been virtually engaged when he sat down at the Albany to play that fateful game of baccarat and that Raffles had conned him into assisting in a burglary of the home of his beloved by making him believe that her family had vacated the house. Alas, things go appallingly wrong. Raffles takes to his heels and it is only thanks to the intervention of his erstwhile fiancée, her lip curling in scorn, that a shame-faced Bunny escapes the long arm of the law. Clearly, any likelihood of their settling down together has taken a nosedive – a supposition confirmed when she coldly sends back his presents without a word – and it is with great sadness, and bitter resignation, that he thereafter embarks wholeheartedly on a life of crime. Raffles, to do him justice, is apologetic and rather glum that the engagement should have been terminated in this fashion.

Thereafter, it is much the same mixture as before – but the element of villainy is played down to a large extent and we are more aware of "gentleman pranksters out on a spree" than of a couple of desperadoes. More often than not Raffles and Bunny bungle things, escaping dreadful fates by the narrowest of margins. When they do manage to rob someone, it is a person with whom we have not the slightest sympathy. Raffles does succeed, admittedly, in robbing a bank vault, by means of concealing himself in a large packing case (with a secret door) which an unsuspecting Bunny deposits there for safe keeping – and he makes use of the same case in a later story, too, as a means of stealing the 'Raffles relics' from Scotland Yard's Black Museum. (He points out to Bunny that he is only retrieving what was rightfully his in the first place, and salutes Charles Peace, a famous Victorian burglar, as "the greatest of the pre-Raffleites".) In a couple of tales, virtually taking a leaf out of Stingaree's book, they do good by stealth. In 'The Criminologists' Club', Raffles outwits a group of gentlemen who had had their suspicions of him – but having taken Lord Thornaby's robes and coronet for sheer devilment, sends his lordship a ticket for their collection from the cloakroom at Charing Cross. In 'The Field at Philippi' he returns to his old school (one bearing a close resemblance to Uppingham) and is instrumental in attracting some additional funds for its bicentenary celebration. In 'A Bad Night' Bunny takes pity on a young man suffering from asthma (Hornung himself) and quite forgets to rob his house – an omission which Raffle soon rectifies. In 'A Trap to Catch a Cracksman' Raffles comes a cropper and has to be rescued by Bunny, while in 'The Spoils of Sacrilege' *both* of them come croppers in an attempt to burgle Bunny's childhood home. (But Raffles manages to retrieve the situation, of course.)

Most curious of the yarns, perhaps, is one entitled 'The Rest Cure', in which Raffles takes a holiday in an empty house while the owners are away. Bunny joins him and, for reasons not readily apparent, dresses up as a woman. The owner of the house, a colonel and a VC into the bargain, returns home unexpectedly and tries to persuade the young lady to tell him where her lord and master is – before realising his mistake. There is something decidedly kinky about this tale, especially when Raffles swoops upon the colonel (who is quite a spirited old buffer in his way) and greatly resents it when the old boy fights back. What has been, up till now, the precursor of a Laurel and Hardy film, suddenly turns very nasty indeed. First of all, the officer is bound and gagged in his chair.

> I thought I had never seen a man better bound or better gagged. But the humanity seemed to have run out of Raffles with his blood. He tore up table-clothes, he cut down blind-cloths, he brought the dust sheets from the drawing-room, and multiplied every bond. The unfortunate man's legs were lashed to the legs of his chair, his arms to its arms, his thighs and back fairly welded to the leather. Either end of his own ruler protruding from his bulging cheeks – the middle was hidden by his moustache – and the gag kept in place by remorseless lashings at the back of the head. It was a spectacle I could not bear to contemplate at length, while from the first I found myself physically unable to face the ferocious gaze of those implacable eyes. But Raffles only laughed at my squeamishness, and flung a dust-sheet over man and chair; and the stark outlines drove me from the room.
>
> It was Raffles at his worst, Raffles as I never knew him before or after – a Raffles mad with pain and rage, and desperate as any other criminal in the land.

The tale has certainly become very vicious, although Bunny promptly finds extenuating circumstances for his friend's behaviour – for Raffles has, after all, been quite seriously wounded by a bottle wielded by the gallant officer. The episode has quite spoilt their holiday, and Raffles and his henchman, now restored to male attire, leave soon afterwards. The point of the whole story, it transpires, is that Raffles (so Bunny thinks) had left the colonel to die, but in fact has sent a letter to the police telling them to rush along to the old gentleman's rescue. He chides Bunny for not having trusted him on this matter. (Could there be any significance, one wonders, in the fact that the colonel – but a colonel of mere sappers – had been a "prison governor or inspector" ever since being awarded his VC at Rorke's Drift? Was savage vengeance being vicariously wreaked on a certain Colonel Isaacson, merciless governor of Reading gaol until July 1896, on Oscar's behalf?)

The Raffles relics having been retrieved from Scotland Yard, Raffles confesses (shortly before they go off to South Africa) that he is sorely tempted to bring his burglary activities to an end. But an even more emphatic termination of his career is at hand. We join Bunny a few months later, after he has come home from South Africa and encountered his old sweetheart in the street, for she writes to him to explain that, after that ghastly meeting in her own home, Mr Raffles had called round to make amends. He had explained that he was solely responsible for having led Bunny astray. She had promptly written to Bunny at the time, forgiving him everything, but the letter (she now realises) had failed to reach its intended recipient. "I hope you are not getting morbid about the past", she concludes.

> It is not for me to condone it, and yet I know that Mr Raffles was what he was because he loved danger and adventure, and that you were what you were because you loved Mr Raffles. But, even admitting it was all as bad could be, he is dead, and you are punished. The world forgives, if it does not forget. You are young enough to live everything down. Your part in the war will help in more ways than one. You were always fond of writing. You have now enough to write about for a literary lifetime. You must make a new name for yourself. You must, Harry, and you will!

And perhaps, she suggests, he might like to call round for a chinwag some day. Dare Bunny yet hope for that which he dare not utter?

Of course he can, and at that point the true Raffles saga comes to an end. Thousands cheered the reprise, especially across the Atlantic. "These latest adventures of Raffles and Bunny are their most thrilling and exciting ones", declared the *Boston Herald*. "The sentimental side of their story has never before been shown so dramatically and romantically, and the suggestion in this book of the final conclusion of their careers cannot but make these stories of greatest interest to all readers."

But nearer home the plaudits were more restrained – and the *Spectator's* critic, in particular, remained firmly unimpressed. "We have already spoken our mind plainly as to Mr Hornung's exploits in this direction," he grimly announced. "As to this present book, which contains a further instalment of the adventures of a thief, we need only say that it is not so mischievous as its predecessors, because it is not nearly so well done." This might have served as a warning, to Hornung, that it would be unwise to mine the Raffles seam any further – but the sales of this latest volume were as sensationally good as its predecessors, and the warning would go unheeded.

17

RELAXATIONS OF A NOVELIST

HORNUNG was thirty-four at the turn of the century and at the time of his great row with Conan Doyle. In appearance he was short, dark-haired and dapper. He had grown a moustache and invariably wore the large pebble glasses to which his brother-in-law referred. He was a quiet man, kept a low profile, delivered no speeches and played a very limited role in public life. He valued his privacy.

He also valued outdoor pursuits (although reflecting, in 1918, that he had probably "led too soft a life, taking very little exercise for its own sake, though occasionally going to the other extreme from an ulterior motive"). Cricket, as we have seen, was one of his great enthusiasms and he was regarded as a recognised authority on the game, but it was a pastime in which he himself could engage only to a modest extent. Lawn-tennis was another pursuit in the early 1890s, but cycling was his chief recreation by 1895. It is probable that Willie and Connie, like Raffles and Bunny in their days at Ham Common, were the proud owners of a Beeston Humber and a Royal Sunbeam respectively and cycled "through Richmond Park when the afternoons were shortest, [and] upon the incomparable Ripley Road when we gave a day to it". They certainly enjoyed swimming, as the letter from Capo Posillipo, quoted earlier, makes clear. A less strenuous pastime was photography, in which they both dabbled, it seems, with some degree of enthusiasm, and experienced no difficulty in attracting an element of human interest into outdoor compositions. "Your honest British rustic", Hornung observed in 1901, "is not the man to reject the favours of the camera, be they never so promiscuous and his chances of beholding its results never so remote."

Motoring also attracted him. Hornung joined the newly-founded Automobile Association in 1906, although it is probable that (like Kipling, who had equally poor sight) he did not drive himself but employed a chauffeur. 'The Man at the Wheel' deals with the experiences of a chauffeur, while Walter Cazalet in *The Thousandth Woman* (1913) hires a chauffeur-driven car for a week in which to take Blanche Macnair on outings. Like Raffles and Bunny, they experience "the glories of the Ripley Road" plus "the grandeur of Hindhead" and then grow even more venturesome:

> The next day they went over the Hog's Back, and the next day right through London into Hertfordshire. This was a tremendous experience. The car was a good one from a good firm, and the chauffeur drove like an angel through the traffic, so that the teeming city opened before them from end to end. Then the Hertfordshire hedges, and meadows and timber, were the very thing after the Hog's Back and Hindhead; not so wonderful, of course, but more like old England and less like the bush; and before the day was out they had seen, by dodging London on the way back, the Harrow boys like a lot of young butlers who had changed hats with the maids, and Eton boys as closely resembling a convocation of slack curates.
>
> Then there was their Buckinghamshire day – Chalfont St Giles and Hughenden – and almost detached experiences such as the churchyard at Stoke Poges, where Cazalet repeated astonishing chunks of its *Elegy*, learnt as long ago as his preparatory schooldays, and the terrible disillusion of Hounslow Heath and its murderous trams.

There are, clearly, some echoes here of the outings Hornung undertook with Constance during the first flush of enthusiasm at owning their very own car.

Visiting Switzerland in the early 1900s, he became a skating enthusiast and a short story, 'The Lady of the Lift', shows that he was well acquainted with the rink at Davos. He would almost certainly have gone tobogganing as well. Switzerland as such greatly attracted him and he clearly stayed at the Riffel Alp Hotel, Zermatt, where the action of *No Hero* is based. He refers to "the stock breakfast of the Swiss hotel, with its horse-shoe rolls and its fabricated honey" and grumbles about "the absurdly early dinner which is the one blot upon the Riffel Alp arrangements". For one with asthma, the climate was a godsend. "Only to lie with the window open", he writes,

> was to breathe air of a keener purity, a finer temper, a more exhilarating freshness, than had ever before entered my lungs; and to get up and look out of the window was to peer into the limpid brilliance of a gigantic crystal, where the smallest object was in startling focus, and the very sunbeams cut with scissors. The people below trailed shadows like running ink. The light was ultra-tropical. One looked for drill suits and pith headgear, and was amazed to find pyjamas insufficient at the open window.
>
> Upon the terraces on the other side, when I eventually came down, there were cane chairs and Tauchnitz novels under the umbrella tents, and the telescope out and trained upon a party on the Matterhorn.... But when I looked it was long before my inexperienced eye could discern the three midges strung out on the single strand of cobweb against the sloping snow.

He was also familiar with Winterwald's "great Excelsior Hotel", which would feature in *The Crime Doctor*. Early in 1909 the Hornungs stayed at Engelberg, where fellow-visitors included the Kiplings and Jeromes. (Jerome K. Jerome found Connie "as cheery and vigorous as ever, but a shade stouter".)

However strained his relationship with his brother-in-law might be, Hornung had no shortage of friends and acquaintances as such. He was extremely sociable and was an amusing conversationalist. It will be recalled that Harry Ringrose "became a member of a club, and got on intimate terms with men whose names and work had become familiar to him in these years. They enlarged his sympathies – they extended his boundaries on every side." Hornung had joined the Reform Club in the mid-1890s and remained a member until his election to the Savile Club in 1913. His membership of the latter body had been proposed by Henry Justice Ford (an artist) and the nine supporters of the proposal included Everard Hopkins (another artist, younger brother of the poet) and Walter Heape (a biologist). Edward Shortt, to whom he dedicated *The Shadow of the Rope*, was a barrister who subsequently became a Liberal MP. Early in the 1890s he would have joined the Society of Authors, founded by Sir Walter Besant in 1884, and in April 1904 was elected to its Council, presided over by George Meredith, and became a member of the Management Committee.

In 1903 Hornung bought a modest country retreat – The Pipkin, East Ruston, near Norwich – but appears to have sold it again in 1906. Of rather more importance, however, was the Hornungs' move from 9 Pitt Street to 7 Hornton Street in 1905 – still in Kensington, but a rather grander abode. The purchase of the lease had cost him £2,850 which was then a very considerable amount of money.

Another close friend was John Millais, son of the artist, who lived near Horsham in Sussex. When Pitt Hornung, now extremely wealthy as a result of his labours for *C.A.M.* and planning to spend more time in England, was introduced to Millais by Willie he found that particular area so attractive that he decided to buy a house of his own there. In 1909 he acquired Compton Lea (with 16 bedrooms) and became much involved with the hunting and shooting set. He also started to build up a string of racehorses. Dividing his time between England, Lisbon and Africa, but with an increasing prediliction for his native land, he eventually found both the house and the stables at Compton Lea too small for his needs and was delighted when the West Grinstead estate, six miles south of Horsham, came up for sale. He acquired the parkland in 1911 and the house in 1913 and Willie and Connie spent many contented weekends with Pitt and his family at West Grinstead during the months immediately prior to the Great War. The two brothers were reasonably close and co-operated in a joint venture of finding jobs for ex-prisoners. Pitt also became friendly with Conan Doyle and (episodes involving false beards notwithstanding) good relations appear to have been formally restored between Willie and his brother-in-law.

An anxious concern, at this time, was the future of his son, Arthur Oscar Hornung. "It is my earnest desire that my son should receive a first class education", he declared when he wrote his will on 1 December 1904. He was delighted, in fact, that the opportunity had arisen to send the boy to the same preparatory school which he himself had attended, which had moved from Moffat to Broadstairs in 1903. While not renowned as a public speaker, he developed a custom of delivering, at least once a year, a little talk, or sermon, at the Chapel of Stone House, Broadstairs, to the assembled pupils. "You know I was a boy at this school myself", he remarked on 12 July 1908, "before the school came here; and I tell you that I have had even greater joy in what I might almost call my second schooldays, of the last five years, than in those days of old that I so love to remember." Oscar left Stone House three months later, his destination being Eton – "The best type of Eton boy," Captain Clephane had declared in *No Hero*, "is one of the greatest works of God . . . . [His poise is] all Eton, except what is in the blood, and it's all a question of manners, or rather of manner." (Uppingham, on this rare occasion, appears to have been out of favour.) Thereafter, in the summer of 1914, Oscar would be moving on to Cambridge.

"He was a poor preacher," remarked Hornung of a vicar who features in *The Shadow of the Rope*, "and no cricketer at all: but in both branches he did his best, with the simple zeal and the unconscious sincerity which redeemed not a few of his deficiencies." This could almost have been his own epitaph.

18

A DEPARTURE

WILLIE'S PERIODIC BREACHES with his brother-in-law were unfortunate, but the two men (despite their valiant efforts to get on with one another) had never been particularly close. Somebody else, however, with whom Hornung had begun to develop an intimate friendship, following their meeting in 1898, was George Gissing. Gissing would have appreciated Hornung because, like himself, he was a self-made man, having been dependent solely upon his own literary exertions for his income – for, unlike Doyle and Wells, neither of them had ever practised any other kind of profession. They had each made their own way in the world. They had maintained spasmodic contact during 1899 but there was a very slight rift between them at the turn of the century, because Hornung had sent Gissing a copy of *Peccavi* and had eagerly awaited his comments. Sadly, response came there none and Hornung complained to Morley Roberts, a mutual friend, about the older novelist's silence.

"It really grieves me to hear what you say about Hornung & *Peccavi*," Gissing wrote from Arachon, in the south of France, to Roberts on 15 December 1901. "I remember so well his telling me about the book long before he wrote it, & gladly would I have read it. But que voulez-vous? I am (with all my charges) miserably poor, & *never* buy a book.... On the other hand, I know that an author canot send presentation copies to an unlimited circle of acquaintances. But I grieve if Hornung thinks that I was idly indifferent to his work – indeed no!" Morley thereupon explained that Hornung *had* sent a presentation copy, and was distressed that it had apparently been ignored. "I am vexed beyond measure that Hornung should have thought me capable of such brutality," Gissing replied on 12 January 1902. "To what address did he send the vol., & when? Yes, give him my address, with all greetings.... *Do* make H. believe that I absolutely never rec[eive]d his book; I am distressed about it – I who reply to every silly stranger who sends me any foolishness."

Good relations were thereupon restored. But Gissing's health was, by this time, very poor and he had virtually worn himself out. Remaining in the south of France to the very last, he died on 28 December 1903 and was buried in the cemetery in St Jean de Luz. "The death of George Gissing", wrote Hornung in a heartfelt obituary published in *The Author* in February 1904,

> came as a complete shock to most of us who mourn him. Delicate he had been for years, but in no such degree as to alarm his friends, who were under the impression that he had derived great benefit from his protracted sojourn at St Jean de Luz. Only a few days before Christmas one heard in delight that there was just a chance of his coming back to live in England. He must have been upon his death-bed at the time. He had been working very hard. Hard work with Gissing meant as much writing in a day and a half as most men accomplish in a week. His book was his life while it lasted; after it had almost been his death, for he scorned to spare himself till the last page was written. His last book was never finished. It was one that he had carried in his mind for many years; it is said that he was within sight of the end; the irony might have been his own. Pneumonia struck him down; in three weeks he was dead.
>
> It is hard to write of a dead man and his living work, especially when one knew the man better than the work, and cared for him infinitely more. There are many who speak of Gissing and his work as though the two were warp and weft. Those who knew him best will be the last to accept that view. The man was one of the most lovable; the work was hardly that. The man had abundant humour; there is little humour in the bulk of his books. He had a glorious laugh – a laugh inconceivable to those who have only read him. There was an appreciative sympathy, a cordial humanity, which it

would be difficult to deduce from his writings. His serious view of life may have been acrid and even savage, but he was certainly not in the habit of obtruding his serious view of life. This, of course, is only to speak of the man as one had the privilege of knowing him; it is not to pretend to have known the whole man, or to have plumbed his depths, but only to have found him all unlike his books, humorous, human, and humane.

On the other hand, there can be no denying that much of his own personality and many of his own experiences found or forced their way into his fiction. Too fine a nature to sit down deliberately to 'make copy' of his joys and sorrows, he was too true an artist not to dip his pen into his own cup as his inspiration urged. At first sight it would appear that his knowledge of life was entirely first-hand, his poverty of mere imagination only compensated by the depth and truth of his extraordinary insight into the secrets of the heart. Yet there is more imagination in *New Grub Street* alone than is ever likely to meet the ordinary eye. It was written in the days when George Gissing frequented the Reading Room of the British Museum. He made that the chief scene of his story, likened the Readers in the wheel of radiating desks to the flies in a spider's web, and drew their imaginary lives. There was, I believe, in the author's mind at least, a flesh-and-blood original of every literary person in the book; and some of them are Readers to this day. Written as the book was, on Gissing's own showing, in six weeks to pay the rent, one of the characters, Reardon, is depicted in the self-same plight; and when, in a candid criticism of Reardon's work, it is claimed for him that his best pages were instinct with a certain "intellectual glow", the self-portrait seems complete. There could be no fitter phrase for the peculiar literary quality which distinguishes the characteristic pages of George Gissing. But the contrasting type, the cynically successful young man of letters, is at least as justly realised, as strongly drawn. And it is difficult to believe that Gissing ever fraternised with such a one in all his literary life.

During the last few years he had made a second reputation for himself as a sane and illuminating critic of Charles Dickens. The immortal works were discussed with equal sympathy and acumen in a monograph and in the introductions to the Rochester edition in a course of publication by Messrs. Methuen. It is greatly to be hoped that all the introductions, so honest alike in their strictures and their enthusiasm, have long been in the publishers' hands. "I didn't relish this critical writing," he wrote with the task in hand; but it is to be doubted whether he ever did anything very much better; for that beautifully veiled autobiography, *The Private Papers of Henry Ryecroft*, brilliantly written as it is, and touchingly eloquent of the man, is in many places marred for his friends by an alien misanthropy and an almost morose perversity of view.

Notable novelist as he was, with a vogue among his peers indubitably dearer to his fine soul than the plaudits of the crowd, there are those who knew George Gissing through and through, and who held that novel-writing was not his true vocation. They say he was a greater scholar than could possibly be gathered from his books, and that he would have been truly great as a scholar pure and simple. He had indeed a passion for the classics, and the very temperament to have taken kindly to a cloistered life; but it is futile to pursue the thought. He spent his life in writing the most modern novels imaginable, in a microscopic hand (a thousand words to the sheet of sermon paper) in keeping with his microscopic observation; and he has left behind him more than one that may well survive as uncompromising transcripts of their time. And a vivid memory of the man, of his fine face, his noble head, his winning kindness, will endure as long as the last of those who knew him. That he retained his great personal charm throughout all the storms of his inner life, is not more extraordinary than the fact that he remained to the last the most acutely sensitive of men. Into the secret of those storms, as into the entire peace of his last years abroad, he admitted only his chosen few; for the rest of us it is enough to know that the storms had long abated, and that the last years were the happiest of his life.

With these moving words Willie took leave of a man whom he had grown, within a short space of time, to greatly admire. And there was destined, as we shall see, to be one final link between the two friends.

19

TRICKS AND CLICKS

A THIEF IN THE NIGHT had been published in 1905. Thereafter, four years went by without the publication of a single new book by E.W. Hornung. An established man of letters, he had also become a gentleman of leisure – and he had, moreover, earned the right to take a rest. But at long last the silence was broken and in September 1909 a new book featuring his most famous creation of all, *Mr Justice Raffles*, published by Smith, Elder & Co., appeared on the bookstalls. On this occasion it was a full-length novel about Raffles, not a collection of short stories. In theory, there was no reason why such a format should not have worked. In practice, the trick did not come off. Certainly, it is nice to have a fresh Raffles yarn to tuck into, and the "gay old rascal" seems to be in sparkling form when the tale begins (seemingly in 1899, which makes nonsense of the dating of the previous tales). But first, there is a glorious camp reunion to get through. "You remember the last time we sat down together?" Raffles asks, after meeting Bunny at Charing Cross.

"You mean that night we had supper at the Savoy?"

"It's only three weeks ago, Bunny."

"It seems months to me."

"And years to me!" cried Raffles.

Then, without a pause, we are told about the man destined to be the chief villain of the tale – a Jewish money-lender who had been sitting at the next table, described by Raffles as a lost tribesman "with the nose like the village pump" and by Bunny as "the great Dan Levy, otherwise Mr Shylock". Raffles, it

190

eventually transpires, had pursued him out to Carlsbad to take the cure and purloin his wife's emerald necklace, had (in disguise as a dirt-begrimed German burglar) been caught in the act, had made his escape, but had then deliberately abandoned the necklace so that Mrs Levy would not be too distressed.

Before all this tale can emerge, however, we have come back to the Albany and are introduced to a brilliant young cricketer, fresh-faced Teddy Garland, whom Raffles greets warmly (much to Bunny's irritation) notwithstanding the fact that Teddy has been caught in the act of trying to forge Raffles's signature on a cheque. For young Teddy, it transpires, is in the same dire straits as Bunny himself had been after that fateful game of baccarat: he is totally skint and at the mercy of Dan Levy, who will be demanding his pound of flesh at noon the following day – at the very moment that Teddy is about to play in the University match at Lords!

Raffles comes to the rescue, out-witting Dan Levy on Teddy's behalf, but Dan soon tumbles to the fact that he has been tricked. It then turns out that Teddy's father is also in hock to the dreadful Dan, who – wreaking his revenge on Raffles, whom he now belatedly recognises as the Carlsbad thief – announces that the Garlands' house belong to him and they must vacate it seven days hence. Once again, it is a case of Raffles to the rescue. He strikes a deal with Levy, whereby he will steal an incriminating letter from a solicitor's office in Gray's Inn on Levy's behalf and Levy, in return, will surrender all financial claims on Mr Garland senior. Raffles fulfils his part of the bargain – one of the few genuinely exciting passages in the book – but Levy, in unsportsmanlike fashion, tries to do the dirty on him. Raffles, incensed, ends up by taking Levy prisoner, and carts him off to a tower in Horace Walpole's empty Gothic mansion at Strawberry Hill. Here he sits in judgment on him – hence the title of the book – and exacts even more onerous terms. Nipping off to the bank to cash the cheque exacted from his prisoner, he is stopped by Bunny.

"Raffles," I said, in a low voice that may have trembled,"it's not a part for you to play at all! I don't mean the little bit at the bank. I mean this whole blackmailing part of the business. It's not like you, Raffles. It spoils the whole thing!"

I had got it off my chest without a hitch. But so far Raffles had not discouraged me. There was a look on his face which even made me think that he agreed with me in his heart. Both hardened as he thought it over.

"It's Levy who's spoilt the whole thing," he rejoined obdurately in the end. "He's been playing me false all the time, and he's got to pay for it."

"But you never meant to make anything out of him, A.J.!"

"Well, I do now, and I've told you why. Why shouldn't I?"

"Because it's not your game!" I cried, with all the eager persuasion in my power. "Because it's all the sort of thing Dan Levy would do himself – it's *his* game, all right – it simply drags you down to his level –"

But there he stopped me with a look, and not the kind of look I often had from Raffles. It was no new feat of mine to make him angry, scornful, bitterly cynical or sarcastic. This, however, was a look of pain and even shame, as though he had suddenly seen himself in a new and peculiarly unlovely light.

"Down to it!" he exclaimed, with an irony that was not for me. "As though there could be a much lower level than mine! Do you know, Bunny, I sometimes think my moral sense is ahead of yours?"

I could have laughed outright; but the humour that was the salt of him seemed suddenly to have gone out of Raffles.

"I know what I am," said he, "but I'm afraid you're getting a hopeless villain-worshipper!"

"It's not the villain I care about," I answered, meaning every word. "It's the sportsman behind the villain, as you know perfectly well."

"I know the villain behind the sportsman rather better," replied Raffles, laughing when I least expected it.

All goes smoothly, except that Levy ("the poor brute") is murdered soon after being released, and Raffles – being genuinely alarmed, for once – rushes off to the Continent, with Inspector Mackenzie apparently in hot pursuit. But the real murderer (another of Levy's victims) owns up just in time, Mackenzie goes back to London and Raffles breathes a sigh of relief. We have learnt, finally, that he has been doing all this *not* for the sake of Teddy Garland and his father but for the sake of the woman to whom Teddy is engaged – Camilla Belsize – for whom he has fallen in a big way. Camilla, for her part, is equally enamoured of Raffles, and has even (without his ever knowing it, for she has sworn Bunny to secrecy) come to the rescue when Levy was on the point of escaping from his imprisonment in the tower. "She's the only woman I ever met", Bunny tells Raffles in an unguarded moment, "who was your mate at heart – in pluck – in temperament." Ten years later, Teddy Garland encounters Bunny in a Turkish bath in Jermyn Street and urges him (on behalf of both himself and Camilla) to tell the full story of what Raffles had done for them, in order to set the record straight. So here it is.

But, in the process, the excitement has gone cold. The tale is simply too tedious to sustain the interest. We begin to long, after a while, for the whole thing to come to an end so that we can turn our attention to something more worthwhile. Perhaps it really was the case that the Raffles and Bunny stories (once again, like the Laurel and Hardy films or even Tom and Jerry cartoons) were better suited for performance in miniature rather than in full-length format. The drama and the rhythms appropriate for a short story are simply coarsened when magnified to fill the space intended for a novel. Only by frenetic stimulants and ever-more improbable twists and turns, the artificial nature of which becomes sadly apparent, was it possible for Hornung to prolong the action and go the whole length of 70,000 words.

There is, in any case, something rather unsavoury about the basic plot of a story in which the villain of the piece spends most of his time tied up, spitting out threats but at the mercy of our heroes. Most distasteful of all, of course, is the fact that the villain is a Jew, for there was a streak of anti-Semitism in

Hornung, just as there was in most of his literary contemporaries at that time (with Hilaire Belloc being the most extreme example). There had been references to "the Jews", with their characteristic hooked noses, going about their business as an army of unscrupulous money-lenders in previous books written by Hornung, and Raffles himself had tangled with them on two or three occasions. But on this occasion the extent to which Dan Levy, or "Mr Shylock", is obliged to stand in the pillory – and then, at the end of it all, just after Raffles has released him, to be stabbed to death by yet another revenge-seeker – is rather too unpleasant to stomach. An attempt is made to keep the balance, for Raffles continually refers to him as a worthy opponent with some traits that are positively admirable, but this is just our dear old cricketing friend trying to play the game in a sportsmanlike way – and to convince us, in the process, that this really is a top-hole yarn. Dan Levy is no Moriarty, any more than Camilla Belsize – appearing on the scene far too late in the day – persuades us that she is another Irene Adler.

It was eleven years since Raffles had created that devastating impression by his initial appearance. Hornung's hand was losing its cunning, so far as plot-writing was concerned, and Raffles as a personality had ceased to shock. This was one curtain-call too many. The initial freshness had gone, although his reappearance was an agreeable enough event for some of the critics to greet him warmly – as they would, say, an old friend at a party who had been out of circulation for some little while. "In these vivacious pages", proclaimed the *Pall Mall Gazette* loyally, "we meet the attractively unscrupulous A.J. once more.... Quite amusing, and will doubtless extend the already large circle of A.J.'s admirers." "Our old cricket-burgling friend", enthused the *Daily Mirror*, "has come to us again" while the *Standard* thought that the story had been "spun very ingeniously. The action never stops for an instant. Raffles and his friend Bunny are tracked and imprisoned" – a wild mis-representation of the plot! – "and knocked about in excellent style." But the fact that the *Standard*'s critic had evidently done no more than glance at it, that the *Mirror* could only highlight "the discovery that Raffles has a heart and a romance" (oblivious, evidently, to the sorry fate of Faustina) and that the *Pall Mall Gazette* had qualified its welcome with the cautious word "doubtless" suggests that, after their initial polite greetings, the critics were looking beyond Raffles to see who else might be in the offing. For the truth of the matter was, alas, that A.J. was now a rather dated figure whose day had come and gone.

"Mr Hornung", remarked *Punch*, "was to be congratulated in the beginning of things for boldly recognising the innate immorality of the reader and allowing his hero-villain no merits but good sportsmanship. But is he to be congratulated either on protracting the existence of the popular idol, or in finding for him a dully virtuous end to justify his charmingly disreputable means? With all its easy style, occasional humour and pleasant seasoning of love interest, *Mr Justice Raffles* rarely rises above the level of everyday criminal fiction... [When] he sits in mock judgment on the melodramatic blood-sucker and rebukes his rather conventional sins in no very original manner, the situation becomes a little ridiculous and Raffles himself something of a prig. Frankly, the reader may feel at the end of the book that, though he would like a lot more of Mr Hornung, he has by now had almost enough of Mr Raffles."

"'I've written my last word about the old boy', says Bunny in the last chapter of his fellow-criminal", noted the *Times Literary Supplement*; "and we confess to a hope that nothing will alter that most laudable determination, for these further doings of the 'gentlemanly' rascal Raffles are neither plausible nor exciting."

Undiscouraged, Hornung now turned his attention to a mystery of a totally different kind. But *The Camera Fiend*, published by Fisher Unwin in February 1911 and running to 76,000 words, is a strange production. The opening chapters suggest that it is a story which could happily have been serialised in the *Boy's Own Paper*, since it tells the adventures that befall Pocket Upton when he leaves his public school to pay a visit to the London specialist treating him for asthma and to stay overnight in town with friends. (His real name is Tony, but he is regarded as a pocket edition of the two elder brothers who had preceded him at school.) He is, of course, a cricket enthusiast, although his asthma prevents him from playing it, and his father (surprise, surprise) is a wealthy ironmaster. (But the family home, for a change, is in Leicestershire rather than Yorkshire.) For one reason and another, however, the people with whom he had intended to stay are unable to put him up – or, to be more accurate, to put up with him – and he decides to camp out in Hyde Park instead. But on waking up he falls into the hands of a Jekyll and Hyde character – a one-time eminent doctor who is now as sinister, and as mad, as they come. Dr Baumgartner is convinced that it is possible to photograph the soul leaving the body at the moment of death. Frustrated at being denied access to people in hospitals at the moment they are about to pass over, or to murderers at the moment they are about to be hanged, he has devised a very unusual camera which is capable of firing a shot and taking a photograph almost simultaneously. He has taken to prowling about London in the early hours of the summer months, searching for expendable victims, and it is on one of these morning excursions – just after shooting a tramp – that he and Pocket Upton come into contact with one another. A prisoner in the doctor's Chelsea home, Pocket makes the acquaintance of his niece, Phillida, and it is for her sake that he remains there when an opportunity to escape presents itself. Meanwhile, his father has hired the services of a private investigator – a very fat gentleman called Eugene Thrush, who is assisted by his manservant Mullins (whom Thrush playfully dubs 'Sherlock' on one occasion). All works out well in the end. In the cause of science, and after three failures to capture the crucial instant, the mad professor shoots himself with his own camera, trusting that on *this* occasion there will be a decent photograph of the soul making its departure which posterity can marvel at. Thrush reunites father and son, and Pocket and Phillida are last seen disappearing into the sunset arm-in-arm. (The camera, alas, falls into the Thames and the photographic plate is ruined.) It is a riveting story, brilliantly told, but nevertheless a very peculiar one.

Phillida is at pains to emphasise that her uncle has not always been the dreadful character that Pocket must think him and is relieved to find, when identifying his corpse in the mortuary, that long-lost attributes have reappeared. "She had steeled herself to look upon a debased image of the familiar face, and she found it startlingly ennobled and refined. Death had taken away nothing here, save the furrows of age and the fires of madness, and it had given back the look of fine courage and of sane integrity which the girl was just old enough to associate with the dead man's prime. She was thankful to have seen him like this for the last time"

It is, of course, impossible to ignore the fact that Hornung's brother-in-law – hitherto the epitome of bluff commonsense – was now becoming interested in spiritualism, which Willie evidently considered an irrational pursuit. When eminent middle-aged (or muddle-aged) gentlemen ventured beyond what might be thought the reasonable limits of exploration then it was time to ring alarm bells. Conan Doyle himself, writing in 1926, states flatly that Willie was "intolerant about Spirit Communion". (One is tempted to assume that 'Baumgartner' was the name that Doyle adopted some eight months after *The Camera Fiend*'s publication, when he donned a false beard *á la* Challenger and went a-calling in Germanic mode.)

The young, asthmatic Upton (who is himself a budding photographer) takes Phillida away from her uncle's house, just as the young, impoverished Overman (who is himself a budding writer) was about to take Ida away from her father's house in '"Author! Author!"', the short story written almost twenty years earlier, and just as Hornung had taken Connie away from her brother's house. The parallels are too obvious to miss.

Hornung still had the poet's eye and a wonderful turn of phrase. Describing a "ragged little garden ... brimming over with moonlight from wall to wall" he adds: "The unkempt grass looked pale and ghostly, like the skin of some monstrous wolf." And later, as the early morning sun comes up over Chelsea:

> Half the streets were raked with level sunlight, but the other half were ladders of dusk with rungs of light at the gaps between the houses. All were dustier, dirtier, and emptier than is ever the case by night or day, because this was neither one nor the other, though the sun was up to make the most of dust, dirt, and emptiness. It was before even the cleansing hour of the scavenger and the water-cart.

The book was greeted with politeness rather than acclaim. "Mr Hornung manages as usual", commented the *TLS*, "to keep alive a certain amount of curiosity as to what is going forward."

But recalling, in the opening pages, his own schooldays at Uppingham had evidently brought back some happy memories, for his *next* book, *Fathers of Men*, published by Smith, Elder & Co. in February 1912, was not a mystery yarn at all but a beautifully sensitive piece of work about life at a public school. It proved to be one of the finest things that he ever wrote – second only, perhaps, to *Peccavi* – and merits a chapter to itself.

20

THE OLD SCHOOL TIES

"WHEN I WAS DOWN here about a year ago", Hornung told his youthful audience in the chapel of Stone House, Broadstairs, on 12 July 1908, "I happened to take a book of verses from one of the shelves upstairs, and quite by accident I opened the book at a poem called 'A Retrospect of School Life'. That, as you know, means a looking-back on school life. It may be that some of you know the poem itself. I can only say that it was new to me a year ago, and it seems to me so true and so fine that none of us can know it too well. 'I go', says the poet – who is about to leave his school like some of you –

> 'I go, and men who know me not,
>   When I am reckoned man, will ask,
> "What is it then that thou hast got
>   By trudging through that five-year task?
> What knowledge of what art is thine?
>   Set out thy stock, thy craft declare."
> Then this child-answer shall be mine,
>   "I only know they loved me there."'

"That is only the beginning of the answer," added Hornung, and went on to consider further verses in the poem, all of which furnished him with ample material for one of his little sermons and a volley of exhortations. "No human boy or man", he concluded, "can be wholly true to his ideals, or wholly 'pure of blame'; but every man and boy can remember the Days of Old and be loyal and faithful to his old school. The first longing of a loyal heart is to do something for those who have done much for us. Well, if you 'play the game' at your public school – you know what I mean – if you lead pure and brave and honest lives there – you *will* be doing something for the school that taught you how."

The poem had provided the theme for his sermon: it also provided the theme for *Fathers of Men*, on which he started work three years later. It is set in an unnamed school which is clearly a fictionalised Uppingham, for the name of the headmaster is Thrale and the name of Uppingham's headmaster had been Thring. Equally clearly, it is set in the early 1880s, for there are references to the music-hall songs of that time and we are told of the "boyish clangour" of the chapel bells, which "ring in the veins after thirty years, and make old blood pelt like young". Mr Heriot has welcomed two new boys to his house, Jan Rutter and a lad called Carpenter, and explains to his sister, afterwards, that the silent, sulky Rutter is actually an ex-stable-boy: his mother had come from a good family, but she had married a coachman and died soon after Jan's birth. Following the death of his father, Rutter's maternal grandfather, a clergyman, had dutifully adopted him, had had him 'crammed' and had now sent him to their school. The boy is evidently going to have a difficult time adapting to his new surroundings, but the tale of his humble origins is at all costs to be kept secret. (Heriot himself is supposed to be unaware of them, and for this reason will be unable to provide any special assistance.)

The book then traces Jan's progress through the school over a period of four years and tells how, despite some rebellious moments, he eventually comes to terms with his schoolmates and with one or two rather awkward masters. It concentrates on his friendship with Carpenter and, more particularly, on his relationship to Evan Devereux, the son of the house when he had been the stable boy. Jan virtually idolises Devereux, who keeps him at arm's length for most of the time but refrains (seemingly) from mentioning his origins to anyone else. For the first half of the book, there is virtually no clue to the fact that Hornung is the author: only in the second half, when cricket looms rather too large on the scene and Jan (a brilliant left-hand bowler) becomes captain of the school eleven, do we find ourselves in familiar territory. Jan eventually comes close to being expelled, much to Heriot's distress, for doing battle with the local ne'er-do-well over an unpaid bill for bottles of champagne. But the powers-that-be ascertain, just in time, that he had been misguidedly battling on Evan's behalf, not his own – and he himself finds out that he did not owe Evan so great a debt as he thought he did. At the very end of the book, he is leaving school and preparing to set off for Australia. There's a final stocktaking interview with Heriot, at which they review what Jan has learnt at the school and how it will, hopefully, stand him in good stead in after life, even in the bush. Heriot presents both him and Carpenter with a book of poems in which 'Retrospect of School Life' appears – but Jan feels that the final line of the verse already quoted ("I only know they loved me there.") should be the other way round. And Hornung had, indeed, rounded off his original sermon with the words: "Say rather in your hearts, 'I only know *I loved them* there', and show it in your lives."

"I have never loved writing anything so much as those closing chapters," Hornung had written to Chichester on 11 August 1911. "I *know* they are good. But they keep me awake at nights! Another ten days should see me through the draft – but weeks of revision etc. will follow. It is the one thing of mine that might not only succeed, but *live*. But it is no good hoping or looking too far ahead; the great thing is for oneself to get as near the top notch as possible, and I know I have never been so near it before."

In one sense, the plot of the book is immaterial. What really comes across is the wonderful richness of its texture, the total naturalness of the dialogue, and the vast crowd of characters with whom Hornung floods his canvas. It seems, however, that in the early stages of its composition the dialogue had presented some problems – to one, at least, of its initial readers. Chichester, who was sent the draft manuscript and invited to be totally free with his criticism, discerned what he claims "was one very big point, which seemed likely to spoil the whole book. When it was put to Hornung, he saw it at once, but it made him wretched; and it led to months of labour and correspondence. The one big change necessitated so many subsequent changes." The flaw in question, which Chichester is careful not to specify too precisely, apparently concerned a mysterious "episode" and the nature of the dialogue exchanged between the boys. There may have been something of a sexual nature about the exorcised material. An unidentified "distinguished Headmaster of very long experience" (who obviously knows more about the matter than we do), writing to Chichester thirty years later, declared: "I feel that you did a real service to all readers of Hornung's works in dissuading him from introducing an episode which would undoubtedly have robbed *Fathers of Men* of the position which it now holds in the very forefront of school stories. In fact the only other successful attempts to reproduce boys' talk, as it actually is, are – in my opinion – *A Day of my Life at Eton*, and that rather unpleasing sketch of Sherborne, *The Loom of Youth* [by Alec Waugh].... As for *Eric, St Winifred's* and even *Tom Brown*, no boys ever talked as their boys did – at least I should hope not!"

Mystifying though these guarded remarks may be, they need not detain us. *Fathers of Men*, as published in January 1912, is an evocation of school life, in both its joyous and its duller moments, which has the ring of truth throughout. Intended primarily for adults, it could have been read with equal enjoyment by children and stands comparison, most certainly, with *Tom Brown's Schooldays*. In many respects, it was an enhanced version of the kind of school-story that Talbot Baines Reed had been writing twenty years earlier and the Religious Tracts Society would have been proud to issue it under its imprimatur. It was serious, compassionate, absorbing and deeply intelligent. The characters of all the leading *persona*, boys and masters alike, are explored with profound subtlety. Chips Carpenter is clearly based on Hornung himself, for he is a small boy and a tremendous cricket enthusiast, but unable to play it to any great effect himself because of bronchial problems – instead, he becomes the cricket commentator of the school magazine and, eventually, its editor. Amiable, patently honest, and slightly garrulous, we feel we know him well by the close of the book – only to be surprised, as Jan himself is, when Chips confesses that he has not always been a paragon of virtue: "You think I've been so straight! So I was in the beginning; so I am now, if you like, but I've not been all the time." He will tell us no more than this, and we do not wish to know any more. Jan also has his dark, despairing moods, and Evan Devereux, despite an engaging manner when he wants something, is evidently a flawed character. But Hornung did not expect his characters to be perfect: he expected them to be human beings.

There are, as always with Hornung, some striking turns of phrase – a thin church spire with a golden cock atop, seen on a summer's afternoon, looks "rather like an inverted note of exclamation on a sheet of pale blue paper" – but on this occasion one remembers the passages of sustained description (clearly based on genuine recollections) more than the odd few words. Here, for example, is an autumnal highlight from the school calendar:

> The paper chase always took place on the last Saturday but one, and was quite one of the events of the winter term. All the morning, after second school, fags had been employed in tearing up scent in the library; and soon after dinner the road under Heriot's study windows began to resound with the tramp of boys on their way in twos and threes to see the start from Burston Beeches. A spell of hard weather had broken in sunshine and clear skies; the afternoon was brilliantly fine; and by half-past two the scene in the paddock under the noble beeches, with the grey tower of Burston church rising behind the leafless branches, was worthy of the day. Practically all the school was there, and quite a quarter of it in flannels and jerseys red or white, trimmed or starred with the colour of some fifteen. Off go the two hares – gigantic gentlemen with their football colours thick upon them. Hounds and mere boys in plain clothes crowd to the gate to see the last of them and their bulging bag of scent. The twelve minutes' law allowed them seems much more like

half-an-hour; but at last time is up, the gates are opened, and
the motley pack pours through with plenty of plain clothes
after them for the first few fields. In about a mile comes the
first check; it is the first of many, for snow is still lying under
the trees and hedges, and in the distance it always looks like a
handful of waste-paper. The younger hounds take a minute
off, leaving their betters to pick up the scent again, and their
laboured breath is so like tobacco smoke that you fancy that
young master in knickerbockers is there to see that it is not.
Off again to the first water-jump – which everybody fords –
and so over miles of open upland, flecked with scent and
snow – through hedges into ditches – a pack of mudlarks
now, and but a remnant of the pack that started. Now the
scent takes great zigzags, and lies in niggardly handfuls that
tell their tale. Now it is thick again, and here are the two fags
who met the hares with the fresh bags, and those gigantic
gentlemen are actually only five minutes ahead, for here is
the high road back past the Upper, and if it wasn't for the red
sun in your eyes there should be a view of them from the top
of one of those hills.

On the top of the last hill, by the white palings of the
Upper Ground, there is a group of boys and masters, and
several of the masters' wives as well, to see the finish; and it is
going to be one of the best finishes they ever have seen. Here
come the gigantic gentlemen, red as Indians with the sun
upon their faces, and one of them plunging headlong in a
plain distress. They rush down that hill, and are half-way up
this one, the wet mud shining all over them like copper, when
the first handful of hounds start up the sky behind them.

And then, a couple of months later:

Christmas weather set in before the holidays. Old Boys came
trooping down from Oxford and Cambridge, and stood in
front of their old hall fires in astonishing ties and wondrous
waistcoats, patronising the Loder of the house, familiar only
with the Charles Cave. But when they went in a body to
inspect the Upper, it was seen at once that the Old Boys'
Match could not take place, for the ground was still thickly
powdered with snow, and a swept path proved as hard and
slippery as the slide in Heriot's quad. This slide was a duly
authorised institution, industriously swept and garnished by
the small fry of the house under the personal supervision of

old Mother Sprawson, who sent more than one of them down it barefoot, as a heroic remedy for chilblains rashly urged in excuse for absence. Indeed it was exceptionally cold, even for a nineteenth-century December. The fire in the hall was twice its usual size; the study pipes became too hot to touch, yet remained a mockery until you had your tollies [candles] going as well and every chink stopped up. Sprawson himself was understood to be relying more than ever on his surreptitious flask; but as he never betrayed the ordinary symptoms of indulgence, except before a select and appreciative audience, and could sham sober with complete success whenever necessary, these entertainments were more droll than thrilling. It was Sprawson, however, who lit up the slide with tollies after lock-up on the last night, and kept the fun fast and furious until the school bell rang sharply through the frost, and the quad opened to dispatch its quota of glowing faces to prize-giving in the big school-room.

On holiday in Switzerland, at the time of the book's publication, Hornung encountered the author of *Stalky & Co.* – who was positively ecstatic in its praise. "I told you on my card that Kipling was keen on my book," a delighted Hornung reported to Chichester on 3 February, "but I could hardly tell you *how* keen he seems: he ran through the hotel to find me when he had finished it, and wrung me by the hand and said more than I ever hoped to live to hear, of any work of mine, from a Master's lips!" And he was able to add, on 15 February, that he had received "some quite wonderful letters from Uppingham men – masters and Old Boys – and *two* ex-captains of that house! They are as keen on the book as you are – and as Kipling is! It is wonderful to me; but now I begin to believe that such a strong opinion, practically unanimous among the first batch of readers, is bound *ipso facto* to be held by many more besides."

The Spectator, which had ignored Hornung's two previous books, devoted almost a page to an enthusiastic review (which Hornung contentedly referred to, on 1 June, as a "nice allusion"). "The picture is vivid", it declared, "and the characterisation fresh and engrossing.... The scene in chapel, the fragment of the headmaster's sermon, and Jan's final interview with the house-master, after everything has been cleared up, are touched with a generous sentiment that escapes effusiveness, and they bring to a fitting close a story which is at once a fine tribute to a great school and a great headmaster [i.e., Uppingham and Thring], and a fresh and penetrating study of that eternal problem – the human boy."

"To the small number of those who can write a readable school-story", added the critic in *Punch*, "must now be added the name of Mr E.W. Hornung, whose *Fathers of Men* strikes me as a more than creditable attempt at a notoriously difficult subject." Then, after summarising the plot, there crept in a slight note of reservation. "It is a beginning rich in promise," he continued, "which is to a very large extent, if not wholly, fulfilled. Jan, with his uncouthness, his mingling of diverse hereditary interests, and his devotion to the handsome but worthless 'Master Evan', is a fine and carefully-studied figure. Perhaps it is all a little too obviously done from the outside."

Once again, as with *Peccavi*, Hornung had surpassed himself. But, again like *Peccavi*, the book fell just short of absolute perfection, for having austerely set out to concentrate on a single issue he had found the task too difficult to sustain unaided to the bitter end. He had once more rested his oars and introduced some extraneous material. He was thereby enabled to cruise on to a conclusion which, while rounding the story off in a dignified, apt and moving manner, was in some respects an unearned increment. "Up to a point", commented a sympathetic critic in the *TLS*, "Mr Hornung has succeeded admirably. Rutter's character, slow, sturdy and shrewd, is vividly presented, and his friend and worshipper 'Chips' Carpenter is also a very clear, sympathetic portrait of an unusual boy. Rutter's early mistakes and gradual progress will be read by all with much interest, but the second half of the story is conventional and lacking in life. The whole episode of Devereux's drinking and Rutter's self-sacrifice is a descent into regions which are both unreal and commonplace in tales of school-life; and the psychological interest which has hitherto distinguished the tale becomes attenuated when

Rutter develops an astonishing gift as a left-hand bowler. Prodigies who bowl out first-class batsmen at will are far too plentiful in fiction; the Jan Rutter of the opening chapters stood out by himself. Mr Hornung makes Rutter and his friend and master, Heriot, acknowledge that this gift has simplified the problem, but it has done worse than that. It also removed the pleasure of watching a boy overcome obstacles, as he was doing, by sheer doggedness of character, and left the reader disappointedly wondering why a story which was so strikingly begun could not have been allowed to pursue its natural course to success."

Even so, it was a pretty good failure.

CB&O

"It was not always intended", wrote Hornung in his Preface to a 1919 reprint, "that the School in this story should be expressly identified with Uppingham. To Uppingham men, indeed, the scenes and customs described were meant to be unmistakable; but the uninitiated were to have taken the picture, had they been so good, for one of public-school life in the early 'eighties, rather than of any particular Public School. An incontinent announcement defeated this project, by parading the names which had been most carefully altered or omitted and perhaps somewhat forcing the special appeal at the expense of the general attempt. At all events it is only at Uppingham, where the keenest criticism was naturally apprehended, that *Fathers of Men* has had much vogue in the eight [sic] years since first publication: and to the many Uppinghamians, of all generations, who have taken the trouble to write to me about the book, I am proportionately grateful for appreciation more generous than I can say. I can only tell them I would not now exchange it for a far wider measure of popularity; for to write about one's old school, and to be taken even half-seriously on the spot itself, is to have appeased the laudable ferocity of the severest critics in the world."

21

SWANSONG OF A NOVELIST

FATHERS OF MEN, running to almost 130,000 words, had been a major achievement demanding a fair degree of concentration. It was the longest book Hornung ever wrote. What followed, in March 1913, was pure relaxation for author and reader alike. It was a collection of eight short stories (averaging about 7,600 words each) published by Hodder & Stoughton and entitled *Witching Hill* – a *jeu d'esprit*, and as fresh, haunting and delightful as anything Hornung ever did. The two main characters are, in a sense, reincarnations of Raffles and Bunny, but in a totally different setting – namely, that of a new housing estate, parts of it still under construction, in a neck of the woods not far removed from Richmond and Kingston. (Although it is, for all practical purposes, Never Never Land.) The narrator, Mr Gillon (whose Christian name we never learn) is a very young Scotsman in charge of the estate office, dealing with tenants' complaints and queries, and he makes the acquaintance of Uvo Delavoye (or should it be de la Mare?), a witty, high-spirited young man with a yellowish complexion who has served in Egypt in his time but is now a semi-invalid living with his sister and widowed mother – just as Hornung had done, of course, in the late 1880s, although the adventures experienced by Gillon and Delavoye take place (so we learn by degrees) during the four closing years of the nineteenth century.

The housing estate is in Mulcaster Park, which formerly formed part of the estate of a wicked Lord Mulcaster who had flourished in the early eighteenth century. The Delavoyes are actually distant but impoverished descendants of his lordship, and as a number of strange events overtake various tenants on the estate so Uvo develops the theory that the baleful spirit of the notorious Lord is still abroad and that it is his own mission in life to do battle against it and, if possible, perform the role of exorcist. Sceptical Gillon tends to dismiss the theory as nonsense, but acts as a loyal Watson in helping Delavoye with his investigations.

In the first tale, 'Unhallowed Ground', they discover a secret tunnel leading from the Delavoyes' garden to the manor house, where the legitimate descendant of Lord Mulcaster, hitherto renowned for his religious proclivities, the pious Christopher Stainsby, is found to be presiding over something not far removed from an orgy. In 'The House with Red Blinds' (which owes something, in title if nothing else, to *The House with Green Shutters*) somebody commits suicide in a house on the site where Mulcaster had driven a disloyal steward to do precisely the same thing. Next, in 'A Vicious Circle', extracts from Wilde's *Ballad of Reading Gaol* (published in 1898) are quoted at length, as a distraught young man tries to work out why he is so depressed nine-tenths of the time and wishing to break off his engagement – the reason, so Uvo realises, being that his fiancée has presented him with a ring which formerly belonged to Mulcaster. In 'The Local Colour' the vicar's prim sister is 'inspired' to write a fictional tale of rapine and violence, intended for the parish magazine, which is a dreadfully accurate account of how the wicked lord had deflowered a young lady from the East End – she reads it aloud to an electrified Delavoye and Gillen, blissfully unaware of the full purport of what she is narrating, until her brother comes home unexpectedly and consigns the manuscript to the fire without further ado. And so the tales go on, a mixture of sly amusement and high drama, with the reader – as soon as one of them has been finished – itching to start the next without delay. But the outbreak of the South African War compels Gillen to enlist. Back on a short spell of leave, he stays with Delavoye and is delighted to find his friend manfully resisting, at the eleventh hour (and at the newly-rediscovered temple of Bacchus), the temptation to carry on with an immensely attractive married woman. Uvo decides to accompany his friend on a trip up north. "By the way," he remarks with the old wilful smile, as the book draws to an end, "I haven't mentioned him since you've been back, but on a last morning like this you may be glad to hear that my old ghost of the soil is laid at last... The rest is silence, if you don't mind, old man."

Sadly, the rest was almost total silence from the critics – although the book did manage to go through at least one more edition. *Punch* conceded that Hornung had had an "ingenious idea" but felt that *Witching Hill* was only good in parts. And that was about it. Yet eighty-six years later, and after two readings, the tales continue to fascinate. Like many of Hornung's others, they certainly merit reprinting.

Thereafter, alas, it was downhill all the way.

The plot of *The Thousandth Woman*, published by Eveleigh Nash in October 1913, is distressingly trite and improbable. Two men travelling to England from Italy, and sharing a cabin, discover that they are both in love with the same woman. One of them, Walter Cazalet, is coming home after ten years in Australia; the other, Hilton Toye, is an American. News reaches them that somebody called Henry Crane, a crooked businessman responsible for the downfall of Walter's father, has been murdered. Walter is far from sorry. Their ship docks at Southampton and they both travel to London, to pay court to Blanche Macnair. But Toye realises that – during four days' absence from the ship, when it was rounding the coast of Italy – Cazalet could have nipped over to England, by means of the railway system, murdered Crane himself, and then rushed back to the ship. It transpires that Cazalet did indeed come to England and was at Crane's house on the night of the murder, but is not himself the guilty party. The real murderer, someone called Scruton ("but more sinned against than sinning"), freshly released from prison and with scores of his own to settle, then comes in and owns up to them both. He is the man whom Cazalet had been shielding, but is clearly not long for this world. The mystery solved, Toye takes his departure and Cazalet prepares to take Blanche back to Australia. He regards her as a woman in a thousand, because she had been prepared to stand by him even though he was accused of murder. End of story.

It ran to only 40,000 words but this was more than enough. Compared, say, to *The Shadow of the Rope*, written ten years earlier, or even (going back a further ten years) to *The Unbidden Guest*, it was an appallingly feeble production. It contained the pleasant account of motoring excursions quoted earlier, and there is a striking reference to Cazalet – "He was tanned a rich bronze about the middle of his face, but it broke off across his forehead like the colouring of a meerschaum pipe." But there was otherwise a dearth of any incidental delights.

The critics were not impressed. "Mr E.W. Hornung has, in the past at any rate, known how to endow his characters with both charm and vigour," commented the *TLS*, "but in his new tale of mystery the capacity for clear and forcible description has deserted him.... The action moves so slowly and there is so much talk which apparently leads nowhere, that although the book is unusually short, it is too long to sustain the interest. Mr Hornung keeps one surprise up his sleeve and the last chapter is much the best; but it comes too late for us to recapture the thrilling sense of mystery and daring which one feels a right to expect from the creator of Raffles."

His next, and final, work of fiction, pointedly dedicated to a well-known American literary agent ("To Curtis Brown, Accessory") was *The Crime Doctor*, running to 70,000 words and published by Eveleigh Nash in July 1914. Once more, we are presented with a batch of eight stories linked loosely together but they contain none of the magic of the *Witching Hill* tales. Written in a competent but detached manner, they have as their principal character Dr John Dollar, a crime doctor – or psychologist – who believes that anyone who commits a crime must be ill. He therefore makes it his business to investigate any crimes that may be brought to his attention, and – when the culprit has been identified – to either invite them to join his establishment, so that he can cure them, or else to mete out appropriate retribution if the villain is beyond redemption. One or two of the stories are mildly interesting, but it is virtually impossible to work up much enthusiasm about the work as a whole. The characters are pasteboard figures and Dollar himself, for all his professed originality (and possible connection with Ezra Pound), seems as conventional, and uninspiring, as so many of the other private detectives who were trying to earn their creators an honest crust in the English fiction market of that time. The other main characters are a Home Secretary called Topham Vinson (presumably based on Winston Churchill), a pair of villains called Scarth and Croucher (the first a sadistic near-mesmerist and the second a snivelling cockney), and a suffragette called Lady Vera Moyle who is about to indicate (just as she comes out of a swoon, and at the second time of asking) her willingness to marry our physician at the end of the final story. While the sadist is preparing to make his exit, the snivelling cockney is busy confessing his sins, ending with the words "Gawd, doctor, wot a fair swine I was!" – "But the crime doctor had even less time to listen to him now; for the eyes of eyes had opened, were gazing up into his; and not one of them had heard the window raised behind the curtains, or the clanging thud upon the iron steps just underneath."

And with this sentence E.W. Hornung's career as a writer of fiction came to an end. It was a dismal conclusion to the career which had begun so radiantly with *A Bride from the Bush*, almost twenty-five years earlier. Like Wilkie Collins before him, his talent for creating fresh and lifelike characters, for weaving ingenious plots, and for telling a compelling story had dwindled away to vanishing point. Whether his batteries would ever have been adequately re-charged must remain a matter for speculation. But he could console himself with the reflection that *Fathers of Men* ("the one thing of mine that might not only succeed but *live*") was continuing to win fresh readers. On 21 October 1913, fresh from a "jolly Sunday" he had spent at Uppingham, he reported to Chichester that he had taken a new boy, "son of the man who supplied me with

Jan's scholastic shortcomings and early battles with Haigh, out to lunch; he had just read the book for the second time. Everybody is still full of it there – they even say it has brought a boy or two to the School. *That* is better than all the shekels for the long effort." And perhaps, after all, *The Crime Doctor*, had its redeeming features? "If our best is never quite so good as we think it," he reflected at the time of its publication, "we may be just as sure that our worst is seldom quite so bad as it seems to the world and to ourselves."

There would be, in fact, one more book of short stories (*Old Offenders and a few old scores*), published by John Murray in 1923, but this was simply a collection of items written in the early 1900s – clever, snappy and enjoyable, each of them having the invariable twist at the end. It was, in any case, a posthumous production, bearing an Introduction by his brother-in-law, and it is improbable that Hornung himself was responsible for bringing this batch of tales together. On *this* occasion, however, Conan Doyle provided an assessment of his capabilities, and achievements, which was far more balanced, and fair – perhaps, indeed, even *too* kind (for Sir Arthur, apparently writing very soon after Hornung's death, would have been conscious of his sister's susceptibilities) – than anything that he would write in *Memories and Adventures*. He suggested, over-generously, that Hornung's literary powers had steadily expanded with every year of his life and had probably not yet reached their full maturity.

> But even as it was, his output was considerable, for from the day that his *Bride from the Bush* attracted attention in the early 'nineties down to the period of the war, he was always at work in his thorough conscientious way, and there was none of that work which could be called conventional, for he always brought to it a literary conscience, a fine artistic sense, and a remarkable power of vivid narrative. At his best there is no modern author who, by the sudden use of the right adjective and the right phrase, could make a scene spring more vividly to the eyes of the reader.
>
> The Raffles stories are, of course, conspicuous examples of this, and one could not find any better example of a clever

213

plot and terse admirable narrative. But in a way they harmed Hornung, for they got between his public and his better work. Some of that work is ambitious, and fell little short of achieving the high mark at which it was aimed. *Peccavi*, for example, is an outstanding novel, deep and serious, while *Fathers of Men* is one of the best school tales in the language, taking the masters in as well as the boys, and thereby perhaps marring the book for the latter. But it was a remarkable achievement, and might well be so, for on the one hand the whole subject of public-school education, and on the other the national game of cricket, were two of Hornung's chief hobbies.... His sympathies were intense, and his point of view clear, and when he focused his powers upon anything which really appealed to him the effect was remarkable.

Hornung had no idea, when he wrote it, that *The Crime Doctor* would be his last work of fiction. Nor did he have any idea that the First World War was close at hand and that he and his wife would be hit, within less than a year, by the most terrible blow imaginable. But, even so, his literary career was far from over.

22

LAST MAN IN

ONE SUSPECTS that Hornung and his wife, while reasonably close to each other, were nevertheless not so intimately entwined as the novelist might have wished. A possible hint of the rather unexciting nature of their married life appears in *The Thousandth Woman*. "There was not, and never had been, the slightest dearth [of conversation] between them," runs the passage in question; "but it was, perhaps, a sad case of quantity. These were two outdoor souls, and the one with the interesting life never spoke about it. Neither was a great reader, even of the papers, though Blanche liked poetry as she liked going to church; but each had the mind that could batten quite amiably on other people." Constance was, certainly, a deeply religious Roman Catholic, and would leave elaborate directions in her will about the saying of prolonged masses, for herself and her husband, at sundry locations for certain specified periods of time. In all probability Hornung was also a Catholic, but – if so – did not go out of his way to advertise the fact; his will is silent as regards masses.

They had, moreover, only the one child, which was rather unusual in that day and age, and it is probable that charting the progress of Oscar Hornung was their one great shared interest. That progress was, indeed, of a nature to make the heart of any parent swell with pride and delight, for he had grown up into a pleasant, frank, fresh-faced lad with an engaging sense of humour who had distinguished himself at Eton, both at work and play, and had a wide circle of friends. Hornung was proud of his son, and – while trying hard not to spoil him – had nevertheless an immense store of love and affection for the lad. One can picture him, without too much difficulty, sucking his pipe in quiet contentment as he read Oscar's latest school report or watched him displaying his prowess on the cricket field.

Arthur Oscar Hornung was enjoying the level of education which Ernest William Hornung had been unable to savour to anything like the full, and the proud father would obviously have experienced a vicarious delight in his achievements. But the father would also have been aware that one should take nothing for granted in this world. A nephew (one of Theodore's sons) had died in Nyasaland in December 1913, aged only thirty-two. The concept of a life cut tragically short was, therefore, one with which the author would have been familiar. In a sermon delivered at the chapel of Stone House, Broadstairs, on 5 July 1914 ('The Game of Life') he reflected on the death, in foreign parts, of another young man – John Keats, who had died in Rome in 1821 believing himself a failure. "Life", he declared, "is the most glorious game of all – right up to the end – if we are men enough to fight Life to a finish. But I do mean this – that in a game we know where we are, but in Life we never do.... God keeps our score, and He doesn't tell us what we have made until we are out. It is better not to think what we are making, better just to try to play the game.... [But] who wants an easy victory? Who wants a life of full-pitches to leg? Do you think the Great Scorer is going to give you four runs every time for these?"

In the same chapel, eight months later, he delivered a sermon ostensibly in the memory of Mary Constance Churchill, wife of the school's headmaster. "The Angel of Death", he observed, after quoting Bright's great metaphor,

has indeed not spared or passed this school. You would have thought he might have spared the house and home, even if the school had sent so many to the war that we could not but expect to lose great numbers there. You would have thought that was enough; but the Angel of Death is one of God's Generals, he has to obey orders like every other soldier; and we – we have to remember that those orders come not only from the God of Battles but from the God of Love. We must believe in that Love to the last, however had it may be. Christianity can never have found it harder than in the last few months. But Christianity as we know it is bearing its present almost unexampled sorrows, not only with resignation, but more cheerfully, more *joyously*, than sorrows were ever borne by multitudes of men upon this earth before. And we of this household and this school, we as a unit of Christ's army are going to bear our heavy sorrow as like that as we can. And the first way – and the first step – as it seems to me, is to *make friends* with the Angel of Death.

Yes; make friends with him! Do not fear him any more; we cannot afford to fear death in England now. There is hardly a little child in England tonight who has not been, or who is not being, educated out of the natural childlike dread of Death. That we owe to the war. It will mean a stupendous change – a change of soul – when the war is over. Some there may be who rebel against it, who will be rebels to the end. They are no use to England now. But you can be of use, every one of you, no matter by how many years you are too young to serve. The youngest boy and the weakest woman here tonight, they both can serve their country in its hour of need. All they have to do is to *be prepared* to submit bravely – proudly – even joyously – to the Will of God. Not to go out and fight and die yourselves, but to do what you may well find far harder; to stay at home and bear courageously your share of the heart-breaks that come your way; and so contribute your share to the common stock of courage by which alone we shall prevail. You have heard of co-operative societies, in which all contribute to the capital and the profits are shared by all: well, our Mother England and her children overseas are at this moment the greatest co-operative society the world has ever seen. Every single man, woman and child, must pay in his or her share of pluck and patience, and contempt of pain or death, and self-sacrifice, and self-control; and you who are young enough will live to share the profits in a simpler, braver, greater Britain than there ever would or could have been without this supreme trial.

He was speaking, of course, in March 1915, seven months after the commencement of the Great War. Four months later his own words may have come back to him – although, as an expression of honestly-held beliefs, and not simply as sentiments proclaimed on a particular occasion, they were already an essential part of the man. And he personally would now be called upon, to the utmost of his endeavours, to contribute a share (and rather more than that) to the common stock of courage to ensure that righteousness prevailed.

Oscar, as noted earlier, had left Eton at Easter 1914, at the age of nineteen. He was due to enter King's College, Cambridge in the autumn and but needed, first of all, to brush up on his History. To this end, he subjected himself to some private coaching at an establishment in Essex. When Britain finally took the plunge in August 1914, and proclaimed she was coming to the rescue of Belgium by declaring war with Germany and despatching her troops to France, Oscar was one of the first to enlist. He became a Second Lieutenant in the 2nd Essex Regiment – albeit attached to the 3rd. There now developed, between Hornung and his son, a wonderful exchange of letters – for Oscar was as fluent a writer as his father. In April 1915 the 3rd Essex Regiment was sent to France. Vicissitudes of war notwithstanding, the animated exchange of letters continued. One dated 5 July 1915 was particularly lively. "It was Oscar talking to us from the trenches," Hornung recalled afterwards,

> talking harder than ever while there was still time, telling us all manner of things in each eager breath! And I was to have talked back next night; there were one or two things I was looking forward to telling him. First, how his nine-and-a-half-months-old Commission had only just arrived in all its documentary glory; and how it began with the King's greeting, "To our Trusty and well beloved Arthur Oscar Hornung"!
>
> Then I had to tell him that I had just been to tea in the room where *Vanity Fair* was written, after pointing out the house to people for twenty years, as one that I never expected to have the joy of entering. It was a last joy. Within the hour came the telegram to say that Oscar had been killed in action on July 6.

"It's all over," Hornung wrote to Shane R. Chichester a few days later. "He was killed last Tuesday – probably on the taking of the Pilkem Trenches, but we have no details yet. He has had many gallant escapades – leading bombing parties, etc, etc – and one had got to think he bore a charmed life, so narrow were some of the shaves. And how he enjoyed them all! Well – you know what it means to us. But we will take it standing up, and saluting God Almighty, whose Will be done on earth." They learned, later, that the youth's last words had been "Is everyone all right?"

The Hornungs' only child was eight months' short of his twenty-first birthday when he died. One is tempted, for an instant, to apply that most heart-rending of all epitaphs to the situation: "They ventured their all in this one frail barque. And, when it foundered, the loss was total." But only for an instant. Hornung was determined to be resolute, to make the best of an appallingly bad job, and to show himself more than equal to the crisis. For, after all, Oscar was not the only young man to have been struck down in the flower of his youth – Cyril Holland, the elder of Wilde's two sons, had been killed two months' earlier – nor, alas, would he be the last. Hornung and his wife counted their blessings, having been privileged to have had a marvellous son for twenty years, and endeavoured to face the future in a positive, realistic fashion. But a life in London no longer held any great attraction for them, and (courtesy of Pitt) they would soon move into a vacant keeper's cottage in West Grinstead Park, where they would be close at hand to other members of the Hornung family. Willie now produced a slim volume, to be printed for private circulation, entitled *Trusty and Well Beloved, The Little Record of Arthur Oscar Hornung*.

The Hornungs were still at Hornton Street on 17 December, however, when Willie sent some glum seasonal greetings to his old friend Frederick Whyte. "I don't remember what I wrote you [last time]", he began,

> but suppose it was about our beloved boy. His little memoir lingers in the Press, and C[onnie] does not want it to synchronise with Christmas cards.

We shall have first to go back to the origin of Christmas, to the Man of Sorrows himself, to bear our own worthily this time.

Do you read Francis Thompson – his *Hound of Heaven*? Or rather, have you read it often enough to find meat and drink in it? I have – not often enough to get the full flavour of it all; or, here and there, the exact sense; but it is about the biggest thing done in our time, and *every* tortured soul finds it so.

And he would have turned, moreover, to his beloved Robert Browning – "There is no Comforter like him in our language," he told Chichester.

Hornung's *Trusty and Well Beloved* was circulated early in 1916. It contained a very brief account of his son's accomplishments but was composed, primarily, of long extracts from the letters which Oscar had written him since joining the army. "And not at Stone House only", it concluded,

is his dear name to endure, but also at Eton, for all the hundreds she has lost. Of their own generous accord, the boys of his Eton House are placing a tablet on the wall of his old room: and for the tablet his revered R[udyard] K[ipling] has written out one of his own stanzas, adding "I like them for Oscar because of the last line." –

"He scarce had need to doff his pride or slough the dross of Earth –
E'en as he trod that day to God so walked he from his birth,
In simpleness and gentleness and honour and clean mirth."

Kipling, too, was fated to lose his only son before 1915 came to an end – an event which plunged him into untold misery and the depths of despair. Hornung's response to his own parallel catastrophe was, however, markedly different: he emerged from the crisis in an almost ebullient frame of mind, determined to demonstrate, if demonstration were needed, that his son's sacrifice had, if anything, spurred him into positive action. His feelings were expressed in a poem entitled 'The Boys' War: Consecration' written at about this time:

Children we deemed you all the days
We vexed you with our care:

> *But in a Universe ablaze,*
> *What was your childish share?*
> *To rush upon the flames of Hell,*
> *To quench them with your blood!*
> *To be of England's flower that fell*
> *Ere yet it break the bud!*
>
> *And we who wither where we grew,*
> *And never shed but tears,*
> *As children now would follow you*
> *Through the remaining years;*
> *Tread in the steps we thought to guide,*
> *As firmly as you trod;*
> *And keep the name you glorified*
> *Clean before man and God.*

For Hornung, in such odd moments (precious few!) as could now be devoted to literary pursuits, had ceased to be a novelist and had become, at long last, a professional poet. As noted earlier, he had longed to be a poet at the very outset of his career, and snippets of rather amateurish verse had fleetingly appeared in several of his books, but the penning of rhymes had been a very subdued, secondary activity. When there was a real need for it, however, he had been fully capable of rising to the occasion, as in 'Forerunners', written in 1900, which had commemorated the deaths of three former schoolfellows in the South African War. In 1913 he had produced 'Uppingham Song', extracts from which have been quoted in the first chapter. Both these poems had been published in school magazines. In the wake of Oscar's departure, he now wrote a poem called 'Last Post', in which he recalled how, "centuries ago", he had waylaid the postman, "So welcome on his beaten track,/The bent man with the bulging sack!" in search of his son's latest letter. But he now waylaid the postman no longer, although "Doubtless upon his nightly beat/He still comes twinkling down our street." Another composed in 1915 was 'Lord's Leave' which began with the words "No Lord's this year: no silken lawn on which/A dignified and dainty throng meanders./The Schools take guard upon a fierier pitch/Somewhere in Flanders." Cricket, he declared, was as Sanscrit to the super-Hun – "Cheap cross between Caligula and Cassius,/To whom speech, prayer, and warfare are all one – /Equally gaseous!" Eighty years on, neither of these poems will stand too close an inspection unless massive allowance is made for the terrible circumstances in which they were written, but they obviously helped Hornung to work some bile and bitterness out of his system. Poetry, for neither the first nor the last time, was proving a useful safety-valve.

These effusions were, in any case, no more than savage diversions from the real job in hand, which was the task of helping to defeat the Germans.

At the very outbreak of the war, Hornung had handed over to the military authorities his latest car (probably a luxurious 15 horse-power Talboys, like the one driven by Dr John Dollar in *The Crime Doctor*). At some stage, he became a member of an anti-aircraft unit. But he wanted to play an even more active part in the proceedings. In 1916 or 1917 (the chronology is not clear) it appears that he started doing voluntary work for the YMCA (the Young Men's Christian Association) for troops home on leave. He cherished, all this while, a hope that he would somehow manage to get to France and visit his son's grave at Ypres so that he could report back to his wife on how it looked. But this would be easier said than done, since the tide of battle had surged back and forth across the zone in question. It might even be that the grave no longer existed.

Early in 1917, at any rate, the opportunity did at least arise to visit another part of the battle front, under the patronage of the War Office and in the company of fellow-writers, and he seized it with alacrity. A poem entitled 'Bond and Free' tells of a car-journey in March of that year along what he subsequently described as the "tight-rope road between Albert and Bapaume, [which] then stretched across a chasm of inconceivable devastation, and only three-parts in our hands; in fact we were industriously shelling Bapaume and its environs when a car from the Visitors' Château dumped two of us, accompanied by a red-tabbed chaperon, in the very middle of our guns". He and his colleague had appreciated that they were in a privileged position as their "car full of favoured mufti" sped past troops heading for the trenches, aware of "just the tail of a scornful eye". For "you gloat and take note in your motoring coat, and the sights come fast and thick". The route, so his poem made clear, was:

A road like a pier in a hurricane of mountainous seas of mud,
Where a few trees, whittled to walking-sticks, rose out of the frozen
flood
Like the masts of the sunken villages that might have been down
below –
Or blown off the face of an earth that God himself wouldn't know!

Not a yard but was part of a shell-hole – not an inch, to be more precise –
And most of the holes held water, and all the water was ice:
They stared at the bleak blue heavens like the glazed blue eyes of the slain,
Till the snow came, shutting them gently, and sheeting the
slaughtered plain.

The poet, according to his own deprecatory account, was much absorbed in framing vivid metaphors with which to depict the scene.

Then we overtook a Battalion ... and I'm hunting still for the word
For that gaunt, undaunted, haunted, whitening, frightening herd!

They had done their tour of the trenches, they were coated and caked
with mud.
And some of them wore a bandage, and some of them wore their blood!
The gaps in their ranks were many, and none of them looked at me...
And I thought of no more vain phrases for the thing I was there to see,
But I felt like a man in a prison van where the rest of the world goes Free.

Three months later he visited a military cemetery, and his moving account of the scene, 'Wooden Crosses', was published in *The Times* on 20 July 1917:

"Go live the wide world over – but when you come to die
A quiet English churchyard is the only place to lie!"
I held it half a lifetime, until through war's mischance
I saw the wooden crosses that fret the fields of France.

A thrush sings in an oak-tree, and from the old square tower
A chime as sweet and mellow salutes the idle hour:
Stone crosses take no notice – but the little wooden ones
Are thrilling every moment to the music of the guns!

Upstanding at attention they face the cannonade,
In apple-pie alinement like Guardsmen on parade:
But Tombstones are Civilians who loll or sprawl or sway
At every crazy angle and stage of slow decay.

For them the Broken Column – in its plot of unkempt grass;
The tawdry tinsel garland safeguarded under glass;
And the Squire's emblazoned virtues, that would overweight a
Saint
On the vault empaled in iron – scaling red for want of paint!

The men who die for England don't need it rubbing in;
An automatic stamper and a narrow strip of tin
Record their date and regiment, their number and their name –
And the Squire who dies for England is treated just the same.

So stand the still battalions: alert, austere, serene;
Each with his just allowance of brown earth shot with green;
None better than his neighbour in pomp or circumstance –
All beads upon the rosary that turned the fate of France!

Who says their war is over? While others carry on,
The little wooden crosses spell but the dead and gone?
Not while they deck a sky-line, not while they crown a view,
Or a living soldier sees them and sets his teeth anew!

The tenants of the churchyard where the singing thrushes build
Were not, perhaps, all paragons of promise well fulfilled:
Some failed – through Love, or Liquor – while the parish looked
askance.
But – you cannot die a failure if you win a Cross in France!

The brightest gems of Valour in the Army's diadem
Are the V.C. and the D.S.O., MC and D.C.M.
But those who live to wear them will tell you they are dross
Beside the Final Honour of a simple Wooden Cross.

'Wooden Crosses' was subsequently published as a tiny booklet in its own right by Nisbet & Co. in April 1918 and sold for the princely sum of sixpence (2.5p); the proceeds, one assumes, went to a serviceman's charity. Also sold as an individual publication, but in America only, was 'The Ballad of Ensign Joy', a narrative poem which falls (let us say kindly) somewhere between the standards of Kipling and Robert Service.

Being able to make these trips, and having the facility to describe them in graphic tones to receptive audiences in England, was something in itself. But Hornung could not rid himself of the notion, while engaged in such forays, that he was doing so in the capacity of a pampered visitor. What he really wanted to do was to play a role, however humble, in the vicinity of the actual combat, and to feel that he was making a genuine contribution to the welfare of the British forces. The ideal opportunity finally presented itself towards the end of 1917. He volunteered to be sent out to France to help man a YMCA canteen a short distance behind the Front Line and, much to his delight, his offer was accepted.

So, at the age of fifty-one, short-sighted, asthmatic and slightly corpulent, but buoyant and determined, Willie Hornung set off for active service on the Western Front.

23

A CAMP-FOLLOWER

WRITING AN ACCOUNT of his experiences in the summer
and early autumn of 1918, at a time when the end of the war
still appeared to be some way off, Hornung was studiously
vague about his movements. The places that he went to, and
the precise identities of the people he met, were shrouded in
secrecy lest the enemy in some way benefit from such
information. His account of his overseas duties with the
YMCA, bearing the title *Notes of a Camp-Follower on the Western
Front*, begins in the dusk of a December afternoon with his
arrival in what was, although he never named it, the battered
remnants of the town of Arras.

With a younger colleague to instruct him, he moved
into the YMCA hut ("the Ark") that was to be his home for the
next three months. Located on what had been a parade
ground, with another hut alongside serving as divisional
cinema, it consisted, in the main, of one large room with a
stove in the middle and trestle tables "with nothing on them
but a dusky polish ... each with a pair of forms in perfect
parallels, and nothing else but a piano and an under-sized
billiard table". The crucial operational area was a counter,
equipped with curtains, behind which were "shelves of
shimmering goods, biscuits and candles in open cases on the
floor, and as many exits as a scene in a farce". One of the
doors opened into a bedroom with two sheetless bunks for
himself and his colleague, reminding him of the bush huts
which he had adored for their discomfort in his teens, and
there was a tiny passage leading to the kitchen. This was
where two scruffy orderlies, both aged about forty (one a

huge giant of a man, a very slow-thinking yokel from Oxfordshire, and the other "a fiery little Londoner with a hacking cough and a husky voice") worked and slept and where all four of them would wash.

At 4.30 the orderlies staggered in with the first urn and the hut then opened up for business, with a stream of soldiers demanding tea in accents from every district and from every class that Hornung had ever known. "They warmed the blood like a medley of patriotic airs, and I commenced potman as it were to martial music. It was, perhaps, the least skilled labour in France, but that evening it was none too light. Every single customer began with tea: the mugs flew through my hands as fast as I could fill them, until my end of the counter swam in livid pools, and the tilted urn was down to a gentle dribble." Initially he simply poured out the tea while his colleague, a "seasoned neighbour", dispensed other goods and managed the till. Each of them took brief breaks and he sat in his bedroom, sipping his own tea and listening with delight to the strange sounds – "the continual chink of money in the till outside; the movement of many feet, trained not to shuffle; the constant coughing of men otherwise in superhuman health; the crude tinkle of the piano at the far end of the hut – the efficient pounding of the cinema piano – the screw-like throb of their petrol engine – the periodical bringing-down of their packed house", presumably by Charlie Chaplin. Then he went back and found himself

> diving into open cases of candles, and counting out packets of cigarettes and biscuits, sticks of chocolate, boxes of matches, and reaching down tinned salmon, sardines, boot-laces, shaving-soap and tooth-paste, button-sticks, 'sticks of lead' (otherwise pencils), writing-pads, Nosegay Shag, Royal Seal, or twist if we had it, and shouting for the prices as I went, coping with the change by light of luck and nature, but doling out the free stationery with a base lingering relief, until my back was a hundred and all the silver of the allied realms one composite coin that danced without jingling in the till. Gold stripes meant nothing to me now; shrapnel helmets were as high above me as the stars; the only hero was the man who didn't want change. Often in the early part I

thought the queue was coming to an end; it was always the sign for a fresh influx; and when the National Anthem came thumping from the cinema, the original Ark might have sunk under such a boarding-party of thirsty tea-drinkers as we had still to receive. I noted that they called it tea regardless of the contents of the urn, which changed first to coffee and then to cocoa as the night wore on: tea was the generic term.

In due course, however, closing time arrived, and green curtains closed the counter despite the wistful faces of those still seeking sustenance: "if I can see them still, it is the heavenly music of those curtain rings that I hear! The mind's eye peeps through once more, and spies the last gobblers at the splashed tables littered with mugs and empty tins; the last dawdlers on a floor ankle-deep in the envelopes of two penny and half-franc packets of biscuits; and a little man broom-in-hand at the open door, spoiling to sweep all the lot into outer darkness!"

So ended Hornung's first day as a canteen assistant.

It was exhausting work but he loved it, and he made a host of new friends in the process – some of them, moving up the line, being close acquaintances for no more than a few hours. Three riflemen, whom he entertained at the counter with cocoa and biscuits one evening, turned out to have been a house-painter from Crewe, a bus-conductor from London, and a builder who operated a bioscope in the evenings. He never saw any of them again. The soldiers from the Highland Regiments (known generically as 'the Jocks') greatly impressed him, and next to them he found the riflemen ('the Gunners') a band of cheery souls. He and his companion were often assisted at the counter by an eighteen-year-old lad from Hull, a private in a Labour Battalion, whose name they never learnt but who slaved away on his free evenings with as great an enthusiasm as themselves.

On Sunday afternoons the hut opened at 4.00 pm instead of 4.30 but there would be a service at 6.30, with the curtains being pulled across the counter for the duration, and thereafter the trade would be confined to tea and biscuits.

Soon [writes Hornung] the shy wintry sun was wearing a veil of frosted silver. The eye of the moon was on us early in the afternoon, ever a little wider open and a degree colder in its stare. All one day our mud rang like an anvil to the tramp of rubicund customers in greatcoats and gloves; and the next day they came and went like figures on the film next-door, silent and outstanding upon a field of dazzling snow.

But behind the counter we had no such seasonable sights to cheer us; behind the counter, mugs washed overnight needed wrenching off their shelf, and three waistcoats were none too many. In our room, for all the stove that reddened like a schoolgirl, and all the stoking that we did last thing at night, no amount of sweaters, blankets, and miscellaneous wraps was excessive provision against the early morning. By dawn, which leant like lead against our canvas windows, and poked sticks of icy light through a dozen holes and crannies, the only unfrozen water in the hut was in the kitchen boiler and in my own hot-water bottle. I made no bones about this trusty friend; it hung all day on a conspicuous nail; and it did not prevent me from being the first up in the morning, any more than modesty shall deter me from trumpeting the fact. One of us had to get up to lay the stove and light the fire, and it was my chance of drawing approximately even with my brisk commander. No competing with his invidious energy once he had taken the deck; but here was a march I could count on stealing while he slept the sleep of the young. Often I was about before the orderlies, and have seen the two rogues lying on their backs in the dim light of their kitchen, side by side like huge dirty children. As for me, blackened and bent double by my exertions, swaddled in fleece lining and other scratch accoutrements, no doubt I looked the lion grotesque of the party; but, by the time the wood crackled and the chimney drew, I too had my inner glow.

So we reached the shortest day; then came a break, and for me the Christmas outing of a lifetime.

For the YMCA had just started what might almost be described as a 'meals on wheels' service to troops in the front line, three miles away from their hut, which consisted primarily of cocoa but which, during the Christmas period, was being reinforced by more substantial offerings. YMCA workers took it in turns to supply this service and on 21 December it was Hornung's turn to go into action for a four-day stint. So, greatly thrilled and equipped with gas-mask, he at last found himself in the trenches – much narrower than expected, with the unbroken chain of duck-boards an unexpected feature, and printed sign-boards so routinely erected that they might have been put up by the London County Council. Progress was slow, if you encountered somebody coming in the opposite direction, and at times he was almost tempted to take a short cut over the top.

> The whole thing put me more in mind of primitive ship-building – the great ribs leaning outwards – flat timbers in between – and over all sand-bags and sometimes wire-work with the precise effect of bulwarks and hammock-netting. Even the mouths of dug-outs were not unlike port-holes flush with the deck; and many a piquant glimpse we caught in passing, bits of faces lit by cigarette-ends, and half-sentences or snatches of sardonic song; then the trench would twist round a corner into solitude, as a country road shakes off a hamlet, and on we trudged through the thickening dusk. Once, where the sand-bags were lower than I had noticed, I thought some very small bird had chirped behind my head, until the other man turned his head and smiled. "Hear that?" he said. "That was a bullet! It's just where they sniped at *me* this morning." I shortened my stick, and crept the rest of the way like the oldest inhabitant of those trenches, as perhaps I was.

Day turned to night and they took refuge in a small hut, sunk well below the level of an adjoining road: a boiler was lit, but it smoked so badly that Hornung and two companions were forced out of it. "The frosty moon was now nearly full, and a grey-mauve sky, wearing just the one transcendent jewel of light, as brilliant in its way as the dense blue of equatorial noon. Upon this noble slate the group of armed men, waiting about in the road above the duck-boards, was drawn in shining outline; silvered rifles slung across coppery leathern shoulders; earthenware mugs turned to silver goblets in their hands, and each tilted helmet itself a little fallen moon. A burst of gun-fire, and not a helmet turned; the rat-tat-tat of a machine gun, but no shining shoulder twinkled with the tiniest shrug."

At midnight their day's supply of water (supplied each morning by a working-party) ran out, and they bedded down in what was, in effect, a tiny dug-out cave, heavily sand-bagged. Not far from Hornung's side a shell had burst a few days' earlier; a few inches away lay the buried body of an unknown British flyer, and Hornung "did not sleep the worse for his honoured company, or for our common lullaby the guns". After a few days, however, the sand-bagged lair, which was none too dry now that a thaw had started, did not seem quite the place for crabbed age. "Youth is welcome to the two beds with the water standing on their india-rubber sheets, and youth seems quite honestly to prefer them; so I make mine on the biscuit-boxes in the shed, turn my toes to the still glowing coke in the boiler fire, press my soles to the hot-water bottle which has distinguished itself by freezing during the day, and huddle down as usual in all the indoor and outdoor garments I have with me, under my share of the blankets, which I have been drying assiduously every evening." At bedtime reading he dipped into *The Romance of War*, by James Grant, which invariably proved an effective means of sending himself to sleep.

But all meals, at least three times a day, were taken at Battalion HQ, which seemed "like the deck-house of a well-appointed yacht after a tramp's forecastle" with "art-green walls and fixed settees, a narrow table, all spotless napery and sparkling glass, forks and spoons as brilliant as a wedding-present" and with the heat coming up an open chimney from the bowels of the earth. The Colonel, at the end of his first visit, took him up to an O.P. (Observation Post) from which he was able to survey the whole of the battlefield: silent on that particular occasion, but bursting into terrible life the following day.

Christmas morning was spent in a hut in the support line, one of the merriest that Hornung ever remembered – the soldiers, being loaded up with their supplies, marvelling at the fact that they should have a Y.M. in their midst, helping to dispense cocoa, cakes and cigarettes. (A sequel to this, three months later, would be a joyful and slightly embarrassing reunion with two inebriated Scots, who hailed him, with much emotion, as their old friend "the Cocoa Man".) At that moment, for the first time, he felt that he had the Front Line like a ball at his feet. The Colonel took him on a tour of inspection, with No Man's Land being viewed through a looking-glass instead of periscope on this occasion: when the going became too dangerous, the Colonel entrusted him to other hands – and the spot where Hornung had been standing was shelled a moment later. His Christmas dinner, that evening, was consumed in an ex-German dug-out with another Colonel and his support staff, enjoying a spell of rest; a curious contrast, he reflected, to the meal which he had eaten at the Carlton Club the previous year.

On Boxing Day a YMCA companion led him through the still-falling snow covering the trenches, so that they "seemed like Gullivers striding between two chains of Lilliputian Alps". Their intended destination was a river where they were due to catch a boat. Hornung's gas-mask was like a real mill-stone round his neck and his colleague insisted on carrying some of his pack, which made him feel his age the more acutely. They walked for a couple of miles without encountering a soul, Hornung uneasily enquiring from time to time whether his friend really did know the way. His guide was confident to begin with but finally came to a halt and confessed – by means of two questions – that he must have taken a wrong turning. The questions were "What would you do if we met a Hun? Put your hands up?" Hornung was stunned by the effrontery of these remarks. His companion retraced their footsteps to find the right route, leaving Hornung for the best part of an hour a short distance from what was (he later realised) the Front Line. "I remember cooling off against the side of the trench, and hearing absolutely nothing all the time. That I still think remarkable. It was not snowing; the sun shone; visibility must have been better than for two whole days; and yet nothing was happening. I might have been waiting in some Highland glen, or in a quarry in the wilds of Dartmoor. I think that particular silence was as impressive, as intimidating, as the very heaviest firing that I heard in all my four months at the front."

But his colleague eventually returned and in due course they reached the river, only to find that they had just missed the boat. "A homeward-bound lorry picked us up at last. And we were in plenty of time for the plain mid-day meal at our humble headquarters in the town. But by then I was done to the world and dead to shame. I suppose I have led too soft a life, taking very little exercise for its own sake, though occasionally going to the other extreme from an ulterior motive. So I have been deservedly tired once or twice in my time; but I didn't know what it was to be done up before last Boxing Day." Back, at long last, in the YMCA hut that was now home, he lay on his bed and listened to the sound of a Christmas concert coming through the walls. "Somebody came in and made tea. It was better than being ill. I lay there till nine the next morning; then went down to the Officers' Baths, and came out feeling younger than at any period of actual but insensate youth."

Incredibly, when taking his turn at the counter for the very first time, a few weeks' earlier, he had encountered some soldiers from his son's own Division. It soon transpired, alas, that there were few survivors from the band of men who had accompanied Oscar during the first ten months of the war, but word gradually got around that Hornung was anxious to visit, if he could, his son's grave at Ypres, sixty miles away, even though there was some doubt as to whether it still existed. The *location*, a shell-blasted farmyard, was known and the body had been buried as deep as possible, but battles had raged in the area since then and the grave could quite possibly have been destroyed. Early in February 1918 an officer in the high command (an old friend) told Hornung that he was free to borrow his car, a powerful limousine, ten days' hence if he wanted to go to Ypres. This gave him time to notify his wife of the intended quest and for Constance, in turn, to send out a package of bulbs and plants.

The Senior Chaplain of Oscar's Division suddenly appeared in Hornung's own Rest Hut (a new building, which we will return to in a moment) the day before he was due to leave. Learning with considerable interest of his host's mission, he told him that he knew the whereabouts of one of the three surviving men, now a bandsman, who had assisted at the burial: he was currently in a nearby rest-billet, and the Chaplain would try to contact him. The following morning the car collected Hornung and made a hopeful detour to the rest-billet where, much to his delight, the bandsman, a young Corporal in a field coat, was indeed waiting. Hornung told him, as they journeyed northwards, that a very distant family friend (whom he had never met) claimed to have discovered the remains of Oscar's grave and had sent him, as relics, a cheap French watch and a boot-strap. The young Corporal instantly dismissed these pieces of evidence: there had been no watch and Oscar had worn ordinary laced boots and puttees, not boots with straps. So it was *not* Oscar's grave that had been disturbed! And, as the car drove on, Hornung marvelled at the fact that he should be accompanied by the one man who could enlighten him on these matters. Yet who had brought him there?

> To be sure, the Senior Chaplain of their Division; but why should the Senior Chaplain, a man I never saw before, have come to my hut in the nick of time to do me this service, so definitely desired? Why should I myself have come to the very place in France where the Division was waiting for me – the one place where I had also an old friend with a car to lend me when the time came? Why had I not gone to Belgium (to be near the boy) as I at first intended? And why, at that very time, should a complete stranger have been making entirely independent efforts to find the grave in Belgium that I yearned to see?
>
> 'Chance' is no answer, unless the word be held to cover an organic tissue of chances, each in turn closely related to some other chance, all component parts of a chance whole! And what sensation novelist would build a plot on such foundations and hope to make his tale convincing? Not I, at

my worst; and there were more of these chances still to come, albeit none that mattered as did those already recounted.

They reached Ypres that evening. The distant family friend had been called away, but his sergeant – a keen amateur gardener, and custodian of the plants which Constance had sent – was there to make them welcome. Next morning, under a leaden sky, the car set out for the farmhouse, with Hornung, the Corporal and the Sergeant being accompanied by a second Sergeant and by a young Catholic Padre from Ypres. They walked on duckboards, through a scene of utter desolation, for two hundred yards. The grave, marked by a new cross, was identified by the Corporal and the last offices read and Holy Water sprinkled. Then narcissus bulbs, primroses, pinks, phlox and saxifrage and a baby rose-tree were planted. The service had been punctuated by explosions from enemy shrapnel, but a British band was playing a long way off and their visit ended to the distant strains of *Auld Lang Syne*. Oscar would have been delighted, Hornung reflected, for the whole difficult thing had been so beautifully arranged. "Chances or accidents, by the chapter, if you will! No man on earth can prove the contrary; and yet there are few, perhaps, who have lost their all in this war, and who would not thank God for such a string of happenings. But one does not thank God for a chain of chances. And if any link was of His forging, why not the whole chain, as two thankful people dare to think?"

Then back he went to Arras, his brief holiday (in the most literal sense) at an end, for there was still abundance of work to be done – and, indeed, a project very dear to Hornung's own heart currently in hand. There had come, from Britain, not only a vast amount of provisions for the troops in the way of food and warm clothing but also hundreds of books. They were heaped up at the YMCA headquarters and gathering dust, for nobody had had time to sort them out. At the beginning of the year someone had suggested that a proper library should be established, and Hornung was the man chosen to organise it. He was given a hut of his own, situated in the grounds of what had once been the imposing town hall. A squad of carpenters erected shelves around the room in double quick time and an inspired artist and decorator got to work with his paint pots (reproducing the flags of the Allies and, as his *tour de force*, "a complete allegorical cartoon of Literature, including many life-size figures in flowing robes busy with the primitive tools of one's trade").

Although sometimes distracted by the need to do battle with passing rats, who "would lope across the floor under one's nose, or dangle their tails from the beams overhead", Hornung and a keen assistant ("an Australian Jock, and of the first water on both sides") set about the task of drawing up a rudimentary catalogue and pasting labels in the first thousand books. (Not *all* from Arras, for he had gone further afield, to Amiens and other localities, on book-raid expeditions.)

> They were a motley herd: the sweepings of unknown benefactors' libraries, the leavings of officers and men, cunning shafts from the devout of all denominations, and the first draft of cheap masterpieces from the base. Classification was beyond me, even if time had been no object.... All authors in alphabetical order seemed the simplest principle; and in practice even that arrangement ran away with days.... The merit of the plan, if any, was that the catalogue order eventually coincided with that of the actual books on the shelves. The drawback was that books kept dropping in or turning up too late for insertion in their proper places. I could think of no better way out of this difficulty than by resorting to a large Z class, or dump, for late-comers.

Opening day had been scheduled for the beginning of February, but it eventually took place on the 20th of that month. With pride, the creator of Robert Carlton surveyed his achievement. Outside the hut was a scraper, possibly the worst in Europe ("I ached for a week from sinking its two uprights into harder chalk with a heavier pick-axe than I thought existed"), so that the mud of war could be firmly dislodged. One then entered the hut, to be confronted initially by pinned-together sketch maps from successive issues of the *Daily Mail* giving a complete picture of the Western Front, the

Line being indicated by the best available red tape. Inside, there were two skylights and side windows shimmering with white material, like permanent snow, to give as much light as possible, and beneath them four trestle tables bearing papers and magazines. There were writing tables under the side windows, two stoves (a luxury, when a hut's normal allowance was one) and around each of them a ring of wicker and canvas arm-chairs, in which soldiers could sink for a doze. Light refreshments and cigarettes would be available and there were ash-trays on the tables. Around the walls, of course, were the newly-erected shelves, there was a platform at the end of the hut from which talks could be given and there was the inevitable piano. A huge motto (from Thomas á Kempis) ran right across the hut: "Without Labour there is no Rest; nor without Fighting can the Victory be Won". (In Hornung's hearing nobody ever commented on it, except for one soldier who dryly remarked "Well, that's logic anyhow!") The atmosphere that Hornung had been striving to attain was that of a club smoking-room, and waking up in bed that morning he had decided to call it the Rest Hut.

The date and time of its grand opening (2.00 pm on 20 February) had been well advertised. Initially, therefore, Hornung was disconcerted when he unlocked the door at the appointed hour and found not a soul in sight. But, after fifteen minutes, the first customers started to trickle in, and after a *further* fifteen minutes the place was packed out. The Rest Hut was a decided success. Hornung and his second-in-command, plus an elderly Frenchwoman who made the tea ("worth all the YMCA orderlies I ever saw") and a hard-working but rather mysterious orderly, had their work cut out to cope with the demands.

The rules of the lending library were simple. A reader could take out one book, but no more, in exchange for a deposit of one franc: he could keep it as long as he liked, and have his franc returned to him when he brought it back. But books would not be exchanged more than once in a day and borrowers were exhorted to bring them back in a reasonable space of time and in a reasonable condition. In addition to this, there was a tiny Reference and Poetry section, at the end of the counter, from which books could *not* be borrowed and a New Book Table ("the apple of the librarian's glasses") on which were displayed, strictly for perusal, copies of the very latest books from fifteen different publishers, which Hornung had obtained as the result of writing fifteen begging letters. This proved immensely popular. The intention was that these books would be absorbed into the lending library after being on display for a fortnight, but it transpired, alas, that most of them disappeared from the New Book Table in far less time than this. When delivering a Sunday sermon a couple of weeks later, therefore, Hornung was obliged to sorrowfully announce "that there had been so many desertions from my crack corps that we were obliged to disband it". Making his way back to the counter, however, he was accosted by one humorist with the words "Beg yer pardon, Mr 'Ornung, but that pinchin' them new books – wasn't a Raffles trick, was it?"

Most of the books lent out were novels (Meredith's *The Ordeal of Richard Feverel* being the very first), and Hornung took a keen interest in assessing the popularity of various authors. Dickens, Stevenson, Kipling and Rider Haggard were in great demand, while "Messrs. Holmes and Watson were the most flourishing of old firms, and Gerard the only Brigadier taken seriously at my counter". Wells, on the other hand, was less popular than might have been expected, while there were insufficient stocks of other authors – Hardy, Meredith, Bennett, Weyman and Galsworthy, for example – for fair comparisons to be made. They had nothing at all by Walter de la Mare, which distressed at least one of their customers. "Thackeray was not fully represented, but we had all his best and they were always out. Of the Brontës we had next to nothing, of Reade and Trollope far too little; but *It is Never Too Late to Mend* enchanted a Sapper, a Machine Gunner, and a Red Cross man in turn, while *Orley Farm* would have headed our first day's list had it been there in time. George Eliot was never without readers, but Miss Braddon had more, and *The Woman in White* only one! After Dickens, however, the most popular Victorian was the first Lord Lytton."

A few of Hornung's own books were among those requested, and while gratified by this fact he suspected that they were borrowed more from curiosity than anything else. Certainly, there was an element of surprise about his identity. "You know that old – that – that elderly man who runs the Rest Hut?" he was told (in the cleaned-up version) one soldier had exclaimed. "He's the author of *Raffles!*" The teller of the tale had intended to amuse Hornung, but the adjective judiciously employed had precisely the opposite effect – "Elderly! One would as lief be labelled Virtuous or Discreet."

A "certain stretcher-bearer, a homely old fellow with a horse-shoe moustache and mild brown eyes" borrowed a copy of *Raffles*, although Hornung expressed grave doubts as to whether he would enjoy it. "He returned it without a word to temper his forgiving smile, and took out *The Golden Treasury* as a restorative. Poetry he loved with all his gentle soul; but when, at a later stage, he asked if I thought he could 'learn to write poetry', the wounds of vanity were at least anointed."

Poetry, in fact, was in considerable demand, as were religious books and works on philosophy. Many of the readers were determined students. A serious young Coldstream Guard, asking in vain for certain items, was obliged "to put up with Anatole France and oddments of Swift and Wilde" – the first and last time that Hornung ever openly mentions *that* particular name in one of his books – "nor do I forget his justifiable disgust on discovering, too late, that our *Gulliver* was a nursery version." With a young man "full of brains and sensibility", a member of the Field Ambulance Corps, he discussed at length Gissing's *The Private Papers of Henry Ryecroft* and took issue with some of the views that Gissing had expressed about the deadening effect of schools. Exchanging thoughts, in this manner and in this place, with a host of readers of every description, was a humbling but uplifting experience for Hornung (who might

well have participated, in a slightly later age, in the Workers'
Educational Association).

> Often and often [he writes] have I looked down the hut and
> compared the splendid fellows I saw before me with the
> peace-time types perceptibly represented by so many. Small
> tradesmen, clerks, shop assistants, grooms and gardeners,
> labourers in every overcrowded field, what they were losing
> in the softer influences of life, that one might guess, but what
> they were gaining all the time, in mind, body, and character,
> that one could see. It did not lessen the heartbreak of the
> thought that perhaps half would never see their homes again;
> but it did console with the conviction that the half who
> survived would be twice the men they would or could have
> been without the war. Nay, they were twice their old selves
> already, if I am any judge of a man who talks to me....

> [The wonderful quality of my fellow-countrymen, as
> revealed in these tremendous years], was there all the time,
> but it took the war ... to make us see it. I might have known
> that rough poor lads were reading Ruskin and Carlyle, that a
> Northamptonshire shoemaker was as likely as anybody else
> to be steeped in Charles Lamb, or a telegraph-clerk and his
> wife to tramp the Yorkshire dales with Wordsworth and
> Keats about their persons. Yet I, for one, more shame for me!
> would never have imagined such men if the God of battles
> had not put me to school in my Rest Hut for one short half-
> term.

For the education had not been a one-way affair. And the
pity of it was, for Hornung and the men whom he served, that
the Rest Hut would last for no more than one month.

24

CLOSE OF PLAY

THE END, when it came, was sudden.

There had been deadlock on the Western Front for more than three years. The Allied Powers and the Central Powers, established in their respective trenches running through France and Belgium, from Switzerland to the sea, had glowered at and bombarded each other. Terrible attempts had been made to break the stalemate: the casualties on both sides had been horrendous, but the aggressor invariably came off worst. The appalling battle of the Somme, in 1916, had been succeeded the following year by the Nivelle offensive and the Passchendaele slaughter. By 1918 the French and British alike were unwilling to take any fresh initiatives. They were content to sit tight in their dug-outs, engaged in a war of attrition, and to wait for the Americans – formal participants in the war since April 1917 but represented, as yet, only by Pershing's advance guard – to send troops to their rescue. By the same token, however, General Ludendorff, in command of the German troops, could not afford to wait. He resolved to make his 'big push' against the Allies and to hurl into the attack all the resources at his disposal – in an effort to win the war before the Americans arrived. His objective was to drive a wedge between the British and the French armies, to decimate the British and to conclude an armistice with the French.

That a major onslaught was being planned had long been suspected by the Allied commanders, but they thought it would be in Flanders rather than the Somme. Haig, in control of the British troops, had therefore kept his reserves concentrated in the north while moving his battle-weary Fifth Army into what was supposedly a fairly quiet sector – the sector which embraced Arras. This, unfortunately, was the pre-destined target of Ludendorff's attack.

In the YMCA Rest Hut, under Hornung's benign control, it had been business as usual. Most of the customers were cheerful, serious men, genuinely concerned with relaxation and study, and their talk was of a reasonable nature, but a Canadian from Vimy Ridge, slightly the worse for drink, was holding forth to his friends one day in an unrestrained manner. "I say, I say!" Hornung called out reproachfully from his counter. "The language is getting pretty thick down there." "Beg pardon, sir. Very sorry," came the contrite response, followed, after a moment's thought, by the remark – "But the shells is pretty thick where we come from!"

"It was", Hornung reflected afterwards, "a better answer than he knew." For the shells, which had spared the town since November, suddenly became very thick indeed. A harbinger had been one which actually bounced off the roof of the Rest Hut, with the sound of a large smack, without leaving a single mark. A prolonged silence followed. "Fritz – range-finding!" said the laconic orderly. A couple of days later, early on the morning of 21 March, the bombardment began in earnest. "It was biggish stuff that was coming in", writes Hornung, "at a longish range; and it was coming in on business, not on pleasure. Its business was to feel for barracks, batteries, and other sound investments for valuable munitions; not to have a sporting flutter here, there and everywhere; much less to indulge in the sheer luxury of pestling a ruined area to powder." Shells, or whizz-bangs, whistled continuously over their heads; four officers were killed in the street. They all donned shrapnel helmets, when venturing out in the sunshine (for the month was more like May than March) and there was much speculation as to whether this really was Jerry's big push. On that one day, apparently, 800 large shells landed on the little town and the bombardment continued during the two days that followed. Hornung commemorated the event in 'Shell-Shock in Arras':

All night they crooned high overhead
As the skies are over men:
I lay and smiled in my cellar bed,
And went to sleep again.

All day they whistled like a lash
That cracked in the trembling town:
I stood and listened for the crash
Of houses thundering down.

In, in they came, three nights and days,
All night and all day long;
It made us learned in their ways
And experts on their song.

Like a noisy clock, or a steamer's screw,
Their beat debauched the ear,
And left it dead to a deafening few
That burst who cared how near?

We only laughed when the flimsy floor
Heaved on the shuddering sod:
But when some idiot slammed a door –
My God!

Incredibly, the Rest Hut continued to function as normal while all this was going on. Hornung was dumbfounded when on the morning of the third day the Padre of the Scots Guards scrambled across the rubble to ask him what he was going to do. Hornung gazed back at him uncomprehendingly, and the Padre explained that many of the troops (including the Jocks) were pulling out and it was likely that all non-combatants would be ordered to evacuate the town before much longer. Hornung was horrified, but the news was soon confirmed from other sources and, like a man in a dream, he started packing his kit-bag in readiness. At lunchtime some senior officers put the same question to him and advised him not to delay too long. But he opened up the Rest Hut for one more day, although the other huts had already closed down. After a while some soldiers drifted in – far fewer than usual, and some of them simply to bring back their books on their way to the battle-front. Behind the scenes, Hornung and his companion parted company with the old lady who made the tea – who had herself been instructed, by the town-crier, to leave her home by 3.30 – and with their taciturn orderly. The Hut remained open until 6.30, by which time most other YMCA personnel had already left the town, and they were reluctantly obliged to shut up shop and evict their few remaining patrons. Hands were shaken as the latter dutifully filed out. "They were pleased with us for having kept open a day longer than any of the other huts. I hope I said the other huts had been closed by order; but I only remember wanting to say a great deal more, and thinking better of it. After all, we had understood each other in that hut to a degree beyond the need of heavy speeches."

The mass-evacuation of Arras was now well advanced. Travelling as lightly as they could, Hornung and his friend boarded the YMCA's little Ford bus and set off for Amiens – once again, feeling guilty as they passed the stream of refugees plodding away on foot. They also passed thousands of soldiers going in the opposite direction, for the straight French road "was choked with strings of lorries and motor-'buses full of reinforcements for the battle-line; silent men, miles and miles of them, mostly invisible, load after load; all embussed, not a single company to be seen upon the march. It was weird, but it was gorgeous: the tranquil moon above, the tossing dust below, and these tall land-ships, packed with fighting-men, looming through by the hundred.... Thousands and thousands of gallant hearts!"

Three or four hours later they reached Amiens, on which were converging from all the surrounding regions vast streams of refugees, including a host of fellow-YMCA workers who had been displaced from their own locations at the Front. Not surprisingly, they were told there were no beds to spare in the town, but somebody recognised Hornung and (piling yet more guilt on his head) smuggled him and his colleague off to the very best hotel – where, indeed, he slept in a bedroom positively palatial. The unaccustomed silence, as he fell asleep, was another luxury, but he awoke to the familiar sound of shells and enemy aircraft – for Amiens too was in danger. After breakfast they sallied forth into the town, to meet the remnants of shattered British divisions – for the Germans were on the march, pushing relentlessly forward, and the Fifth Army had lost 150,000 men. It was the morrow of a great catastrophe and the scene was one of chaos, yet there was also a strange air of exultancy among the survivors. For it was widely recognised that Ludendorff, in winning the battle, had lost the war: the German losses had been almost as heavy as those of the British, and it would be impossible for him to keep up the momentum. To gladden Hornung's heart in particular, a company of Australians suddenly appeared on the scene, heading for the Front:

> They were marching in their own way; no stride or swing about it; but a more subtle jauntiness, a kind of mincing strut, perhaps not unconsciously sinister and unconventional, an aggressive part of themselves. But what men! What beetling chests, what muscle-swollen sleeves, what dark, pugnacious, shaven faces! Here and there a pendulous moustache mourned the beard of some bushman of the old school; but no such adventitious aids could have improved upon the naked truculence of most of those mouths and chins…. In the day of battle, could there have been a better sight than this potential band of bushrangers and demon bowlers? Not to my glasses; nor one more bitter for the mate of the Rest Hut, thrice rejected from those very ranks.

They wandered round the town, constantly meeting familiar faces (including those of the two inebriated Scotsmen, who sang the praises of "this ol' feller" the Cocoa Man), and compared notes with YMCA colleagues. (Hornung would be at pains to stress that many of them, several even more advanced in years, had been through far more gruelling ordeals than himself.)

It was, in a sense, a strange kind of holiday, for the work of the YMCA in this particular region was suspended while the crisis lasted. The poor Fifth Army, greatly outnumbered and already exhausted by labours elsewhere, were falling back and dragging the rest of the Front Line with them. Amiens was under threat, and it was time for the YMCA workers to depart. On the evening of 26 March 1918 they boarded a train to an army rest-camp: ten minutes after leaving, the station was bombed and the train – with a cargo of hymn-singing passengers, squatting on their luggage in bare trucks – was obliged to take refuge in a wood. Eventually they reached the rest camp, "on a chilly plateau at the mouth of the Somme", and a month or so later Hornung arrived back in England.

He rejoined Connie in the keeper's hut in West Grinstead Park and, once again, was a frequent guest at his brother's dinner-table. Another of his neighbours, by this time, was Hilaire Belloc, living at King's Land, who also enjoyed Pitt's hospitality. Willie's niece observed that, on the whole, they got along quite well, but that there was sometimes trouble at the dinner-table because "both were ready talkers and each liked to hold the floor. If H.B. won, as he usually did, Willie was inclined to sulk, but this rivalry in no way damaged their friendship." He wrote *Notes of a Camp-Follower on the Western Front* in August and September of that year, but as soon as the Armistice had been signed, in November 1918, he resumed his work with the YMCA and went, this time, to Germany itself, for it was in Cologne that he re-established his Rest Hut and library for the use of British troops.

Notes of a Camp-Follower was published by Constable in 1919 and amply demonstrated (as the extracts quoted above will have shown) that his marvellous descriptive powers remained undimmed. "There are parts of it", Conan Doyle acknowledged in 1923, "which are brilliant in their vivid portrayal." It was a graphic, gripping account of his experiences, but shot through with a humour and compassion which did much to reveal the character of the man who had written it. "To meet some authors, whose books one has liked", wrote Chichester in 1941, "often means disappointment, if not disillusionment. Not so, however, with Hornung. Appreciative readers of his books ... rejoiced to find in the man the keen, enthusiastic, loving and kindly characteristics so often portrayed in his books. Great as the latter were, the words Hornung once used of Kipling are indeed true of him also – 'that he was so much greater than anything he wrote'."

Later that year Constable published a slim volume of his collected verse, *The Young Guard*, consisting in all of twelve poems. Constables also brought out a second edition of *Fathers of Men*, to which Hornung supplied an introduction recalling his own days at Uppingham.

Hornung probably returned to England in the spring of 1919, his work with the YMCA complete. Normality of a kind was now being resumed, but he and Constance had no desire to return to London. Their house in Hornton Street, Kensington was sold but the West Grinstead keeper had also come back from the wars and needed his cottage again. Pitt, however, who had started acquiring vacant houses in the area and doing them up for various members of his family, was able to make Midway Cottage in the nearby quiet hamlet of Partridge Green available to them. Pitt's daughter later described it as "less than a house and more than a cottage, with a little land attached to it". So they remained in close proximity to Hornung's brother and West Grinstead, where Constance – and sometimes, no doubt, her husband – attended the Roman Catholic church of Our Lady of Consolation and St Francis.

Midway Cottage was ideal for their modest requirements, but one luxury to which Willie treated himself (emulating Bernard Shaw) was a revolving hut in the garden where he could tuck himself away in seclusion for his writing activities. In theory he was not be disturbed, but he had reckoned (so his niece recalls) without the Belloc children, who had scant regard for such rules. "Bicycling over from King's Land. they would rush into the garden at Midway, and rout Willie out with cries of 'Raffles! Raffles! you've been working too long, come out of it!' It may be noted here that, although Willie's younger relations were on excellent terms with him, not one of them would have dared to disturb him at work!"

For Willie had, it seems, started a new novel. He told Chichester that it was going to be the best he had ever written, and read parts of it aloud to him. (But the manuscript, alas, does not appear to have survived.)

His *Who's Who* entry, from 1920 onwards, ceased to mention any recreations – skating and motoring having been a legacy from pre-war days – for he was, in a sense, in retirement. His niece, Bertha Collin, considered (debatedly, perhaps) that he had not really taken much interest in life since the death of his son. One thing in which he took a very keen interest, however, was the form of the War Memorial to be erected at his old school. "These are *my* choice (and I have carried them through) of Watchwords to go under the seven panels of names – three columns in each panel – in the Uppingham Shrine", he wrote to Chichester, adding that there was a doubt about the first:

1. What are these which are arrayed in white robes?
2. A People that jeoparded their lives unto the death in the high places of the field.
3. They were a wall unto us both by night and day.
4. Their sound went out into all the earth.
5. Therefore they shall be mine, said the Lord of Hosts, in the day when I make up my jewels.
6. Thine, O Lord, is the greatness, and the power, and the glory and the victory.
7. Make them to be numbered with Thy Saints in glory everlasting.

He took a similar interest in the War Memorial to be erected at West Grinstead – although, as a relative newcomer to the area, it is not clear whether he would have had much say in the matter.

The likelihood is that his health had not benefitted from his sojourn on the Western Front – Peter Haining, for one, has asserted as much – but neither Chichester nor Conan Doyle have portrayed him as an invalid at this time. It was Constance's health which was giving cause for concern in

February 1921, in fact, and Hornung took her to the South of France for a holiday. He caught a sudden chill on the train journey, however, which turned into aggravated influenza and pneumonia, and he died on 22 March 1921, three months' short of his fifty-fifth birthday. He was buried in the cemetery at St Jean de Luz, a few feet away from "dear old Gissy". The grave bears the words 'Trusty and Well Beloved' and on the side of it there is an inscription to the memory of Arthur Oscar Hornung, killed at Ypres on 6 July 1915.

"He had always been delicate", Conan Doyle would reflect, "and it was only his quiet courage which prevented his friends from constantly knowing it. He was loved by many, and as I dropped flowers upon his newly-turned grave at St Jean de Luz, where he lies with only a gravel path between him and George Gissing, I felt that the tribute was from many hearts besides my own."

Constance survived her husband by just over three years, dying in a nursing home at Beckenham on 8 June 1924, the day after Hornung's birthday, at the equally early age of fifty-six. She was buried in the churchyard of Our Lady of Consolation and St Francis. She had made a will on 20 November 1923 in which Chichester, who appears to have been her husband's closest friend for many years, was named as one of the two executors and trustees; in a codicil dated 8 March 1924, however, she revoked this appointment and left him the sum of £100 instead of the £250 originally intended. Her effects totalled £17,461. The sum of £200 was set aside for masses to be said in memory of herself, her husband and her son at the West Grinstead church once a month for a period of five years. Without in any way creating a trust or imposing any legal obligation or responsibility, she asked her chief executor (Clennell Wilkinson, Willie's nephew) and his successors "to pay to the caretaker of the cemetery at St Jean de Luz, France a sufficient sum to ensure that my husband's grave there be kept in good order". By 1990 the condition of the grave had seriously deteriorated and the cemetery authorities were considering its removal. Pitt's grandson, Stephen Hornung, learnt of this and was able to have it restored; he hopes that it will now be safe for a little while longer.

ଓଃ৪ଠ

Seventy-eight years have passed since the death of E.W. Hornung and there is now barely anybody alive who still personally remembers him. It is more than a century since the very first Raffles story appeared in *Cassell's Magazine*. The seventeenth biography of Sir Arthur Conan Doyle was recently published but the present volume is the very first to celebrate his brother-in-law. Certainly, as indicated at the beginning of this book, he has become something of a Person Unknown so far as posterity is concerned. When mentioned at all, the same sparse handful of facts has been recycled remorselessly – and not altogether accurately, since it has been asserted time and time again (except, to its credit, in the *Australian Dictionary of Biography*) that Hornung's father was a solicitor.

The fame of A.J. Raffles, on the other hand, has continued unabated. The short stories have been constantly re-published (although a tactful veil has been drawn over *Mr Justice Raffles*, unseen since pre-holocaust days). As we shall see, there have been stage plays (in one of which Graham Greene took a hand), films, television and radio productions. All of Hornung's other works have been forgotten, with the possible exception of *Stingaree*, but the cricketing cracksman continues to enthral.

All of which, it must be concluded, is a pity. The Raffles tales are, by and large, first rate, and easily stand comparison with those of Sherlock Holmes, but Hornung produced other books which were far better (and a few, it must be acknowledged, which were much inferior). His style is curiously elusive, for he tried on various shoes for size, and comparisons have been drawn, in the preceding pages, with Bret Harte, Henry James, Stevenson, Ouida, Hardy, Kipling and Chesterton, to name but a few. The hallmark of a novel by Hornung at his very best is that of a calm, measured narrative, steering clear of sensationalism but with a surprise or two in store for the reader and marked, above all, by some wonderful descriptive passages. There are at least half-a-dozen of his "unknown" books (not to mention a host of brilliant short stories) which, in the worldly-wise days of the late twentieth century, would still bear reprinting.

Of Hornung himself, it is clear that he was a kind, sensitive, gentle man, endowed with a subtle sense of humour and capable, when the occasion demanded, of rising to do his duty, in however exalted or lowly capacity he might be needed. He could also exert firmness and was not afraid of declaring his adherence to Christianity. His two greatest enthusiasms were cricket and the public school system – two sides of the same coin, perhaps. "Play up, play up and play the game!" was his rallying cry, in vigorous endorsement of Sir Henry Newbolt's sentiments. By the same token, he was a firm believer in the merits of military discipline as a means of bringing out the best in a man rather than subduing it. His only fault, seemingly, was a slight tendency towards loquaciousness.

He was probably a homosexual, in the days when homosexuality was the deadliest of sins. So far as he dared, he had indicated in the pages of his novels a close affinity with Oscar Wilde. It was men, rather than women, who engaged his warmest sympathies and to whom he opened his heart. There was his budding friendship with George Gissing, cut short by the latter's untimely death, and in later years there had been the cordial friendship with Chichester. He had always been acutely conscious of the colour of men's eyes – brown or blue usually being remarked upon – and he had sung the praises of boys and young soldiers ("magnificent young life; bodies at their very best, perfect instruments in perfect tune"). In contrast, although heroines dutifully figured in most of his books, he had precious little to say about individual women or the female anatomy. His relations with Constance appear to have been close, and they evidently stayed good friends, but one hesitates to say that they were a couple ardently devoted to one another.

In the present state of our knowledge about Willie Hornung, this is as far as one can go – or needs to go. We may note that Chips Carpenter in *Fathers of Men*, "a wild impulse burning in his eyes", declares that he has not always been so "straight" as his friend supposes, but stops short of saying any more. Clearly, Hornung was *not* a sphinx without a secret. But we should also take heed of Mr Upton in *The Camera Fiend* – "I like a man's secrets to die with him" – and, above all, of the final words of Uvo Delavoye in *Witching Hill*: "The rest is silence, if you don't mind, old man."

25

AFTERWARDS – AND AFTERWORDS?

YET NOT TOTAL SILENCE, it would seem – or not, at any rate, so far as Conan Doyle was concerned.

This present chapter is, in a sense, a postscript to the twenty-four which have preceded it and something of an 'optional extra'. Readers sceptical about psychic matters, seances and communications with those in the 'spirit world' may well prefer to skip the next five pages. It is hoped, however, that those prepared to concede that some convincing evidence for an after-life has accumulated during the past century or so, the undoubted existence of fraudsters, gullibility, self-deception and wish-fulfilment notwithstanding, will find its contents of interest. Certainly it can be argued, as Brian Inglis did convincingly on several occasions, that the onus now rests with those who disbelieve in such a possibility to prove that communication is *not* possible.

Hornung himself, during his lifetime, was a staunch disbeliever and viewed his brother-in-law's increasing fascination with spiritualism as an unhealthy aberration. Doyle found him "intolerant", with Constance equally so. Spirit messages from Oscar Hornung, which he endeavoured to pass on to the boy's parents, were (he tells us) flatly rejected by them "on religious grounds". Doyle's wife developed psychic powers in the early 1920s, becoming (much to her own astonishment) a writing medium, and in 1924 this developed into semi-trance inspirational talking. At a sitting on 21 July 1921 Doyle communicated with his eldest son, Kingsley, who had died in 1918, and asked "Are you in touch with Willie Hornung?" "Yes," was the reply, "he came over all right to us... He is heavy and tired. But he will improve. Already he is better. His mind is more open. He is sorry, and he realises things now." There was a long pause, and then Hornung piped up for himself.

EWH: I am Willie. I am here. I am so glad to be here. Arthur, this is wonderful. If only I had known this on earth, how much I could have helped others. However, it is too late. I am with Oscar. It is so glorious. I am working and feel so well. It is nice to be free from my asthma.

ACD: You are happy then?

EWH: It is a wonderful life – so high and fine in all ways. Worth living for. If only people knew! There is such heaps and heaps I want to say to you, Arthur. First of all, to tell you that I love you all. I have learned a lot since I came over here.

ACD: Is your present work literary?

EWH: Yes, of a kind. It is most interesting. I prefer it to my work in the world. It is so much more vital. It really counts.

ACD: Could I finish any of your work here?

EWH: Not much, thank you. It does not matter. We will leave it so.

ACD: I wrote a preface about you in your posthumous volume.

EWH: I saw it. For a time it is better not to speak to my people about this.

ACD: You remember that Oscar sent messages?

EWH: Several times. But we would not listen. Oh, the pity of it! Oh, the pity of it! If I had my time over again how different I would be. But it is too late.

ACD: The knowledge was not given you.

EWH: No, but I'll progress here. I am doing so.

ACD: Well, I always admired you.

EWH: Yes, I know you honestly admired parts of me. It's hard to break off. It is such a joy to come back the first time.

ACD: You are very welcome.

EWH: Thank you, dear old fellow. My love to all.

ACD: What's the use? They won't believe it.

EWH: Never mind. Plod on. You will win through. Right is might. Goodbye. God bless you!

A few days later, he paid a return visit.

EWH: This *is* good. I had been hoping to get through again. I feel rather selfish, for there are so many others who wish to communicate, but they made me come....

ACD: I am so glad you have taken this up.

EWH: I am fearfully interested. I hate to think of not having had it all this time, but now I am going to make up.

ACD: Have you active amusements?

EWH: Rather. And I am no longer handicapped by my horrid old asthma. You would not recognise me. I am much improved in appearance.

ACD: Any good my telling Pitt?

EWH: None whatever. He is even worse than I was. He will learn in time. But a little too late.

ACD: Could you help in psychic photography?

EWH: I'm not sure that I can.

There was a third visit some weeks later (on 14 October, apparently).

EWH: Hello! I'm Willie. This *is* good.

ACD: You enjoy coming?

EWH: Isn't it natural that I should, considering that I have been cut off from you all so long? I do so love getting through to you, but I am so new at it all. Jean has two fine guides – one a very high guide who has come to help her in this work. So many are here. By the way, there is a fellow here who played cricket with you upon earth. He has just come over. He has never seen or heard of this earth telegraph and is greatly interested.

ACD: Can you get the name?

EWH: Names are terribly difficult. You see a name does not represent any sort of an idea. It is an indigestible chunk. You can't suggest it to the Medium's brain. But I will try.

This resulted in the medium writing down a series of letters which made no sense but ended with CINI.

ACD: If that is a name it is an Italian name. I never knew an
     Italian who played good class cricket.

EWH: Well, he is here and sends his regards.

"This was most evidential," Doyle comments. "[P.J. de]
Paravicini, who played for Middlesex, had died two days
before [on 12 October], and neither the Medium nor I were
aware of it. I can't remember playing with him, but it may
have been so."

Ever since his wholesale conversion to spiritualism in 1915,
as distinct from the mere dabbling and speculation of earlier
years, Conan Doyle had been a tireless campaigner for the
cause. In 1920 he had toured Australia, proclaiming the
proven existence of an afterlife, and he visited America in
1922 with the same fervent message. At a seance in Toledo,
Ohio, the medium provided him with a brief message from
Willie. Back in London he experienced, at another seance, the
wholesale appearance of Oscar – "I saw his materialised form
with every feature clear as plainly as ever in life" – and a little
while later Oscar's father again made contact.

EWH: I am Willie Hornung.

ACD: Hello! I have not touched you since Toledo.

EWH: It is true, old man. We were there.

ACD: Should we go to America again?

EWH: Yes, rather. The seed needs sowing in many places.

ACD: You know that I saw Oscar?

EWH: Yes, he was awfully pleased that you saw him then, and
     that you are always so ready to get into touch with him.
     He is getting on so well over here in many ways.

ACD: What about Constance?

EWH: I fear it is no good, old chap. She is too much in the grip
     of the church. Alas! She will be so dreadfully sorry. God
     bless you a thousandfold and keep you in His care – all of
     you in this blessed home, the centre for all of us on this
     plane.

"From that time onwards", writes Doyle, "we heard
occasionally from Hornung, always in the same characteristic

strain, but presently the advent of Pheneas" – an Arabian gentleman who tended to hog the spiritual airwaves – "displaced the other Communicators." Before that advent, however, and before he departed on a second American tour, there was, on 11 February 1923, another aural encounter with Oscar Hornung.

ACD: You remember the London sitting?

OH: Rather. I loved hearing the children's voices. I know you saw me. I'll show myself again to you both.

ACD: I have never seen your father.

OH: And you won't for a long time.

ACD: Your mother will learn, I hope.

OH: It won't be very long, I am thankful to say.

Oscar's mother died sixteen months later, on 8 June 1924. But she does not appear to have sent any messages to her brother. (Perhaps, despite everything, she remained "in the grip of the church" and resolutely refused to participate in what she had regarded, during her lifetime, as highly questionable activities.) And whether Conan Doyle ever experienced a materialisation by Oscar's father, before his own death on 7 July 1930, must remain a matter for speculation. As, indeed, must the contents of the whole of this chapter.

26

RAFFLES TRIUMPHANT

THE CREATOR of A.J. Raffles was dead. The creation itself, however, would not only live on (despite having officially met his end in 1900) but would actually go from strength to strength – destined to become, in fact, a star of stage, cinema, radio and television and the hero, twice over, of a string of totally new stories. He gave his name, moreover, to what was launched as a particularly stylish brand of cigarettes.

As far back as 1903 Raffles had started to pursue a career of his own, for it was in that year that Hornung collaborated with Eugène Presbrey in writing a four-Act play entitled *Raffles, the Amateur Cracksman*. But one suspects that, although Hornung is credited as joint-author (and received a large share of subsequent royalties), his contribution to the venture was minimal. Almost certainly, he simply ran an eye over the finished product to ensure that it did not depart too drastically from the characters and plots of his stories – although, even so, dramatic liberties were taken to so great an extent that it is a totally unprofitable exercise to try to reconcile the stage versions of Raffles and Bunny with those which had appeared on the stories. What Presbrey did, in effect, was to cobble together two of the tales ('Gentlemen and Players' and its sequel 'The Return Match') and throw in bits and pieces from some of the other yarns for good measure. He also killed off Inspector Mackenzie (casually referred to in passing as a deceased "English detective", which may raised some hackles north of the Border) and, for the benefit of New York audiences, replaced him by an American sleuth. T h e curtain rises on the graciously-attired world of an Edwardian house-party in which A.J. Raffles and Harold Manders – despite schoolboy connections – scarcely know one another. They are, in fact, rivals for the hand of the fair Gwendoline Conran (with Raffles well in the lead, much to Bunny's intense annoyance). Inevitably, Miss Conran is a niece of Lady Melrose. For we are at Milchester Abbey, Dorset, on an evening in September, and while the excitement of a cricket match is the ostensible purpose for this select gathering, it turns out that the chief topic of conversation is the true identity of someone known to all and sundry as the Amateur Cracksman, responsible for a host of burglaries at stately homes in the area. But Curtis Bedford, a retired American detective ("once the Sherlock Holmes of New York"), fortuitously residing in this part of the world, has been hired at colossal expense by Lord Amersteth (our host) to keep an eye on Lady Melrose's diamond necklace and is looking forward to an encounter with the Amateur Cracksman. In the course of idle chit-chat about the Cracksman's possible identity, Mr Raffles playfully regrets that, despite having been a guest at most of the stately residences in question, he would be regarded as a harmless lunatic if he went to Scotland Yard and claimed to be "our famous Cracksman" because the police would simply check his bowling averages and throw him out. The remark is greeted with much mirth by nearly all the others. But Bedford, significantly, thinks it an interesting theory. Even more interesting is the fact that Mrs Vidal, an unpopular fellow-guest endured as the widow of somebody's cousin, claims to have actually met the Cracksman on one occasion (when he stole the Kaiser's pearl from a handsome young Prussian officer on a steam liner in the Mediterranean) and would definitely know him again. She looks pointedly at Raffles as she says this.

Night falls, and the cast officially retire to their slumbers – although most of them find it difficult to sleep and continually come downstairs again for private *tête-à-têtes* with Raffles. Mrs Vidal, being A Woman Scorned, threatens to reveal his true identity to Gwendoline, and is challenged to do her worst. Bunny then comes in and laments that, apart from being ignored by Gwendoline, he has lost heavily to Lord Amersham's son at piquet and is virtually ruined. Raffles reassures him that all will be well on both counts. Bedford perambulates, then settles down near the safe. But the necklace is not really in the safe at all, for Lady Melrose (with Bedford's permission) has taken it to her room.

The audience has already caught a glimpse of Crawshay, the professional burglar, in furtive discussion with Maria, a French maid (his confederate) at the very outset of the play, and the action now speeds up at a satisfying pace. Crawshay breaks in and Maria throws him the jewels, but he is promptly apprehended by Raffles – who filches the necklace in the course of raising the alarm and handing Crawshay over to Bedford. Crawshay is borne away, vowing vengeance on his captor. Next morning, Raffles announces that he has to return to London – where Bedford is also heading – but very nobly renounces all claims to Gwendoline (philosophising, in passing, about the lonely path of the transgressor) and recommends her to look kindly on Bunny instead. Alas, Gwendoline – despite heavy hints from Mrs Vidal – misunderstands his elliptical utterances and concludes that *Bunny* is the Cracksman, much to the consternation of both that young man and his mentor. (Gwendoline, it seems, is not of the brightest.) Crawshay meanwhile escapes from the local police station and Bedford's suspicions deepen as regards the true identity of the Cracksman.

After the Interval, the audience is transported to those famous bachelor quarters at the Albany, where Raffles plays debonair host, as it were, to the rest of the cast during another couple of Acts. He is menaced by Bedford on the one hand and by Crawshay on the other, but remains totally unperturbed. Suffice to say that Bunny (after being shocked and horrified on learning that his revered old school chum is none other than the Amateur Cracksman) gets his money and the girl, that Mrs Vidal gets her come-uppance, that Lady Melrose gets her necklace back, that Crawshay (with the aid of Raffles) gets away and that Raffles, after promising

Gwendoline and Bunny that henceforth he'll lead a better life, also gets away, and that Bedford gets frustrated – until, gazing out of the window to see whether he can spot his elusive quarry in the London fog, he breaks into a broad grin and hopes that Raffles will make it because, when all's said and done, he's really a pretty decent chap.

This splendid piece of nonsense was performed for the first time in New York in October 1903, with an American matinée idol, Kyrle Bellew, as Raffles. It proved a considerable success and there were, in all, 168 performances. The silent movies were, by this time, proving to be a flourishing industry and Bellew starred in a film of the same name (*Raffles, the Amateur Cracksman*) made by Eagle Films of New York in 1905, although the subtleties of the plot can scarcely have been adequately conveyed in the space of only ten minutes! The Vitagraph Company of America, impressed by what was evidently its great popularity with the public, went one better and immediately made a feature film with the same title starring J. Barney Sherry.

The London *première* of the play was at the Comedy Theatre on 12 May 1906. Curtis Bedford was played by Dion Boucicault, Crawshay by Laurence Irving and Bunny by Graham Browne. But in the central role was thirty-three year-old Gerald du Maurier (son of George and about to become the father of Daphne), whose relaxed portrayal of the audacious conman, ever resourceful in moments of crisis, would prove to be the stunning success of the season. The rave reviews were everything that he (and Hornung) could have desired. Audiences flocked to see *The Amateur Cracksman* (Henry James being among their number on one occasion) and there were, in all, 351 performances. Du Maurier's famous reputation as a matinée idol was virtually established by his performance in this one role. (Previously, he had been known primarily as the Captain Hook of Barrie's *Peter Pan*.) Although he privately claimed, in July 1906, that he "loathed acting and actors", he played the role until well into 1907 and then went on to star in *Brewster's Millions*.

In 1909 Hornung collaborated with Charles Sansom in writing a sequel, *A Visit from Raffles*, although it does not appear to have been performed to the same extent as its predecessor. Two years later an Italian film company, Vita Studios, made a six-part serial of some of the stories. The first major film (again, bearing the familiar title of *Raffles, The Amateur Cracksman*) was made by the Hiller-Wilk Studio in 1917 and starred John Barrymore. House Peters starred in a remake produced by Universal Pictures in 1925 (which on this occasion was simply called *Raffles*).

In 1930, with the 'talkies' having arrived on the scene, Samuel Goldwyn produced for United Artists what was undoubtedly, at that time, something of a prestige version of *Raffles*. The star was Ronald Colman, an English actor who was beginning to specialise in romantic, debonair roles in Hollywood films and played them all (whether it was to be Raffles, Bulldog Drummond or Sidney Carton) in exactly the same cheerful manner. The film is set in a contemporary London, with taxis having replaced hansom cabs, and Raffles (as noted earlier) has now been provided with a manservant who greets his employer's accomplice in crime with the immortal words "Good morning, Mr Bunny". (Sidney Howard was the scriptwriter responsible for this and other abominations.) But, as before, the great topic exercising the public's imagination is the true identity of the Amateur Cracksman (who has now taken, obligingly, to leaving notes at the scene of his crimes, lest there be any doubt as to their perpetrator). Newspaper placards periodically proclaim "Amateur Cracksman Strikes Again" and Colman, attired in opera hat, smart overcoat and elegant evening suit, glides gracefully through London fogs, utters witty repartee and continues to be a hit with the ladies. Only occasionally do we glimpse him actually cracking a safe – and, almost invariably, it will ultimately be for A Good Cause.

An English-made sequel of 1932, *The Return of Raffles*, starred George Barraud and appears to have enjoyed box-office success. For the fact remained that there was still a great public who thrived upon escapist romance and delighted in seeing the noses of Scotland Yard inspectors being perpetually tweaked by lovable rogues. In effect, Baroness Orczy was doing exactly the same thing with her adventures of the Scarlet Pimpernel, for here was Sir Percy Blakeney – another jolly member of the upper classes, and a brilliant master of disguise – continually outwitting the teeth-gnashing Chauvelin and leading two totally separate existences. Or, going back even further than the French Revolution, one could enjoy the exploits of Robin Hood (as personified by the Douglas Fairbanks or Errol Flynn of the day), a light-hearted daredevil who invariably got the better of the Sheriff of Nottingham (and was, moreover, really the Earl of Huntingdon all the time).

Most of Hornung's books were reprinted at least once during the 1920s, but the Raffles tales were more in demand than any of the others – and by the 1930s, apart from the occasional revival of Stingaree (whose adventures had also been dramatised), it was the Raffles books alone which were being republished. Arguably, they could be perused time and time again, for their original freshness remained undimmed, but it must be remembered that the entire Raffles corpus amounted to only 26 short stories and one rather unsatisfactory novel. For those longing to know more about the great man, this was a frustratingly small stream at which to slake their thirst.

Understandably, therefore, there was considerable interest in 1933 when a totally fresh batch of short stories about Raffles was published – the English edition being entitled *Raffles after Dark* and the American version, more appropriately, *The Return of Raffles*. These were the work of Philip Atkey (1908-85), writing under the pseudonym of Barry Perowne. Their success encouraged him to churn out a stream of sequels, both novels and short stories, about the cricketing conman. In the first instance, readers were regaled with *Raffles in Pursuit* (1934), *Raffles under Sentence* and *She Married Raffles* (both in 1936), *Raffles' Crime in Gibraltar* and *Raffles vs. Sexton Blake* (both in 1937), *The A.R.P. Mystery* (1939) and *Raffles and the Key Man* (1940). Then came a temporary cessation, Atkey having departed on some active service of his own, but nobody could complain, any more, that Raffles stories were in short supply.

If anything, Atkey had rather overdone things. As always, the narrator is Bunny Manders, A.J. Raffles is his usual charming, Sullivan-smoking self and the Albany continues to be their base camp, but any resemblance or relationship to the stories of E.W. Hornung (apart from a passing reference to the 'Ides of March') is otherwise more by accident than design. There is a superabundance of whirlwind activity in these new tales and we soon become aware that our heroes have left the 1890s far behind them and (as in the Hollywood portrayals) have moved into the world of the 1930s. Cars, planes and telephones loom large in the action. When the curtain rises on *Raffles after Dark* in 1933, Bunny is discovered at the wheel of a Rolls Royce; later, he and Raffles will be pursued by the Flying Squad. Glamorous girls flit in and out of the action, there are fiendish foreign villains, punch-ups, murders and exclamation marks galore. It is all very slick and streamlined, with convoluted, wildly improbable plots and barely a moment to draw breath – for we are in the highpowered world of Bulldog Drummond and Simon Templar (and almost, indeed, the era of James Bond) rather than that of the amateur cracksman. But it was one to which Raffles and Bunny adapted admirably, however much the purists might lament that this new batch of stories, while readable enough so far as they went, were grossly inferior to the great originals.

Certainly, George Orwell gave no indication of being acquainted with them when he penned his celebrated essay, 'Raffles and Miss Blandish', for the October 1944 issue of *Outlook*. He was disdainful enough about the original tales as it was, although acknowledging that Hornung was "a very conscientious and on his level a very able writer", and lamented that Raffles and Bunny were devoid of religious belief and had "no real ethical code, merely certain rules of behaviour which they observe semi-instinctively". But they came, nonetheless, from a golden age, for "the Raffles stories, written from the angle of the criminal, are much less anti-social than many modern stories written from the angle of the detective. The main impression that they leave behind is of boyishness. They belong to a time when people had standards, though they happened to be foolish standards. Their key phrase is 'not done'. The line they draw between good and evil is as senseless as a Polynesian taboo, but at least, like the taboo, it has the advantage that everyone accepts it." (He then turned his gloomy attention to what was, in contrast, "the cesspool" of *No Orchids for Miss Blandish*).

In the meantime, with recording techniques having advanced considerably since the days of the earliest talkies, Hollywood had yet another crack at portraying Raffles on the big screen. In 1939 Goldwyn and United Artists made what was almost a carbon-copy of their 1930 success, with David Niven (in his first starring role) reprising Ronald Colman's performance. There was a strong supporting cast, including Dame May Whitty as Lady Melrose and Olivia de Havilland (fresh from *Gone With the Wind*) as her niece, while John van Druten and F. Scott Fitzgerald were among the squad of writers brought in to polish up Sidney Howard's 1930 dialogue. William Wyler directed some of the scenes. In the event, however, the film was something of a disappointment. Niven was adequate in the role, but it failed to break any fresh ground. It was painfully obvious, to cast and critics alike, that this latest *Raffles* was basically a re-make of the 1930 production – except that the Hays Office was distressed at the idea that Raffles should escape scot-free at the end of the film and demanded some last-minute changes. Richard Mallet, reviewing the finished product in *Punch* in April 1940, confessed that most of the film had bored him. He acknowledged that Niven had walked gaily through the part, that de Havilland was as beautiful as ever and that Dame May had done all she could with her limited opportunities, but "even the moments that should have been full of suspense fell pretty flat. For American audiences I suppose the picture's revelation of the quaint habits and manners of the English gives it the charm of strangeness; but for English audiences there is merely its revelation of Hollywood's quaint ideas about England, and we were tired of those already."

That was the end of the line so far as American films were concerned. Raffles and Bunny had been dragged into the 1930s but after 1939 there was nowhere left for them to go. In the age of Cagney, Bogart and Robinson (not to mention Miss Blandish and her tormentors) the 'amateur cracksman' had already been something of a genteel anachronism, and while Hollywood now saw nothing wrong in producing a series of films in which Holmes and Watson (as personified by Basil Rathbone and Nigel Bruce) turned their attention to defeating the Nazis it was clear that their criminal class counterparts had no further role on the contemporary scene. This was the main thing (but by no means the only one) which had been wrong with the Barry Perowne books – and, on reflection, Atkey evidently reached this conclusion for himself. From 1945 onwards, having attained years of greater maturity, he made a conscious attempt to emulate Hornung's style and penned a series of more leisurely short stories which returned the two protagonists to their natural *milieu* of the 1890s. These were published in *Ellery Queen's Mystery Magazine*, the *Saint Magazine* and *John Bull*. They were not collected into book form until the 1970s, forty years after the appearance of the original 'Barry Perowne' stories (which had now been mercifully forgotten), and were greeted with a fair degree of critical acclaim. *Raffles Revisited* was published in New York in 1974 and in London the following year. An agreeable collection, it was followed by *Raffles of the Albany* (1976) and *Raffles of the MCC* (1979) – the tales in these sequels being taken, so it was indicated, "from the Clandestine Papers, newly discovered, of Raffles's Confederate, Manders".

It soon becomes clear that the main reason why the Manders papers have been kept secret for so long is that a Famous Person features in almost every one of the stories. Amazing to relate, Raffles and Bunny had been acquainted with virtually every leading light of the 1890s. They encounter, on a visit to Portsmouth, a Dr A. Conan Doyle, author of the newly-published *A Study in Scarlet*, and his friend Mr James Watson, secretary of the Portsmouth Literary and Scientific Society; on a visit to India they meet up, inevitably, with a young newspaper correspondent called Rudyard Kipling; they visit Stevenson and his wife in Samoa; as escaping prisoners of war in South Africa, they seize a train and are thereby indirectly responsible for helping Mr Winston S. Churchill, another well-known newspaper correspondent, to make his own escape from the Boers. Their paths also cross those of John L. Sullivan, Lord Kitchener, Mata Hari, Lillie Langtry, George Bernard Shaw and P.G. Wodehouse.

Perhaps the most intriguing story of all, bearing in mind earlier conjectures in the present volume, is one entitled 'Dinah Raffles and Oscar Wilde'. Atkey had taken it upon himself to provide Raffles with a long-lost sister, brought up in Australia, with whom Bunny is naturally much smitten but for whom Raffles intends to find, if he can, a wealthy suitor. In this particular yarn, set in 1898 or thereabouts, there is an unpleasant clash in a London restaurant with the Marquess of Queensberry, who vows to avenge himself on Raffles. In a café in Paris, a little while later, they encounter the debauched Sebastian Melmoth, alias Oscar Wilde, with whom Raffles courteously exchanges pleasantries. Dinah is much attracted by Wilde and also by his companion, Aubrey Beardsley. After they part, Raffles realises that a couple of thugs hired by Queensberry are pursuing Melmoth with murderous intent: he follows them all to Venice and is able to send the blackguards off on a false trail. Melmoth, after expressing his gratitude, sets off in the opposite direction and a little while later Dinah draws the attention of her brother and Bunny to the fact that an exquisite fair-haired young man, namely Lord Alfred Douglas, has just arrived on the scene and is obviously in search of his old companion.

The stories contained in these three volumes are competently written and moderately entertaining. They are also, alas, unlike their turn-of-the-century predecessors, instantly forgettable. Occasionally Atkey manages to introduce a real element of suspense into his yarns, so that one wonders, with genuine curiosity and mounting excitement, how our heroes are going to extricate themselves from a particular situation. But such moments are rare, although at least one of Atkey's admirers bravely contends that the stories are "exciting, exotic, and frequently more richly evocative of the gaslit era of the 1890s than Hornung's originals". Certainly, he had written at far greater length about Raffles than Hornung himself had ever done, although he had transformed him, in the process, into a knight errant – a high-spirited and light-hearted young man keen on adventure, who goes about righting wrongs and coming to the rescue of impoverished friends. Justice invariably prevails once Raffles has become involved. Now and then, admittedly, he helps himself to a spot of commission, but this is no more than his due, and we are left with the feeling that, in a properly-regulated society, he would be rewarded for his labours with an OBE. Atkey had made Raffles and Bunny more socially acceptable – an exercise which Hornung himself had tentatively ventured upon in *Mr Justice Raffles* – and had undoubtedly polished up their images. But the world painstakingly depicted in his countless tales is strangely unreal, in contrast to that of the original stories: paradoxically, the cumulative effect of introducing so many 'genuine' characters is that we cease, ultimately, to take that world seriously, for there is a limit to the extent to which belief can be suspended. Cosiness and complacency have replaced tension and drama. In the last analysis, it is improbable that the stories would ever have been published if Atkey had given the two leading characters different names and left them to sink or swim on their own merits.

Hornung's own Raffles stories, with the exception of that unhappy novel of 1909, continued to be regularly reprinted during the post-war period. There were, among others, Penguin editions and Everyman editions. In 1984, however, the Souvenir Press broke fresh ground by publishing *all* the short stories in one volume, an event which Graham Greene (a Raffles enthusiast, as we shall see very shortly) hailed as "a splendid idea". Penguin books followed suit soon afterwards, with a Raffles Omnibus.

From time to time (most recently in 1995, with Nigel Havers at the microphone) some of Hornung's Raffles stories were broadcast on BBC radio. In December 1945, in particularly venturesome mood, the BBC serialised them in dramatised form, with Frank Allenby as Raffles and Eric Micklewood as Bunny. The tales were adapted for radio by Beatrice Gilbert and the series produced by Leslie Stokes. ("When Tees-siders listened in last night to the latest episode of the Raffles series", enthused the *N.E. Daily Gazette* on 11 December, "few would be aware that they were listening to the work of a local author.") The experiment was not repeated. On 10 September 1975, however, by which time colour television had been firmly established in Britain, Yorkshire TV scored a palpable hit by *premiering* a one-hour production of *Raffles* (regrettably, yet again the tired old saga of Lady Melrose and her diamond necklace, plus Crawshay's arrest and escape, rather than 'The Ides of March'). But with the waters tested, and public reaction having proved favourable, they went on to present a thirteen-part series of Raffles tales which ran from 25 February to 20 May 1977. In the main role was Anthony Valentine and Bunny was played by Christopher Strauli. No expense was spared and there was conscientious attention to detail. The world of the 1890s was lovingly recreated and Philip Mackie, the adapter (unlike his Hollywood predecessors) kept as close as he could to the spirit and dialogue of the original stories. 'The Ides of March' became *The First Step* and 'The Criminologists' Club' (with Tony Britton and Peter Sallis as its leading members) became *The Gold Cup*, but there were also some familiar titles in the saga such as *A Costume Piece* (with Alfred Marks as Reuben Rosenthall and Brian Glover as Purvis), *The Spoils of Sacrilege*, *A Chest of Silver*, *The Last Laugh*, *A Trap to Catch a Cracksman* (with Robert Hardy as Lord Ernest Belville, the evil Rational Drink fanatic scheming to become another Raffles) and *The*

Gift of the Emperor. Even *Mr Justice Raffles* was pressed into service, and the series concluded with *An Old Flame* – with Raffles on the run from an ardent Lady Poulton (as Jacques Saillard has now become), played by Caroline Blakiston, and deciding that only by faking his death can he give his admirer (who Knows All) the slip.

In one crucial respect, however, the saga was simplified. A.J. Raffles, the well-known cricketer, remains firmly at the Albany until almost the last moment, for *The Gift of the Emperor* is just one self-contained episode among many. Never, at any point, is the Amateur Cracksman unmasked by Scotland Yard, and Raffles is never obliged to dive off the German liner, swim to Elba for safety and endure, for several years, the shadowy half-life of Mr Maturin. Had it not been for Lady Poulton's intervention, so we gather, he would have continued to flourish unchecked. It was on this note that the series came to an end – a jocular enough conclusion, certainly, however unflattering to the undoubted charms of Ms Blakiston, but not the one which Hornung had devised. But by the late 1970s it was no longer morally imperative for Raffles to be brought low by officialdom, however indirectly, and for Bunny to do time at Pentonville or Wormwood Scrubs. The television series studiously eschewed the darker side of the tales, but the two basic characters remained unchanged and were, indeed, brought more accurately to life than in any previous representation. The audiences, and the critics, were delighted. "The voice of the amateur cracksman is heard once again in the land," enthused David Pryce-Jones in *The Listener* (3 March 1977); "*Raffles* has become a serial. In Anthony Valentine, what is more, Raffles has been splendidly personified, a lean, dark figure with a smile at once engaging and slightly saturnine. The eye is cold, the manner debonair. He looks as if he could well play cricket for England and would steal any tiara without compunction.'

At long last, the ideal actor had been found. The splendid personification was much overdue for there had been some uncertainty, over the years, as to what Raffles actually looked like. This was never a problem in the case of Sherlock

Holmes, where an aquiline face surmounted, more often than not, by a deerstalker, conveyed an instant impression of who it was that the artist or the actor was endeavouring to portray. In the case of Raffles, however, there had been a perpetual element of mystery. Hornung, after referring to his indolent, athletic figure, had described him as having pale, sharp, clean-shaven features, with curly black hair and a strong, unscrupulous mouth. John H. Bacon, the first artist to show him in action (in *Cassell's Magazine*), adhered quite faithfully to this description (although Bunny, in contrast, adorned with a drooping moustache, fair hair and a perpetually worried expression, appears to be a much older man). But Cyrus Cuneo, illustrating the final batch of short stories (in the *Pall Mall Magazine*) showed a lantern-jawed, ruthless, determined man with whitish hair – an undoubted rogue, one would conclude. Du Maurier and Barrymore were both clean-shaven, while having little else in common with Hornung's description, but both Colman and Niven had elegant, pencil-line moustaches and theirs were the images that passed into common currency. When Edwin Phillips came to illustrate the Barry Perowne stories for *John Bull* in the mid-1950s, therefore, he showed a handsome, mustachioed man who could easily have passed muster, in a dim light, as Robert Taylor – or even Clark Gable. The television adaptations, however, restored Raffles to a much closer approximation to what Hornung had in mind. The TV Raffles was slim, dark-haired, pale-faced and clean-shaven (while Bunny, despite having an earnest, anxious expression, was fresh-faced, fair-haired and slightly chubby and clearly a few years younger than his chief). Simon Cadell, who portrayed Raffles in a revival of the original Presbrey play in 1984, was also slim and clean-shaven – and his slightly twisted mouth would have added an extra dimension of evil to the character.

From time to time, there had been good-natured 'spoofs' of the Raffles tales. The earliest of these, in 1905, was by an American, John Kendrick Bangs, who produced a dozen short stories for *Puck* which were published in book form by Harper & Brothers that same year under the title *Mrs Raffles, Being the*

Adventures of an Amateur Crackswoman. He also supplied *Harper's Magazine* with ten short stories which were published by Harper in 1906 ("With Apologies to Sir Arthur Conan Doyle and Mr E.W. Hornung") under the title *R. Holmes & Co., Being the Remarkable Adventures of Raffles Holmes, Esq., Detective and Amateur Cracksman by Birth.*

The latter described how Sherlock Holmes, called in by Lord Dorrington in 1883 to investigate the theft of a famous ruby seal, narrowed down his chief suspects to Miss Marjorie Tattersby and her father, the Reverend James Tattersby, retired missionary of Goring-Streatley-on-Thames. Holmes discovers that Miss Tattersby, a young lady of astonishing beauty, is totally innocent of the crime and that her father is, in reality, none other than A.J. Raffles, the famous cricketer, who is also guilty of purloining some valuable plate from Cliveden. Disguised as a young American clergyman, Mr Dutton, Holmes wooes Miss Tattersby and then confronts her father (whom he had met previously at Dorrington Hall when he himself had been Dutton and Tattersby had been Raffles). The dialogue that follows, recording an encounter of a truly unique nature, is worthy of permanent preservation.

Holmes and Raffles went at once to Tattersby's study.

"Well?" said Raffles, impatiently, when they were seated. "I suppose you have come to get the Dorrington seal, Mr Holmes."

"Ah – you know me, then, Mr Raffles?" said Holmes, with a pleasant smile.

"Perfectly," said Raffles. "I knew you at Dorrington Hall the moment I set eyes on you..."

"I am glad," said Holmes. "It saves me a great deal of unnecessary explanation... [But] the presence of the seal in this house will involve you in difficult explanations. Why is it here? How did it come here? Why are you known as the Reverend James Tattersby, the missionary, at Goring-Streatley, and as Mr A.J. Raffles, the cricketer and man of the world, at Dorrington Hall, to say nothing of the Cliveden plate – "

"Damnation!" roared the Reverend James Tattersby, springing to his feet and glancing instinctively at the long low book-shelves behind him.

"To say nothing," continued Holmes, calmly lighting a cigarette, "of the Cliveden plate now lying concealed behind those dusty theological tomes of yours which you never allow to be touched by any other hand than your own."

"How did you know?" cried Raffles, hoarsely.

"I didn't," laughed Holmes. "You have only this moment informed me of the fact!"

There was a long pause, during which Raffles paced the floor like a caged tiger. "I'm a dangerous man to trifle with, Mr Holmes," he said, finally. "I can shoot you down in cold blood in a second."

"Very likely," said Holmes. "But you won't. It would add to the difficulties in which the Reverend James Tattersby is already deeply immersed. Your troubles are sufficient, as matters stand, without your having to explain to the world why you have killed a defenceless guest in your own study in cold blood."

"Well – what do you propose to do?" demanded Raffles, after another pause.

"Marry your daughter, Mr Raffles, or Tattersby, whatever your permanent name is – I guess it's Tattersby in this case," said Holmes. "I love her and she loves me. Perhaps I should apologise for having wooed and won her without due notice to you, but you will doubtless forgive that. It's a little formality you sometimes overlook yourself when you happen to want something that belongs to somebody else."

What Raffles would have answered no one knows. He had no chance to reply, for at that moment Marjorie herself put her radiantly lovely little head in at the door with a "May I come in?" and a moment later she was gathered in Holmes's arms, and the happy lovers received the Reverend James Tattersby's blessing. They were married a week later, and, as far as the world is concerned, the mystery of the Dorrington seal and that of the Cliveden plate was never solved.

"It is compounding a felony, Raffles," said Holmes, after the wedding [which was *not* performed by the Reverend

Tattersby], "but for a wife like that, hanged if I wouldn't compound the ten commandments!"

The fruit of this unlikely union, born the following year, was a boy christened Raffles Holmes, who takes up residence in New York in 1905 and promptly goes in search of a reasonably prosperous journalist who might be in need of a few fresh ideas. He alights upon a Mr Jenkinson, gaining access to his apartment by a spot of breaking and entry so that he can first of all cast an eye over his royalty statements. "I want a literary partner," he declares, "a man who will write me up as Bunny did Raffles, and Watson did Holmes, so that I may get a percentage on that part of the swag." Jenkinson agrees. In the agreeable little collection of tales that follows, this curious young man displays hereditary traits inherited from both his illustrious forebears. He is perfectly capable, depending upon which particular type of adventure he is involved in, of solving a crime or cracking a crib – and Jenkinson does his best to confine this Jekyll and Hyde character to the nobler side of his ancestry. "There are days", he declares, "when you are the living image of your grandfather Raffles, but that is only when you are planning some scheme of villainy. I can almost invariably detect the trend of your thoughts by a glance at your face – you are Holmes himself in your honest moments." Bangs thus contrived to have the best of both worlds.

Another improbable union occurred in 1984, when Willie Rushton brought together A.J. Raffles and Dr Watson in a splendid yarn both written and illustrated by himself – *W.G. Grace's Last Case*. But the spoof which proved even more wonderful was that perpetrated by Graham Greene, whose three-Act play, *The Return of A.J. Raffles*, was *premièred* by the Royal Shakespeare Company in December 1975 with Denholm Elliot in the main role. It was billed as "An Edwardian Comedy/in Three Acts/Based Somewhat Loosely/on E.W. Hornung's/Characters in/The Amateur Cracksman" and Greene confessed, in an Author's Note, that he had taken some minor liberties with both fact and fiction.

First of all, he endeavours to convince us that Bunny did *not* accompany Raffles when the latter set out for the South African War and had falsified history in order to conceal the fact that he himself had been in Reading Gaol at that time, where he made the acquaintance of Oscar Wilde. The curtain rises on that famous apartment in the Albany, which Raffles had left to Bunny in his will – for Raffles is supposed to have been officially alive until killed at Spion Kop – and we are intrigued to find that Bunny's closest friend is none other than Lord Alfred Douglas. Bosie, it transpires, is seeking revenge on his father and wants Bunny to put his safe-breaking skills to good use by carrying out a break-in at Queensberry's country house. Bunny, however, is less than enthusiastic about the proposal, claiming that it would be no fun without Raffles. In the meantime, bewhiskered Inspector Mackenzie has arrived and insists on prowling around the flat in search of possible incriminating evidence. He disappears into the bedroom, but emerges a little while later – and lo and behold, it is Raffles all the time! He proclaims himself in great need of a Sullivan, which Bunny hastens to produce.

RAFFLES: The first I've had in eighteen months. You've always been inclined to dispose of me prematurely, B u n n y . You remember when I drowned in the Mediterranean under the eyes of old Mackenzie? By the way, these tweeds are quite his style, aren't they? I spotted them in a second-hand clothes shop in Harwich when I landed this morning. So this is Lord Alfred Douglas [*offering his hand*]. I've read a lot about you, sir, in the *Cape Times*.

BUNNY: But Raffles ... Spion Kop ... that will stained with your blood...

RAFFLES: Not my blood, Bunny. The poor devil beside me had his face blown off, so I took the opportunity to exchange papers before the Boers got to me. Some of the blood was his, though just in case I had used a lot of tomato sauce on the paper the night before. I didn't think that they'd check the genuineness of blood on a battlefield.

LORD ALFRED: And the Boers got you, Mr Raffles?

RAFFLES: The Boers got me, Lord Alfred, but they were no cleverer than poor old Mackenzie. In fact I took a souvenir away with me. [*Raffles takes a gold watch from his waistcoat pocket.*] General Botha's, inscribed by President Kruger himself. I had to leave the chain behind.... And now, Lord Alfred, what's all this about your avenging Mr Wilde?

Indubitably, A.J. Raffles has returned and is very much back in business. What matter that things don't go strictly according to plan, that there are some startling complications, that, before the evening is out, we encounter again the real Inspector Mackenzie, as well as a German spy, and that the Prince of Wales has to intervene to prevent Raffles from being arrested? For the dialogue crackles with life and the changes are rung in a dazzling fashion which Hornung himself couldn't have bettered. (Retribution is, moreover, emphatically dealt out to the Marquess of Queensberry.) The Prince presents Raffles with a gold box containing diamonds, in exchange for valuable services rendered, and exacts a reluctant promise, as he takes his leave, that henceforth England will know only Raffles the cricketer, and not Raffles the amateur cracksman.

Greene had produced a little gem of a play and one which ought, ideally, to be admitted to the official canon. Sadly, he never recycled it in the form of a short story, but six years later, in 1981, Methuen Paperbacks Ltd tried to atone for this oversight by publishing Peter Tremayne's *The Return of Raffles* (a title originally used, of course, by Barry Perowne in 1933). Far from being a spoof, however, it is presented as a straightforward continuation of the memoirs of *Henry Manders*, who is now married to Alice Devenish. The year is 1904. A guest in the empty house of his brother-in-law, Lord Toby Devenish, with all the servants having been given the night off, Bunny apprehends a burglar cracking the family safe – and faints away, not surprisingly, on discovering that it is none other than dear old Raffles, whom he last saw lying splashed in blood "on the sunbaked veld [sic] before Mafeking" while a sergeant dragged him away assuring him that "the awficer be dead, sor". But it now transpires that

Raffles was simply shot through the shoulder, although it was a nasty enough wound at the time, and had regained consciousness in a makeshift Boer hospital. "Not only that but while I had lain unconscious someone had looted my belongings, including all my identification.... Well, the first thing the Boers asked me was what my name, rank and number were. It suddenly occurred to me that the war might be over soon and a dead A.J. Raffles might have some distinct advantages over a live one."

So he calls himself Arthur Roberts, cousin and heir to A.J. Raffles. He is once again living in the same apartment at the Albany (unoccupied, it would seem, since 1893) and is once again hard up. No sooner has he persuaded Bunny to assist him in burglaring the house of a Jewish banker, than they are apprehended by Chief Inspector Mackenzie – who bears them off to meet the Solicitor-General, Sir Edward Carson, and the Prime Minister, A.J. Balfour. For these are desperate times. The King has written some injudicious letters, containing disrespectful remarks about the Czar, and the letters are now in the German Embassy and about to be whisked off to Berlin. Raffles, as the greatest cracksman in the land, is required to retrieve them – in return for which he and Bunny will be handsomely paid and (much to Mackenzie's evident annoyance) nothing more will be said about their misdemeanours.

The yarn which follows is, in many respects, a good one – far better, indeed, than *Mr Justice Raffles*. It contains some ingenious twists and turns and a few surprises. But it is marred by some unfortunate mistakes. Bunny's literary style has deteriorated to an alarming extent, for he twitters and expostulates like a maiden aunt, and a cause for concern is the strange manner in which the eyes of his leader change colour: they are brown in the first chapter, grey in the third and blue by the twenty-third. We are told, in passing, that "Lord Macauley" used to live at Albany – for the definite article is zealously omitted. (Quite properly, indeed, for an erudite article by Anthony Davis in *TV Times* on 10 March 1977, which Mr Tremayne had evidently digested, had pointed out that both Macaulay and Hornung were wrong to refer to it as *"the Albany"* – but for Harold/Henry Manders to suddenly take belated account of such niceties is dreadfully out of character.) If it had not been produced with such carelessness, the book would have made a more lasting impact. But, notwithstanding all its blunders, the personality of Raffles comes across quite effectively – an improvement, certainly, on the sanitised version produced by Perowne, and almost equal to Greene's recreation.

According to Tremayne, Raffles (with Bunny in tow) is off to join the Secret Service on a permanent basis; according to Greene, he is simply going to transfer his safe-cracking operations to the Continent – for his promise to the King did not extend beyond the shores of England – and possibly masquerade as "one of the obscurer Rockefellers". Perhaps, indeed, he was able to pursue *both* vocations.

ை

On 7 October 1996 a contestant in BBC Television's *Mastermind* chose as her special topic 'E.W. Horning and his Raffles stories'. At about the same time, Oxford University Press published yet another omnibus edition of the tales under the title *The Collected Raffles Stories*. With the centenary of his first appearance in *Cassell's Magazine* already behind us, it is a pretty safe bet that the fame of the Amateur Cracksman will continue unabated until well into the twenty-first century. Or, as the great man (in Fielding's sense of the term) might gleefully have remarked, "Not a bad score, Bunny, old boy! We've come out of the twentieth century with a good deal less credit than when we went in. But, by Jove, we're jolly lucky to have come out of it at all!"

APPENDIX:
THE WORKS OF E.W. HORNUNG

(**NB** So far as initial publications of short stories in magazines is concerned, this bibliography lays no claim to completeness: it simply lists information currently known to the present author.)

(A) Books

1890
A Bride from the Bush (London: Smith, Elder & Co.; New York: US Book Co.)

1892
Under Two Skies (London: A. & C. Black; New York: Macmillan & Co.)

1893
Tiny Luttrell (London and New York: Cassell & Co. Ltd)

1894
The Boss of Taroomba (London: Bliss, Sands and Foster; New York: Scribner's [*in 1900*])
The Unbidden Guest (London: Longmans, Green & Co.; New York: Longmans)

1896
The Rogue's March (London: Cassell & Co. Ltd; New York: Scribner's)
Irralie's Bushranger (London: Neville Beatman Ltd; New York: Scribner's)
My Lord Duke (New York: Scribner's; London: Cassell & Co. Ltd [*in 1897*])

1898

Young Blood (London: Cassell & Co. Ltd; New York: Scribner's *[in 1899]*)

Some Persons Unknown (London: Cassell & Co. Ltd; New York: Scribner's)

1899

Dead Men Tell No Tales (London: Methuen & Co. Ltd; New York: Scribner's)

The Amateur Cracksman (London: Methuen & Co. Ltd; New York: Scribner's)

1900

The Belle of Toorak (London: Grant Richards; New York: Scribners *[in 1901]* as *The Shadow of a Man*)

Peccavi (London: Grant Richards; New York: Scribner's)

1901

The Black Mask (London: Grant Richards; New York: Scribner's as *Raffles, Further Adventures of the Amateur Cracksman*)

1902

The Shadow of the Rope (London: Chatto & Windus; New York: Scribner's)

At Large (New York: Scribner's)

1903

No Hero (London: Smith, Elder & Co.; New York: Scribner's)

Dennis Dent (London: Isbister & Co; New York: Stokes)

Raffles, the Amateur Cracksman (a play, written with Eugéne W. Presbrey, premièred in New York and performed in London in 1906)

1905

Stingaree (London: Chatto & Windus; New York: Scribner's)

A Thief in the Night (London: Chatto & Windus; New York: Scribner's)

1906

Raffles, The Amateur Cracksman (London: Eveleigh Nash) [combining *The Amateur Cracksman* and *The Black Mask*]

1908

Stingaree, the Bushranger (a play, premièred in London)

1909

Mr Justice Raffles (London: Smith, Elder & Co.; New York: Scribner's)

A Visit from Raffles (a play, written with Charles Sansom, premièred in London)

1911

The Camera Fiend (London: T. Fisher Unwin Ltd; New York: Scribner's)

1912

Fathers of Men (London: Smith, Elder & Co.; New York: Scribner's)

1913

Witching Hill (London: Hodder & Stoughton; New York: Scribner's)

The Thousandth Woman (London: Eveleigh Nash; Indianopolis: The Bobbs-Merrill Co.)

1914

The Crime Doctor (London: Eveleigh Nash)

1916

Trusty and Well Beloved, The Little Record of Arthur Oscar Hornung (privately printed)

1917

The Ballad of Ensign Joy (a poem, published in New York by Dutton)

1918

Wooden Crosses (a poem, published in London by Nisbet)

1919

The Young Guard (a collection of poems, published in London by Constable & Co)

Notes of a Camp-Follower on the Western Front (London: Constable & Co.; New York: E.P. Dutton & Co., the American edition incorporating most of the poems included in *The Young Guard*)

1923

Old Offenders and a few old scores (a posthumous collection of short stories, published in London by John Murray)

(B) Serialisations and short stories

1890

'A Bride from the Bush' – *The Cornhill Magazine* (July – November)

1891

'The Luckiest Man in the Colony' – *Strand Magazine* (April) *[Author allegedly 'S.W. Hornung']*
'The Notorious Miss Anstruther' – *Strand Magazine* (May)

1892

'Strong-Minded Miss Methuen' – *Strand Magazine* (March)
'The Romance of Sergeant Clancy' – *The Idler* (April)
'Kenyon's Innings' – *Longman's Magazine* (April)

1893

'"Author! Author!"' – *Strand Magazine* (March)
'The Burrawurra Brand' – *The Idler* (November)
'The Voice of Gunbar' – *Pall Mall Gazette* (December)
'A Literary Coincidence' – *Strand Magazine* (December)

1894

'The Unbidden Guest' – *Longman's Magazine* (May - October)
'"Galloping Jess"' – *Temple Bar* (December)
'The Star of the *Grasmere*' – *Strand Magazine* (December)

1895

'The Man that shot Macturk' – *Pall Mall Gazette* (September)

'Irralie's Bushranger' – *Cassell's Family Magazine* (December)

1897

'A Demon of Revenge' – *Cassell's Family Magazine* (June)

1898

'The Ides of March' (**R**) – *Cassell's Magazine* (June)

'A Costume Piece' (**R**) – *Cassell's Magazine* (July)

'Gentlemen and Players' (**R**) – *Cassell's Magazine* (August)

'Nine Points of the Law' (**R**) – *Cassell's Magazine* (September)

'The Return Match' (**R**) – *Cassell's Magazine* (October)

'The Gift of the Emperor' (**R**) – *Cassell's Magazine* (November)

1900

'The Saloon Passenger' – *Strand Magazine* (June)

'The Jackeroo on G Block' – *Strand Magazine* (April)

1903

'No Hero' – *Pall Mall Magazine* (January - May)

'Chrystal's Century' – *Strand Magazine* (June)

1904

'A Voice in the Wilderness' (**S**) – *Strand Magazine* (September)

'A Bushranger at Bay' (**S**) – *Strand Magazine* (October)

'The Honour of the Road' (**S**) – *Strand Magazine* (November)

'The Black Hole of Glenranald' (**S**) – *Strand Magazine* (December)

1905

'Out of Paradise' (**R**) – *Pall Mall Magazine* (January)

'The Real Simon Pure' (**S**) – *Strand Magazine* (January)

'The Chest of Silver' (**R**) – *Pall Mall Magazine* (February)

'To the Vile Dust' (**S**) – *Strand Magazine* (February)

'The Rest Cure' (**R**) – *Pall Mall Magazine* (March)

'The Villain Worshipper' (**S**) – *Strand Magazine* (March)

'The Criminologists' Club' (**R**) – *Pall Mall Magazine* (April)
'The Moth and the Star' (**S**) – *Strand Magazine* (April)
'The Field of Philippi' (**R**) – *Pall Mall Magazine* (May)
'A Bad Night' (**R**) – *Pall Mall Magazine* (June)
'A Trap to Catch a Cracksman' (**R**) – *Pall Mall Magazine* (July)
'The Spoils of Sacrilege' (**R**) – *Pall Mall Magazine* (August)
'The Raffles Relics' (**R**) – *Pall Mall Magazine* (September)

(**R**) indicates a Raffles story and (**S**) indicates a Stingaree story

SOURCES AND SUPPLMENTARY INFORMATION

So far as the early history of the Hornung family is concerned, *J.P. Hornung, A family portrait* by Mrs B. M. Collin (privately-printed, 1970) contains much useful information and there is also a slim folder of information on the Hornung family in the Middlesbrough Reference Library.

It should be noted that Theodore Hornung, despite his father's bankruptcy, was able to re-establish the family business of iron exportation and develop it into a thriving concern. He filled his father's old post of vice-consul for Denmark, Sweden and Norway, established Middlesbrough's music society and was elected to the town council in 1901. He moved to London in 1905.

Erdely, complete with tower room, still exists (as No. 404 Marton Road) but is now greyish-white rather than brick red. It housed the Convent of the Holy Rood from 1923 until 1934, when the sisters moved into new adjacent buildings, but they retained Erdely until the late 1970s and used it first as an orphanage and later as a nursing home. It is now a NACRO hostel.

Hornung's Preface to the reprint of *Fathers of Men*, published by John Murray in September 1919, contains some recollections of his schooldays at Uppingham and a vivid sketch of its headmaster. But his memories of the RA painting of the charge of the Light Brigade, and attending test matches at the Oval, will be found in *Notes of a Camp-Follower on the Western Front*.

Apart from Hornung's own semi-fictionalised autobiographical recollections, the work most helpful to the present author has been *E.W. Hornung and his Young Guard 1914*, compiled in 1941 by Shane R. Chichester (who dedicated it to the Young Guard of Today), the profits from which went to the YMCA. It contains a brief memoir and some of the addresses which Hornung delivered at the Chapel of Stone House, Broadstairs (in effect, his old school, St Ninian's, Moffat, re-established in somewhat different surroundings). "I

285

agree with you", wrote Chichester to Mrs Collin (Pitt's daughter, Bertha) on 16 October 1941, "that it is a mercy that E.W.H. and your father have been spared this further awful War. The former foreshadowed it in a letter to me when my Oscar was born. He was always very devoted to your father, for whom he had a great admiration besides affection.... I would love to come and examine those manuscripts when it can be arranged. Thank you so much. I wonder if there is amongst them the book which he was writing after the last War, and which he told me was going to be the best novel he had ever written! I feel it ought to see the light of day: he read me bits of it. But there are other things too of his, which I should like to see published." (Letter in the possession of Mr Stephen Hornung.) A short leaflet on *Fathers of Men*, which Chichester compiled in August 1942, was also extremely helpful.

Frederick Whyte's *A Bachelor's London* (1931) contains some useful scraps of information about Hornung (pp. 30-33). The extracts from Gissing's diary, quoted in Chapter 8, are taken from *London and the Life of Literature in Late Victorian England: The Diary of George Gissing, Novelist* edited by Pierre Coustillas and published by the Harvester Press in 1978 (pp. 486-9 *passim*), and the quotations from his letters are taken primarily from Volumes 7 and 8 of *The Collected Letters of George Gissing* (1995 and 1996), edited by Paul F. Mattheisen, Arthur C. Young and Pierre Coustillas. (A puzzling footnote by the editors on page 336 of Volume 7 states that Hornung was living at 36 Edwardes Square in 1899, which – if correct – could only have been for a very brief period.) Bernard Shaw's diary entry for 14 September 1886, quoted on p. 46, will be found in *Bernard Shaw: The Diaries, 1885-1897* (1986), edited and annotated by Stanley Weintraub (vol. I, p. 198).

Quotations from Conan Doyle's letters have been taken primarily from the biography by Pierre Nordon, published in Paris in 1964 (*Sir Arthur Conan Doyle: L'Homme et L'Œuvre*) (see pages 191 and 197-8); an English translation by Frances Partridge was published in 1966. In the second of the two furious letters which he wrote to his mother in the summer of 1900, Conan Doyle referred to Hornung as 'William' rather than 'Willie' – an obvious indication of just how annoyed he was. A brief extract from that letter, quoted by John Dickson Carr in his 1949 biography of Conan Doyle (p. 183), confirms that 'William' was the name used on this occasion. Although *Old Offenders* was not published until May 1923, Conan Doyle's Preface was evidently written soon after his brother-in-law's death. The information about his spirit-world communications with Willie and Oscar will be found in *Pheneas Speaks* (1927) (see pages 12-19, 43 and 52). (Constance and Pitt are circumspectly referred to, therein, as 'Cynthia' and 'Bute'.)

The playful disposition evinced by Hornung when it came to bestowing names upon his fictional creations almost merits a Holmesian monograph. The folk of Middlesbrough appreciated that some of his nobility (e.g., the Marquess of Maske and Lady Kirkleatham) originated from the Tees-side area, while some of his leading characters (e.g., Methuen and Dent) were evidently distant connections of certain publishing houses. 'Tahourdin' could be an oblique reference to Houdini, while 'Langholm' is basically 'Hornung' with the syllables reversed. 'Erskine Holland' derives his nomenclature from Oscar Wilde, who masqueraded as 'Mr Melmoth' and thereby encouraged Raffles to masquerade as 'Mr Maturin'. 'Uvo Delavoye' would seem to echo Walter de la Mare, with 'Uvo' roughly equivalent to 'eau' just as 'Walter' is roughly equivalent to 'water'. The English Dr Dollar, preaching revolutionary doctrines as regards the rehabilitation of criminals, is perhaps the opposite number of the American Mr Pound, preaching revolutionary doctrines as regards the development of poetry. (And, on a slightly different tack, it should be noted that Deedes Major, the antithesis of Holmes, mischievously engages a Captain Watson, owner and skipper of the *Mollyhawk*, to assist him in making a sea-going getaway. Clearly, they would have been steering into deep waters....)

The two final sentences of Chapter 26 are adapted from the closing remarks uttered by Raffles in 'A Costume Piece'.

The entry on Hornung's Raffles stories in *Edwardian Fiction: an Oxford Companion* (1997, pp. 192-3) suggests that "both the figure of the hero and his story's narration by an admiring schoolfriend owe something to a popular novel of a previous generation, *Guy Livingstone* (1857), by G.A.Lawrence (1827-76)". The book referred to, now almost forgotten, is a long-winded melodrama containing many classical allusions and sententious reflections. Livingstone, a gallant but hot-tempered Byronic figure, is jilted by his true love (Constance Brandon) when discovered in the evil arms of another (Flora Bellasys). Bitter and reckless, he retires to Paris to engage in a life of debauchery, and re-encounters his scheming *femme fatale*. Summoned home by Constance, so that she can bid him farewell from her deathbed, he sees the error of his ways and is never the same man again. He renounces both Flora and profligacy, tracks down the murderer of his best friend, Charles Forrester, and dies bravely after a hunting accident, apologising to the narrator for both his perverse temper and his inclinations towards wrong-doing. The narrator is indeed a younger schoolfellow, upon whom the dashing Guy (a masterly football player, held in great esteem by other boys) bestows a kindly word, thereby saving him from a group of bullies. Levinge, the highly unpleasant grandson of a "prize-fighting Israelite", is contemptuously killed by his opponent in a duel, after firing his own gun too soon, and "a vacancy in the most luxurious set of chambers in the Albany" is created as the result of another character's death. It must be acknowledged, therefore, that the creator of C.J. Forrester and Dan Levy might well have been familiar with Lawrence's book, but – apart from their sporting prowess – it is difficult to discern any direct parallels between the wealthy but hot-tempered Livingstone (who was law-abiding) and the impecunious but cool-headed Raffles (who was not).

INDEX

(a) to people, places, subjects, organisations, titles, etc – i.e., anything of a factual nature

(b) to fictional characters
* denotes fictional character created by Hornung